CW01474875

Britain, America and Rearmament in the 1930s

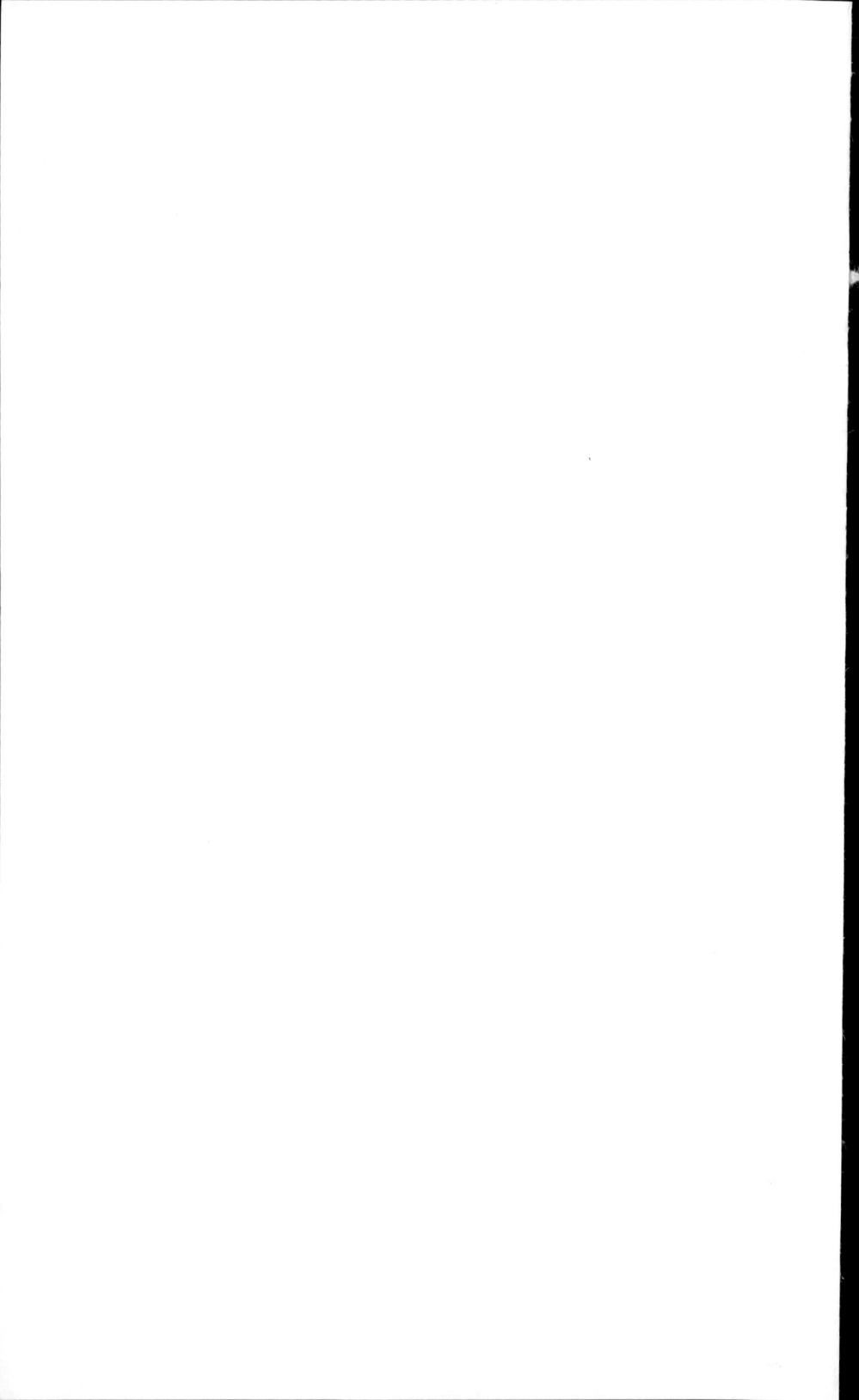

Britain, America and Rearmament in the 1930s

The Cost of Failure

Christopher Price
Postdoctoral Teaching Fellow
University of York

palgrave

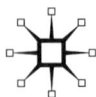

© Christopher Price 2001

All rights reserved. No reproduction, copy or transmission of this publication may be made without written permission.

No paragraph of this publication may be reproduced, copied or transmitted save with written permission or in accordance with the provisions of the Copyright, Designs and Patents Act 1988, or under the terms of any licence permitting limited copying issued by the Copyright Licensing Agency, 90 Tottenham Court Road, London W1T 4LP.

Any person who does any unauthorised act in relation to this publication may be liable to criminal prosecution and civil claims for damages.

The author has asserted his right to be identified as the author of this work in accordance with the Copyright, Designs and Patents Act 1988.

First published 2001 by
PALGRAVE
Houndmills, Basingstoke, Hampshire RG21 6XS and
175 Fifth Avenue, New York, N. Y. 10010
Companies and representatives throughout the world

PALGRAVE is the new global academic imprint of
St. Martin's Press LLC Scholarly and Reference Division and
Palgrave Publishers Ltd (formerly Macmillan Press Ltd).

ISBN 0–333–92292–1

This book is printed on paper suitable for recycling and made from fully managed and sustained forest sources.

A catalogue record for this book is available from the British Library.

Library of Congress Cataloging-in-Publication Data
Price, Christopher, 1964–
    Britain, America, and rearmament in the 1930s : the cost of failure / Christopher Price.
        p. cm.
    Includes bibliographical references (p.) and index.
    ISBN 0–333–92292–1 (cloth)
    1. Chamberlain, Neville, 1869–1940—Views on military policy.
    2. Great Britain—Foreign economic relations—United States.
    3. United States—Foreign economic relations—Great Britain.
    4. Foreign exchange—Great Britain—History—20th century.
    5. Great Britain—Military policy—History—20th century.
    6. Great Britain—Politics and government—1936–1945. 7. Great Britain—Defenses—History—20th century. 8. Great Britain——Economic conditions—1918–1945. 9. World War, 1939–1945——Causes. I. Title.
    DA585.C5 P75 2001
    941.084'092—dc21
                                                          2001024550

10   9   8   7   6   5   4   3   2   1
10   09 08 07 06 05 04 03 02 01

Printed in Great Britain by Antony Rowe Ltd, Chippenham, Wiltshire

For my mother and in memory of my father

'Defence expenditure had increased from £160 million in 1936–37 to £263 millions in 1937–8 to £343 millions in the coming budget; and in the next two years, it would probably be greater still. These figures could not be reached unless we turned ourselves into a different kind of nation.' Sir John Simon, chancellor of the exchequer, 6 April 1938

'Wollen sie Realpolitiker sein? Oder sind sie Theoriemensch?' Adolf Hitler

Contents

The Fall of Sterling, 1938–39 and International Events

The following graph illustrates events described in Chapters 5, 7 and 8 of this book. It portrays the concurrence between the international events of 1938 and 1939 and pressure on sterling's rate of exchange with the dollar. The British authorities were in no doubt that a connection existed between the two, and four distinct phases can be observed.

Before March 1938 the pound–dollar exchange and the level of reserves were stable. It should be noted that even at this stage Great Britain was running a substantial current account deficit, thus weakening the argument that subsequent changes were primarily influenced by this deficit, as would be expected according to classical economic theory.

Between March 1938 and January 1939, both the level of gold and foreign currency reserves and the sterling exchange rate against the dollar fell, as reserves were spent to mitigate the pound's decline in preference to the institution of formal exchange controls. These movements began with the *Anschluss* and gathered pace through 1938. The Munich Agreement afforded scant respite.

Between January 1939 and August 1939, the pound–dollar exchange rate was stable. However, in January the bulk of the gold in the Issue Department of the Bank of England was transferred to the Exchange Equalisation Account for the purpose of supporting the currency. Thus, although the pound was stable, continuing and unabated pressure on the exchanges is indicated by the accelerated decline of gold and foreign currency reserves. The sums involved were more than considerable. The total reserve loss of more than £400 million in the period covered in the graph can be measured against a total budget for the British Army of £81 million in the financial year 1937–38.

Finally, as war became imminent, the threat of total loss of reserves forced abandonment of support operations and an instant depreciation of sterling to $4.03. Exchange controls were finally introduced on the outbreak of war and this exchange rate became official for the duration of hostilities.

Sources

Figures for holdings of gold and foreign currency are taken from: Susan Howson, *Sterling's Managed Float: the Operations of the Exchange Equalisation Account, 1932–39* (Princeton, 1980), Table A-3, p. 62.

Figures for the sterling–dollar rate of exchange are taken from: *Journal of the Royal Statistical Society* 101 (1938), p. 274; 102 (1939), p. 166; 103 (1940), p. 149.

The Fall of Sterling 1938-39
And International Events

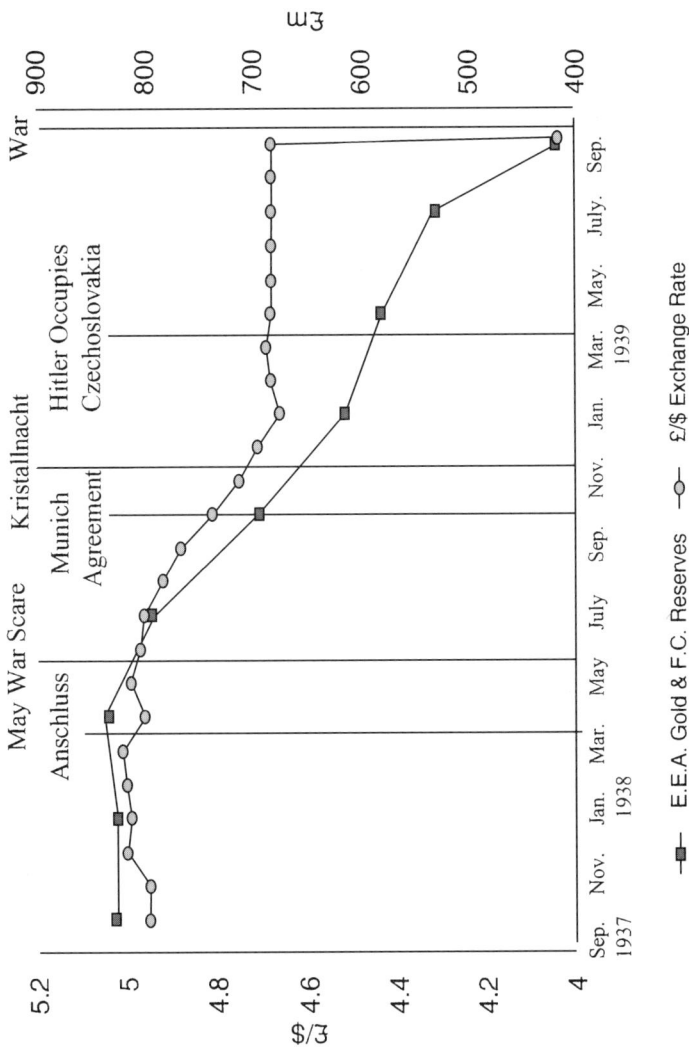

Preface

This book examines a current orthodoxy: that Britain's diplomacy before the Second World War was compromised by her inability to create and sustain vast armaments. This view was encapsulated in Sir Thomas Inskip's enduring assertion that economic stability could 'properly be regarded as a fourth arm in defence, without which purely military effort would be of no avail'.[1] Chamberlain's modern defenders thus 'attempt to turn the tables on the critics by charging them with having adhered to illusions',[2] chiefly a wild overestimation of Britain's economic capacity between the wars. In the face of this argument, critics of appeasement have remained silent.

Indeed, it is argued that to ask: 'Could more have been achieved if the canons of sound finance had been abandoned?' amounts '[i]n some ways' to 'an unfair question'.[3] It was 'untrue that "deficit finance" capable of being applied as if by magic by Keynes, or those who "listened" to him, could have increased the resources available for rearmament'.[4] It follows that bare survival in 1940 was the best that could possibly be achieved by the rearmament process,[5] a meagre return itself credited to the 'extra year' gained by appeasement.

No effective counter to the enduring fourth arm argument has yet been attempted. The dated Churchillian thesis rests on 'the traditional yardstick of balance-of-power politics',[6] which criticises Chamberlain's diplomatic record and simply assumes Britain's economic ability to rearm. A development of this theme attempts to turn the tables yet again by demonstrating that economic weakness made still greater the enormity of Chamberlain's diplomatic blunders.[7] Such perspectives leave the fourth arm argument untouched as a justification for prudence in policy. Significantly, favourable assessments of the inter-war imperial economy made by economic historians have not been used to effect in the diplomatic and political fields of study,[8] and this is no coincidence.

Middlemas has realised that having 'relied most heavily on Government archives, there is a danger that the conclusion might be one which the Government itself would have wished to perpetuate'.[9] An excellent example of this tendency can be seen in the uncritical, and indeed often favourable, reception given by historians to Sir Richard Hopkins' incredible apologia to Cabinet in July 1939 for the failings of the fourth arm policy, assailed bitterly and at length by the secretaries of state for war and air.[10]

Chamberlain argued that 'until our armaments are completed we must adjust our foreign policy to our circumstances'.[11] But what were Britain's circumstances? The stark fact of the matter, as officials admitted amongst themselves in private weeks before the outbreak of war, was that the government had no idea what was actually possible in the field of rearmament.

This book argues that, had the will to rearm existed, British resources were effectively limitless, and moreover that after 1931 a system to develop them effectively was in place. The particular culpability of Chamberlain's government lay not in inactivity but in the active destruction of British-imperial war potential. In this area history has certainly been written by the victors, and revision is long overdue.

This study uses previously unconsidered documents in British and American archives to demonstrate that Britain's best hope was known to lie in the maintenance and strengthening of the Ottawa system, which had delivered six years of world-beating growth. Chamberlain chose instead to liberalise British trading practice with two objectives in mind. Firstly to appease the Americans, whose dearest wish, aggressively pursued, was to penetrate imperial markets and liquidate the sterling bloc, and secondly to keep the lid on defence expenditure by constructing an imaginary yet plausible threat to sterling from unbridled rearmament in free market conditions. Chamberlain's government did not rearm because it did not want to.

Chamberlain's faith in the likely success of his appeasement policy left him reluctant to provide unnecessary armaments. His genius in formulating this policy was to draw together the various strands of liberal thought, inside and outside government, whose commitment to free trade was stronger than their fear of Hitler. This coalition included the American Secretaries of State and Treasury, Hull and Morgenthau, who became daily participants in the British political process.

A fundamental and glaring misapprehension is still repeated, namely that: 'It was clear by early 1938 that the Ottawa agreements were not benefiting Britain, something underscored by renewed pressure on the pound.'[12] This was by no means clear in 1938 because it was not so. A speculative attack on sterling began in March 1938, which led to the catastrophic loss of half Britain's war chest of gold reserves. As this book demonstrates, though, this was known within government to have absolutely nothing to do with the state of Britain's trade or economy, but as the date implies was the result of political panic beginning with Hitler's move into Austria.

Sterling's fall and the reserve drain could have been halted at any moment by exchange control, a measure appropriate to the reality of undeclared war, yet Britain's war potential continued to be smashed in the international markets right up to the actual outbreak of hostilities, bewildering the Americans who refused to believe that such profligacy in precious metal could possibly continue.

America, though, gained massively from British policy. Morgenthau's instinctive brilliance in letting the gold come, despite his and his Department's fear of international financial collapse, and the final triumph of Hull in concluding the Anglo-American Trade Agreement, sealed Britain's fate as a world economic power.

The following chapters tell this story in full, and shed light on the forces behind Britain's precipitate collapse and America's swift recovery as war approached. It is not pleasant reading for believers in British democracy, involving weakness, folly and something as harmful as treachery at the apex of Britain's government. It is sobering to reflect that had it not been so easy to deceive Parliament and people, and to exercise power without constitutional authority, many of the horrors and humiliations subsequently endured before and after the defeat of Hitler might not have occurred.

Acknowledgements

Thanks are due to many people who helped the book along its course. I would like to thank the University of York for providing essential funding. I am also indebted to the Franklin and Eleanor Roosevelt Institute for awarding a scholarship to work in the Franklin D. Roosevelt Presidential Library, and to the staff at the Library who were unfailingly helpful and friendly.

On a level between the personal and the official I should like to thank Bill Trythall, for his help and encouragement and for his open-minded interest in what must at first have seemed a rather peculiar project.

Friends and acquaintances who provided much appreciated assistance along the way are too numerous to mention, so I shall try to be specific. I remain indebted to Pat and Art Costello and family of Hyde Park, New York, for their marvellous hospitality, especially during the blizzard and its aftermath when the English visitors must have been a heavy burden. I should also like to thank Dr Steve Casey, whose company and knowledge of American ways were an enormous help.

I should like to thank Dr Heidi Schubert and Dr Ralph Vocke for their friendship and support over a number of years. I am similarly grateful to Fay Bound and Andy Hopper, who also provided invaluable help in proofreading. Thanks are also due to Martin Knudsen for his indispensable help and generosity during the editing process, and to Rachel Hadfield for her support and managerial skills at the same stage.

Finally I wish to express my continuing gratitude to my mother, Margaret Price, and my late father, John Price, without whose understanding, encouragement and support the book could not have been attempted.

List of Abbreviations

BT	Board of Trade Papers, PRO
CAB	Cabinet Office Papers, PRO
CEI	Economic Advisory Council, Committee on Economic Information
CID	Committee of Imperial Defence
DBFP	*Documents on British Foreign Policy, 1919–1939.* Second and Third Series
EEA	Exchange Equalisation Account
FDR	Franklin D. Roosevelt Library, Hyde Park, New York
FO	Foreign Office Papers, PRO
FRUS	*Foreign Relations of the United States, 1936–1938.* Various Volumes
MD	Morgenthau Diary, FDR
PREM	Prime Minister's Office Papers, PRO
PRO	Public Record Office, London
SD	General Records of the Department of State RG.59, National Archives, Washington DC
T	Treasury Office Papers, PRO

1
New Rules for an Old Game: the Shaping of Fourth Arm Concepts in a Fluid Environment, 1919–31

The conviction that Britain's economic stability and financial credibility amounted to a fourth arm of defence was deeply rooted in liberal intellectual and administrative tradition. Its success in 1938 is ample testimony to the resilience and cohesion of classical economic ideals. These survived the movement generated during the Great War in the direction of an autarkic imperial economic system, forcefully advocated in the exhaustive 1917 report of the Dominions Royal Commission.[1] Its conclusions were thought extreme: in fact they were at the opposite extreme to the fourth arm policy eventually adopted. Between 1918 and 1938 therefore, a polar transformation of policy occurred, the origins of which can be found in developments between the end of the Great War and the collapse of gold in 1931.

After 1918 CID planning was influenced by the retention of external finance in the hands of the Treasury and the Bank of England during hostilities. They had been able to maintain essentially peacetime financial machinery by the expedient of huge borrowing in America, and it was assumed that such a policy might in future be repeated. Furthermore, continuing civilian control enmeshed war finance in the bitter controversy between the 'familiar shibboleths of protection and free trade'.[2]

In this debate, war was a defining issue. What one liberal economist of the inter-war years described as the 'intellectual holiday of the War'[3] reinforced the protectionist case, and it was a concern of liberal thinkers to contain the unwelcome economic concepts of war within its temporal boundaries, completely excluded from peacetime economic debate. In the planning of war finance, the entrenched position of the champions of free trade in the government machine was of deep significance. This was true before and after sterling's eviction

1

from the gold standard in September 1931. The steps taken during and after this emergency, though effective measures of crisis management, gave a misleading impression of the ideological conversion within government, caused by the initial relief of officials at the economy's survival and the silencing of their liberal convictions in the face of the obvious success of a floating pound, protection and imperial preference.

Even at this stage, however, it was clear that as soon as the crisis passed, traditional modes of thought would begin to reassert themselves. In 1931 the report of the Macmillan Committee noted uneasily, as Britain faced eviction from the gold standard, that 'there are "rules of the game", which, if not observed, will make the standard work with undesirable rather than beneficial consequences'. It added that: 'It is difficult to define in precise terms what is meant by the "rules of the game". The management of an international standard is an art and not a science.'[4] After the crisis, liberals looked forward to the day when play could be resumed. Quiet work done in the 1920s ensured that despite the fragmentation of the world economy in the 1930s, a liberal recovery was possible in Britain, and that domination of rearmament policy would be central to it.

1.1   Peace, war and a new concept of financial control

The British were quick to utilise experience gained in the Great War. Introducing the Fifth Annual Report of the CID's Advisory Committee on Trading and Blockade, the chairman, Lord Salisbury, described it as 'the latest stage of an Inquiry that has been going on for more than nine years. In February 1920, a number of Sub-Committees were appointed to overhaul the experiences of the late War over a wide range of subjects while the memory was still fresh.'[5] War finance was among them.

In this sphere it was later observed that there existed during the war 'two separate torrents of emotion', which 'were driving the peoples and their statesmen'.[6] One was 'the torrent of war fury', which 'carried on its surface the ideas of "economic defence", – of national or imperial self-sufficiency'. The other was 'the torrent of peace fervour' which 'carried on its surface the theory of an international economic order'. Autarkic ideas prevailed and were officially adopted by the Imperial War Cabinet and the Imperial War Conference in April 1917. The technicalities were encapsulated in the *Final Report* of the Dominions Royal Commission, which had over five years documented the extent of imperial resources and the progress made in their development. Its conclusion was that:

> In our opinion it is vital that the Empire should, so far as possible, be placed in a position which would enable it to resist any pressure which a foreign power or group of powers could exercise in time of peace or during war in virtue of control of raw materials and commodities essential for the well being of the Empire, and it is towards the attainment of this object that coordinated effort should be directed.[7]

When peace returned it was easy for liberal commentators to traduce these sentiments as advocating 'the economics of siege . . . as permanent policy on an imperial scale',[8] and most damagingly as an attempt by the Empire 'to secure exclusive supply for itself'. These absurdities were to become mainstays of the internationalist case that imperial self-sufficiency constituted an incitement to war on the part of 'excluded' powers. In fact, imperial defence required guaranteed, not exclusive, supply from the Empire, what the *Final Report* called 'the maintenance and development of supplies of commodities'.[9] In any case, for the Empire to 'use its monopoly powers to impose "sanctions" on behalf of its own interests' it would in the first place have to be trading with its potential victim.[10] Indeed, where imports were concerned the Commission's ideas were just as likely to work against monopoly, because 'if supplies cannot be obtained from British sources it is clear that in the general interests of the Empire its civil and military industries should draw their supplies from as many sources as possible, and not depend on a single foreign country for their requirements'.[11]

The Committee on Commercial and Industrial Policy After the War was far from seeing imperial self-sufficiency as a means of excluding foreigners in peacetime. Its *Interim Report on Certain Essential Industries* noted that it was 'essential to the safety of the nation that tungsten should be manufactured within the Empire after the war on such a scale as to supply domestic requirements and afford a margin for export so that any sudden increase in our own requirements may be readily met'.[12] Thus, even extreme selfishness scarcely amounted to the economics of siege. The *Final Report* of the Committee, despite listing first of '[t]he main subjects discussed in this report' its concern with 'the manner in which Imperial resources may be further developed and the supplies of raw materials assured',[13] noted that any attempt to make the Empire self-supporting in respect of them all would probably be both impracticable and economically unsound. Some selective policy will be necessary, which shall have regard to relative importance, whether industrial or military, and to the sources of supply and the likelihood of their disturbance in times of war.[14]

This was far sighted, as assured supply could be expressed essentially in the willingness of suppliers to accept sterling without condition in payment for their goods. The advent of the sterling area would broaden this category beyond the formal empire, and such sources of supply were not necessarily any more prone to interruption than those under direct British control.

Nevertheless liberal orthodoxy won the peace, led by public demands for economy from, amongst others, the Northcliffe press under the umbrella of an 'anti-waste movement'. The perspective encapsulated in the slogan 'back to 1914' dismissed imperial economics as representative of a time 'when the spirit of wartime unity in the Empire was at its height'.[15] A crucial distinction was drawn between the infringements on a liberal economy necessitated by war, and the requirements of peacetime trade. This was made manifest in decisive fashion by representatives of the government, the Bank of England, and selected financiers on the Committee on Currency and Foreign Exchange After the War (the Cunliffe Committee).

The *First Interim Report* of the Committee, published in August 1918, asserted that its members were 'unanimous',[16] in their conclusions, chief amongst which was that 'it will be clear that the conditions necessary to the maintenance of an effective gold standard in this country no longer exist, and it is imperative that they should be restored without delay'.[17] To express support for the gold standard was implicitly to advocate a return to the laissez-faire economic system of which gold was an integral component. It also meant that the credibility of the financial system would be rooted in *external* financial stability, so deeply in fact that this attitude would survive the end of the gold standard itself, with profound consequences as the next war approached.

Although the liberal economic machine would normally be expected to run itself, in 1918 it was clearly in need of repair. In this respect, time was of great importance to the Committee which, eager for its conclusions to be translated into policy, could not 'too strongly emphasize our opinion that the application, at the earliest possible date, of the main principles on which they are based is of vital necessity to the financial stability and well being of the country'.[18] The Cunliffe Committee was able to push the government into policy commitments to satisfy an essentially spurious requirement for haste. In the event it would prove impossible to reintroduce the gold standard, and it was formally suspended in 1919. However, a commitment to future return was sufficient to enforce a liberal economic regime in the interim.

With the eventual return to gold assumed, numerous further measures could be implemented immediately to hasten the day. A balanced budget was thought the most important prerequisite for a gold standard economy, and in 1918 the main obstacle to it was clearly the war effort. In accordance with the demands of the Cunliffe Committee, therefore, public expenditure was reduced by extraordinarily rapid demobilisation. In 1919 Lloyd George formed a Finance Committee, in effect a senior inner Cabinet, and this soon turned its attention to 'various suggestions for securing economies in the spending of public Departments, with special reference to the functions of the Treasury'.[19] Lloyd George explained that 'not only in view of the state of public opinion, but because of the financial situation of the country, ruthless cutting down of expenditure was imperative'. It was the Committee's problem to 'fix on the specific items of waste and extravagance which should be eliminated, and it was here that the Treasury should be able to help the Committee'.

The Treasury was, therefore, instructed 'to prepare for the Committee an analysis of the abnormal and temporary expenditure of the chief spending Departments and particularly the War Office, the Admiralty and the Ministry of Munitions'.[20] This task was performed with relish, and the Treasury quickly formulated an analysis of the 'national balance sheet'[21] as a basis for drastic economies and the restoration of a balanced budget. This document was duly presented to the Committee and not for the last time in such analyses it painted a 'terrifying picture' of insolvency. The Cabinet of 1919 was made of sterner stuff than its successors, however, and elements of creativity in the Treasury's accountancy were subjected to detailed criticism.

The most obvious cavil was that the figure for debt expenditure included the whole £50 million of annual interest payable to the USA, but this was not balanced on the revenue side by the £80 million owed annually by Britain's debtors. Also, the planned replacement for the excess profits tax was expected to yield £50 million annually, but not in 1920–21, because of the time lag involved in collection. The chancellor, Austen Chamberlain, 'said in reply to the Prime Minister that if payment of £50,000,000 to America were omitted and the proceeds of the excess profits' tax added, the deficit would disappear'. When during further criticism of the Treasury's figures, its permanent secretary (and head of the Civil Service) Warren Fisher was asked to defend the high level of expenditure on pensions, the prime minister felt it necessary to intervene. He 'said that he hoped the Treasury Officials understood that the criticism that had been made in the Meeting bore no reflection whatever on their hard-working Department. It was fully realised what an extremely difficult task they had to undertake.'[22]

Nevertheless, the Treasury was forced to produce answers to the questions raised by the Committee and to revise its report. When these were produced, the Treasury justified its position on the grounds of the hallowed accounting principle of prudence. However, the document produced was supposed to give an impression of conditions prevalent in a normal year, which was hardly the case. Despite this, it was produced as a White Paper, and the budgetary measures implemented produced impressive surpluses. They enabled 'a deficit of £1690 million in financial 1918–19' to be 'transformed into surpluses of £237.9 million in 1920–21, £45.7 million in 1921–22 and £101.5 million in 1922–23'.[23] Despite the caution in interpretation necessitated by fluctuating price levels at this time, these were impressive and arguably excessive surpluses.

The Finance Committee was told by the secretary of state for war that daily costs were falling drastically and that, 'broadly speaking, it was true to say that the Army had melted away as rapidly as available shipping and political conditions had permitted'.[24] The zeal with which a return to balanced budgets was pursued through military economies set a precedent for a particular and dangerous feature of later financial crises, which could, as in 1938–39, be induced by diplomatic dangers requiring a show of force.

In addition to immediate constraints on armed strength it soon became clear that preparations for any future war would not be permitted to interfere with normal economic activity, as the introduction of the 'ten-year rule' at the Treasury's request in 1919 indicated. Though this measure could be taken to mean that the forces should prepare for a major war in 1928, economy was maintained until the rule was placed on a rolling daily basis. The 'Geddes Axe' of 1923 imposed the tightest possible definition of the concept that national defence should be organised within balanced budgets. War economics were to be strictly contained within wartime, while peacetime probity redeemed the budgetary and trade deficits of war past and future.

In 1925 this attitude was embodied in a Treasury memorandum circulated to the CID by the chancellor, Winston Churchill.[25] Noting that: 'Fighting departments are always apt to take the standpoint of sons who think their fathers' purses inexhaustible', it claimed that Britain was 'only qualified to bear' the financial burden of the Great War by

> our prudent financial policy in the years before the war. The principal factors were:
>
> 1. A substantial sinking fund.
> 2. Moderate taxation.
> 3. A sound currency.
> 4. Large private savings.
> 5. Highly organised financial markets (including the stock market, the discount market, the foreign exchange market, the insurance markets, &c.).
> 6. Large foreign investments.

The memorandum then demonstrated its intricate composition with the observation that the 'various factors are related together. The markets and the foreign investments were the result of the savings. The savings were increased by the sinking fund, and were not encroached on by taxation.' There was, though, a foundation to this system of interrelationships: 'A sound currency was made possible by a sound budget and was a prerequisite condition of everything.'

However,

> by being used during the war, all this financial machinery was strained. Now we can only maintain a sinking fund by means of very heavy taxation. Heavy taxation falls on profits, and depletes the fund out of which savings are made. Our currency has been depreciated. Our financial markets have declined, partly owing to the decline in savings, partly owing to the adverse effect of an unstable currency on credit operations.

This litany of woe, added to a 'debt so heavy as to be overwhelming' led according to Treasury logic to an inevitable conclusion: 'Recovery from this condition of things cannot be other than slow.' This was because Britain's 'disposable margin of resources . . . is small'. Disposal of debt could only result from the expenditure of a budgetary surplus, or the freeing of profits untaxed because of a balanced budget. At the heart of the Treasury's argument, therefore, was the classical precept that all expenditure amounted to the taking of slices from a cake of fixed size. This axiom of the mid-1920s was to have vast repercussions for rearmament, though by 1938 it would be known within the Treasury to be false. The message to the CID, that any requests for additional funds would upset even the prevailing glacial pace of financial recovery from the previous war, was reinforced by implications for the future. The sum available annually for financial redemption was 'small in proportion to the total debt, but it accumulates at compound interest, so that *the rate of progress increases* [italics in original]. Therefore, the effect of any additional burden placed upon this country's finances is itself cumulative; it prolongs the period of recovery to an extent disproportionate to the amount of money involved.' This was a stroke of genius, sufficient to justify the most pettifogging exercises in budgetary control.

Here was the first articulation of the fourth arm concept, for excessive military expenditure was not only a threat to prosperity: 'even if the question of the material welfare of the people be left on one side and nothing be taken into consideration except the prospect of this country winning the next war, expenditure on armaments in excess of what is absolutely necessary would be highly injurious'. Although the Treasury stated that: 'This conclusion is quite independent of any psychological reaction of armament expenditure on financial markets', nevertheless it was 'a matter on which City opinion has become very sensitive', as evidenced by the 'fact' that: 'Foreign Governments which spend money on increases of armaments find great difficulty in borrowing in London.' The memorandum's concluding sentence neatly combined the threats that military expenditure would pose to both peacetime prosperity and preparedness for war: 'Any suggestion that this country would take part in a new competition in armaments would have a most disastrous effect upon confidence, and greatly weaken the progress of the financial recovery necessary before we can face another war.'

This statement of Treasury policy in the defence sphere was a confident exposition of the doctrine which had arisen from the post-war ideological triumph of the Cunliffe Committee and the concomitant success in reestablishing budgetary orthodoxy. The Treasury was now seeking to establish the firmly liberal doctrine that the economic imperatives of war and peace were distinct, and that it was dangerous to attempt to combine them. Peacetime fiscal probity was portrayed as the bedrock of the economic ability to sustain war.

The logical bases of this argument, which accounted for the success of its coercive power have, however, been misinterpreted. It has recently been argued, accurately, that in the early 1920s, statesmen's 'views were similar to the later doctrine that finance was the fourth arm of defence, although this argument was not specifically adopted until 1926. The government regarded finance as a more important element of power than armed force.'[26] These views were not only similar to the fourth arm doctrine, but the foundation of it. The inference has then been drawn, however, that such an attitude 'misunderstood the relationship between economic strength and military power' as components of national strength to the detriment of the latter, and 'overrated the strategic value of Britain's economy' by 'assuming that whenever necessary this could sustain whatever rearmament its security might require'.[27] This analysis is itself rooted in misunderstanding. The conflict that damaged British military effectiveness was not between the 'distorted . . . importance of financial compared to military factors in power as a whole', but as the documents quoted specifically state, between financial and economic factors.[28]

The two terms are distinct and not interchangeable, a fact understood in Germany which traditionally maintained separate financial and economic departments of state, with the latter as the senior partner. In Britain, the relative importance of the two factors was reversed. The inability of the British Empire to create and sustain massive military power was to be the result of a determination, in the name of sound finance and the restoration of the international trading system, to ignore great economic possibilities in the rearmament field. Churchill's Treasury memorandum was quite clear in seeing 'financial power as the basis of economic power'. Although 'economic power had to be pushed up to the maximum and maintained there', nevertheless 'economic strain was felt above all as a *financial* strain'. This was orthodoxy, which stated the 'supreme importance of financial power as the basis of economic power, and of economic power as the base of military power'.

As war plans were formed in the 1920s, the liberal stranglehold on policy became increasingly apparent in the relationship between the

twin pillars of economic war strategy: blockading the enemy into submission and ensuring British 'staying power' while this policy took
effect. This was an essentially attritional concept appropriate to experience in the First World War. The blockade aspect of this concept had
an obvious military dimension and was covered by the CID's Advisory
Committee on Trade Questions in Time of War. This Committee busied
itself with largely technical questions relevant to blockade, such as
neutrals' rights and the provision of bunkering facilities for warships.
However, it did consider the financial implications in the reports of its
Advisory Committee on Trading and Blockade.

In the Committee's Third Annual Report in 1926, Ralph Hawtrey
at the Treasury[29] set forth his views on these matters in the context
of war against Japan. These were later given general application to all
potential enemies and appeared in the Financial Section of the Fifth
Annual Report in 1929, remaining unchanged thereafter as the basis of
official policy. The gist of this advice was that the function of finance
as a weapon was: 'To employ the dominant position of the London
financial market' to damage the enemy.[30] Hawtrey, though, had little
enthusiasm for such activities. Under the heading 'Remarks', he noted
that:

> Control of the London Market to influence neutrals may drive
> business from the London market and seriously affect our dominant
> position both during and after the war. The whole question must
> be carefully balanced before any control through the London market
> is exercised. The situation would be studied in the first place by the
> Advisory Committee on Trading and Blockade in conjunction with
> the Treasury, who would be instrumental in the formation of the
> Committee, subject to the directions of the Minister.

Hawtrey's comments revealed clearly the division between military
and financial problems, and at the same time suggested a limit to the
authority of the CID, beyond which lay the Treasury's domain. For to
interfere with the London market was to raise concerns about Britain's
own financial position, or 'staying power', and this was the Treasury's
ground.

The Treasury's appropriation of all the financial aspects of defence
ensured that a critical component of war planning was no business of
military experts. Even in the blockade sphere, the strictly technical
nature of the CID's planning was stressed. In his introduction to the
Advisory Committee on Trading and Blockade's Fifth Annual Report,

Lord Salisbury took pains to 'emphasize, however, that the report is entirely without prejudice to the question of policy, which would, of course have to be decided by the Government of the day in accordance with the circumstances of the moment'.[31] If this was not clear enough, Salisbury refined his argument to define his report

> as being in the main a work of codification, and, upon the analogy of the codification with which we are familiar in legislation, implies no judgement on the merits of the thing codified, but merely assembles in a convenient form the experience of the late war. Further than this it would not be right for the Committee to go. It is not for the Committee to determine policy. . . .

The Treasury felt no squeamishness in proffering its advice to successive governments and its dominance ensured that defence needs were never likely to drive financial and economic policy, even in conditions of some danger, and furthermore that planning in war finance and economics would conform to a classical liberal model.

The Advisory Committee on Trading and Blockade noted in its Third Annual Report that the 206th meeting of the CID approved the view of its Standing Sub-Committee on the Co-ordination of Departmental Action on the Outbreak of War: 'That all Sub-Committees enquiring into matters connected with War preparation plans should be instructed to bring their work up to a stage not less than that existing before 1914 before the submission of their next annual report.'[32] It was pointed out in the report that: 'No similar organisation existed in 1914 and the blockade machine had to be developed as the war proceeded under the stress of war conditions.'

The Treasury, though, was in a position to ensure that the next war would be paid for on the assumption that financial conditions would match those that prevailed even before 1914. Crucially, however, the official image of the pre-war financial world was nostalgic and idealised, and the British war plan would be rooted in the premise of the model classical economy, even when pressing and obvious circumstances laid bare the absurdity of its assumptions. Consequently, an analysis of British defence capability between the wars must consider how the official perception of economic well-being was shaped after the Great War, and how this survived the crises of the 1920s and early 1930s to become an integral component of the fourth arm argument as a new war approached. It is a narrative best shaped in terms of gold.

1.2   British attitudes to gold between war and crisis

At the outbreak of the First World War Great Britain was the hub around which the international financial system revolved. Britain was evidently no longer the workshop of the world, but there was no disputing her position as its banker. Thus, although 'Britain's share of world income in 1913 was only about 13 percent [*sic*]',[33] the British held 'nearly one half of the total international investments',[34] and had 'the highest ratio of foreign trade to national income'. These facts, along with the financial impartiality implied by Britain's commitment to free trade, and the convenience of settling international accounts in sterling, helped to ensure that the pound 'provided a very close substitute for gold'.[35] In these circumstances the British influence on the operation of the international gold standard was inevitably great, but the British perspective was that the gold standard worked automatically, according to a theoretical model.

During the nineteenth century all the world's major currencies had become convertible into gold at fixed prices and their values were thus pegged in relation to each other, within narrow limits. It was assumed that imbalances within individual economies would be corrected by automatic inflows and outflows of gold. This mechanism, based on Hume's price-specie flow model,[36] was accepted in its most simplistic form by the Cunliffe Committee, and it has been suggested that this was because of Lord Cunliffe's limited but happy experience of buoyant pre-First World War financial conditions, beginning in 1911 as deputy governor and then from 1913 governor of the Bank of England.[37] However, the Cunliffe Committee's stress on the intellectual purity of the mechanism was mistaken.

Before the First World War the gold standard was not a concept perfectly realised, but an effective system that had developed and expanded as the nineteenth century progressed. It has been observed that it could 'properly be called a "gold standard" system, in so far as the arrangements of the several countries fitted together in a reasonably coherent way, even though no one had consciously designed it, and even though no international agency administered it, assisted it, or brooded about it'.[38]

The Bank of England, because of the sheer scale of international holdings of sterling and London's position as 'the world's premier money, capital and commodity market',[39] could exert an enormous 'pull on the exchanges'[40] and ensure that movements in the British balance of payments responded directly to rises and falls in its discount or 'Bank' rate. This meant that in British eyes the gold standard appeared to work as perfectly as the model suggested, it being 'thought at the time, and afterwards, that Bank Rate was a weapon of immense power, able to pull gold from the ends of the earth'.[41] The model, however, was simplistic in the extreme and took no account of the potentially dangerous limitations of actual British reserves of gold and foreign currency, which were disguised by London's ability to command assistance from other central banks in times of financial crisis.[42]

The success of the British monetary authorities in getting by on low stocks of gold at a time of international monetary cooperation was to prove unrepeatable in the fractured world after 1918. But equally importantly for British war potential, low stocks of gold and foreign exchange in pre-war Britain, when measured against London's power to attract funds, revealed a disinterested attitude to the metal itself. In the British official mind gold was valued because it made the system work, not for its intrinsic monetary worth, and from a position of monetary equilibrium the accumulation of gold was no more to be desired than its loss. Experience appeared to teach that the true value of gold lay in its utility or even its symbolic value, as monetary adjustments often occurred in the mere expectation of gold movements. The gold standard achieved its mythical status over years of operation until, as Ralph Hawtrey, writing in 1926, observed: 'Economists have been inclined to teach that this usage is so firmly established that it approximates to a moral principle, as if the use of a metallic currency were somehow essential to honest dealing.'[43]

A fact of critical importance for the inter-war years was that Britain had not been forced to use its gold as a hoard of wealth during the First World War, because of the availability of loans in the United States. These were used to help finance the war effort of Britain and her allies, but also to support sterling, an activity disliked by the Americans who made 'frequent and urgent requests that the British find some other way to support the rate than through the use of American advances'.[44] Such requests fell on deaf ears and the use of American money, together with the fact that the cost of insuring gold for shipment became prohibitive with the growth of the U-boat menace, ensured that Britain's reserves, actually smaller than in 1939, proved sufficient.

This peculiar set of circumstances would not recur, as war debt default provoked the Johnson Act of 1934 forbidding US loans to war debtors, a situation reinforced by the subsequent Neutrality Acts. In the 1920s, however, it seemed that the best way to secure supplies from the US in future war was to pay the colossal debt and restore Britain's international financial reputation. No precedent existed to suggest that Britain's gold reserves might actually be needed for their intrinsic worth, to buy where sterling was not accepted. There was also the attraction that dependence on US supply did not involve any compromise of liberal ideology. With the return of peace the undamaged prestige of gold overwhelmed the concept that imperial resources should be developed to the point where a vast dollar debt need not again be incurred.

The attitude of 1918 to the gold standard was a strange parody of the pre-war perspective. A functional mechanism had been raised to the status of a law of nature, whilst the cheerfully utilitarian attitude to gold as a metal was retained.[45] The consequences of this belief would be very grave, especially in conjunction with another manifestation of the 1918 mental framework, the inherited tendency to equate sterling with gold. Confidence in the pre-war status of sterling 'as a close substitute for gold' did not simply mean that it performed some of the same functions by proxy, but that it possessed as well many of the attributes that made gold universally convertible. The sheer presence of sterling as the currency of the largest Empire in human history ensured that it had to be used for the convenience of world trade, and was desirable to hold because it was backed by obvious and enormous physical wealth.

Sterling was not a complete substitute for gold because its value depended on the strength it was seen to represent, while the intrinsic value of gold lay in its scarcity. This fundamental distinction was most obviously manifest in times of crisis. Whereas the value of gold would naturally increase during a crisis threatening British power, that of sterling would naturally fall, unless determined political steps were taken to preserve that power and control the exchanges. The First World War did not make this fundamental relationship clear, although the cost of its concealment was the mountain of dollars borrowed to support sterling.

To equate gold with sterling was to link the gold standard to British prestige. The emotional appeal of such a system was great, as it went without saying that Britain's well-being was indissolubly linked to the economic health of the world. The Cunliffe Committee, in rejecting the appeals of its witnesses to consider economic practices current in other countries, stated that 'we would point out that these countries have not in practice maintained the absolutely free gold market which this country, by reason of the vital importance of its position in international finance, is bound to do'.[46]

In the years before 1931 the weaknesses of the gold standard as a regulator of international trade would be revealed fully, and its collapse in September of that year left ample time for an economic system to be evolved which was more closely fitted to the core economic strength of the Empire and more able to face the challenge of the multi-polar world of the 1930s. Unfortunately, the grave danger of employing liberal ideology as a basis for war finance remained hidden in the government machine until Hitler uncovered it.

1.3   American attitudes to gold and the onset of crisis

The British authorities understood that the post-war world was much changed, and the emergence of the United States as the dominant economic power was evident. However, Americans prized the gold standard as highly as the British and were equally keen to see its restoration worldwide. Nevertheless, the price of gold at $20.67 an ounce was too low to induce gold producers to sell to central banks, so that the amount of gold available to back the currencies of the world economy was essentially fixed at a level inadequate for the purpose.[47]

This scarcity led to the development of a 'gold exchange' standard, pushed hard by the British but disliked by the Americans, whereby the reserves of many of the world's central banks were held in currencies legally convertible into gold, a means of economising on the metal that would suffice unless holders of these currencies exercised their right to convert. If this happened, the monetary authorities of gold standard countries would be deluged with demands for gold unconnected with the state of their own economies but which, according to gold standard theory, would have to be met by contraction of their money supplies to match the loss of gold and, hopefully, reverse the process.

The inadequate supply of monetary gold was compounded by its maldistribution. The British knew that the United States had captured a sizeable proportion of the world's gold during the war. The Cunliffe Committee was told that the Federal Reserve's holdings increased nearly tenfold from $48,264,000 in December 1914 to $415,798,000 in December 1918,[48] and though large movements of gold in and out of the US occurred between the wars the legal reserve requirement of the Federal Reserve ensured that a vast amount remained consistently in America as backing for the huge American money supply. In addition, post-war international conditions favourable to American finance ensured that: 'In the 1920s the United States thus became a gigantic sink for the gold reserves of the rest of the world.'[49]

Technical problems with gold were compounded by economic nationalism, exacerbated by the war. This led to 'the attempt of each of the main powers to secure for itself a disproportionate share of the world's limited stock of monetary gold'.[50] Throughout the 1920s America in particular pursued its national interest with insufficient regard for new financial responsibilities, and its accumulation and sterilisation of gold risked a deflationary contraction of the money supply amongst its debtors. Washington failed to perceive these dangers, and believed by the mid-1920s that in the 'three interlocking components' of the 'Dawes Plan, the debt settlements, and the gold standard'[51] it had established lasting machinery for 'European recovery on an open-door, capitalist basis, conducive to U.S. economic penetration'.[52] In Europe, Uncle Sam became 'Uncle Shylock'.[53]

The British, experienced and internationalist, were conscious of the US Federal Reserve's 'slim qualifications for the world monetary leadership that fate had thrust upon it'.[54] The return to the gold standard in November 1925, therefore, gave London every chance to prove the thesis developed in 1918, that the influence of British finance and the effectiveness of the gold standard mechanism could restore order to the world economy. Indeed, the return to gold was an initial success in terms of the immediate objectives of the British authorities, which were the 'attainment of sterling parity, the reversal of the gold flow to the United States, and the realignment of United States and British prices'.[55] The deflationary effect of the overvalued parity of $4.86 on the British economy was obscured by renewed confidence in London as a centre of international trade. The events of the late 1920s, however, would expose the structural weaknesses of the gold standard system and test beyond endurance the British belief that their economic health depended upon its operation.

While the US exercised an irresistible pull on the world's capital through its gold holdings, trade surplus and creditor status, British finance could do little to compete and this became more true after 1928 when the effects of the stock market boom in America and the pegging of the French 'franc Poincaré' below its real value made themselves felt. These events led to a drain of the world's capital to the USA and much of its remaining gold to Paris, where French reserves increased by £80 million in 1929 alone, a figure 'the equivalent of the world's output of new gold for a year'.[56] This situation was sustainable only as long as the USA was willing to lend further funds to its debtors in order that they might remain on a gold exchange standard and avoid a catastrophic contraction of their currencies.

When the Americans perceived in 1929 and 1930, under the influence of their own accelerating financial crisis, that their debtors were in an increasingly poor position to repay further loans, they simply stopped lending, and in 1931 the United States actually imported a net $756 million of capital.[57] The consequences of American policy were then revealed in the form of an unstoppable collapse in world prices, as the currencies of US debtors imploded. Many of these nations were primary producers, and the approaching crisis manifested itself in a sharp decline in world agricultural prices.

The consequences of the American withdrawal of credit for primary producers were grim, as they had to 'repay, rather than fund, earlier borrowings at a time when their foreign exchange earnings were beginning to decline'. In the absence of American credit a 'large and sustained outflow of gold from the debtor to the creditor countries' occurred, with South America alone losing $369 million, more than a third of its stock, between the end of 1928 and the end of 1930. By April 1930 nine countries had been forced off the gold standard to prevent the immediate collapse of their currencies, as the world economic crisis fed on itself.

In world agriculture, 'prices fell by about 50 per cent between late 1929 and mid-1931',[58] and a series of bank collapses in Europe and the US led to a huge demand for short-term funds in order to stabilise the world economy. Before the Great War, any such development would have been offset by advances of short-term credit from London balanced by British borrowing from creditor nations. At this time, however, only Great Britain was willing to extend credit and conduct normal financial business, and consequently the whole burden of rescuing the world economy from a disaster of biblical proportions fell on London.

1.4   A chance to rebuild

In the crisis of 1930–31, London was called upon to play its traditional role of alleviating the forces of world depression by providing short-term funds to tide struggling nations over their time of crisis. On this occasion, however, the scale of the problem was unprecedented and the British financial position was weaker than ever before. The British response to pressure for credit was usually automatic and involved separate processes, whereby long-term foreign investment would be reduced in favour of short-term investment, while interest rates were raised to attract foreign capital which was then lent in turn to those demanding credit. The first of these processes was accomplished as before, but the attraction of sufficient foreign investment proved impossible.[59]

In the first place, foreign capital was hard to come by as creditor nations were not lending and banking crises were freezing British claims abroad, for example in Germany where the closure of the banks immobilised £70 million of British short-term assets.[60] Secondly, British interest rates could not be raised to a level sufficient to attract such foreign capital as was available. The British domestic economy had been badly hit by international events, and as more British capital was now invested at home a rise in interest rates would do further damage to the economy. In the absence of foreign capital the international demand for credit fell on existing British reserves which were in no way adequate to bear the burden. These stood at £430 million in June 1930, but between this date 'and December 1931 London lost £350 million of foreign funds',[61] and in the summer of 1931 the rate of loss was phenomenal: 'Between July 15th (the last phase of the sterling crisis) and September 1st 1931 about 200 m. of funds were withdrawn from London.'[62] This was unsustainable, and on 21 September: 'When the gold standard was suspended, the Bank was holding only £134 million in gold and £16 million in foreign exchange.'[63] It was also faced with the repayment of emergency credits worth £130 million at gold standard rates of exchange, received from the United States and France.[64]

In fact, by apparently failing to preserve the order of international finance, the British authorities had stabilised the system and created a new basis for the conduct of international trade. The sense of doom that accompanied sterling's departure from gold dissipated with remarkable rapidity when immediate economic collapse failed to occur. On 15 October 1931 the prime minister was informed by the Treasury that there was 'absolutely no sign of either inflation or hoarding',[65] and in addition to this heartening domestic news the prime minister had been told as early as 6 October by E.R. Peacock, a director of the Bank of

England, that 'on the whole, since we had come off the gold standard, the £ had behaved much better than had been expected' and that sufficient foreign money 'was returning to keep things steady'.[66] A month later, despite the uncertainties produced by a general election, the controller of finance and supply services at the Treasury, Sir Richard Hopkins, was able to tell MacDonald that during the campaign, 'the pound had kept remarkably steady & on the whole surprisingly high'. He concluded that 'there does not appear at the moment to be ground for worry'.[67] Sterling had stabilised with a 30 per cent devaluation against the dollar, ending the reserve drain and improving its competitiveness, a benefit not exclusively British but common to all sterling-based economies.

India and the British colonies were compelled to follow sterling, and the Dominions, with the exception of Canada, were too intricately connected with the British economy to follow any other course. Apart from Canada, 'Australia and New Zealand had already suffered exchange depreciation, and needed to link to sterling to maintain competitiveness in the British market', although the independently minded South Africans suffered a period of economic agony before 'being forced to devalue and peg to sterling for similar reasons'.[68]

Many non-Empire countries shared these imperatives. The benefits of remaining with sterling complemented grave risks in pursuing alternative courses of action: Portugal alone had £50 million of government money in London when sterling came off gold and was typical of a number of smaller independent states in that it pegged to sterling, 'because it was trapped'.[69] In this piecemeal way, the sterling bloc was created, as separate authorities entered a common system to alleviate their shared difficulties.

The British authorities were quick to perceive these consequences of sterling's float. In January 1932 Hopkins, about to become second secretary at the Treasury, responded to a question from the new chancellor, Neville Chamberlain, about 'the possibility of a revival of prosperity starting here (rather than in the United States) spreading to other countries as a prelude to a general revival'.[70] Hopkins' attitude was positive: 'The specific effects of depression in the United States are mainly felt in countries whose currencies are closely linked through the gold standard to the dollar.' Because of this he felt that 'depression in the United States might exist with a very fair degree of general prosperity in the rest of the world'. The agency of this world prosperity could only be Britain, which was 'off gold' and 'to a large extent insulated from depression in the States. Greater prosperity in this country would be shared by the countries from whom we purchase and with whom we are closely linked, especially the Empire, South America and the East.'

British abandonment of the gold standard wrested the economic initiative from the USA and the British authorities knew it. They had, however, washed up in uncharted ideological territory. In the context of British rearmament it has been stated that 'the days of Keynes' "General Theory" were not yet'.[71] The 1930s, though, were quintessentially the days of Keynes before and after the publication of his most famous work, and not just in Britain. He 'was widely respected in Germany by virtue of his well-known position concerning the treaty of Versailles. The Nazis and their entourage were also fond of quoting him at current economic discussions.'[72] Despite Keynes' influence in Germany, a number of German economists were keen to stress an independent and traditional development along the same lines. It has been observed that: 'In 1932 Ernst Wagermann emphasized the independent development of German monetary theory in a reference to Keynes: "Keynes would drop his eyes in shame if he had the opportunity to look into the important writings by Adam Müller, Adolf Wagner and others."'[73]

The independent development of German economic theory was very significant, because while Keynes' ideas conformed with such thinking on the domestic level, in matters of international trade Keynes was a liberal, and his German equivalents very definitely were not. Extreme nationalists, they felt that a national economy should serve the state within a capitalist domestic framework based on private property. From their ideas the Nazi system of autarky was famously developed by Hitler's economics minister Dr Schacht, whereby strictly regulated foreign trade, together with imposed price and wage controls, would end the free convertibility of the state currency in international markets and shield the domestic economy from external pressures.

This policy depended upon the existence of sufficient economic potential within the currency area, and the British already had this on the grandest possible scale. The pound sterling, as its recovery in late 1931 demonstrated, possessed great natural strength as the medium of exchange for a massive global empire which contained much of the world's population and natural riches. The smoothly functioning sterling bloc, the largest and most dynamic of the world's new currency areas, can be contrasted with Hitler's early attempts to create

Mitteleuropa. Initial Nazi efforts at 'the opening up of new markets while hoping to prevent the industrialisation of agrarian countries',[74] were received with an understandable lack of enthusiasm by primary producers supplying Germany who 'quickly grew tired of having to accept typewriters, aspirins and mouth organs in return for their grain'.[75]

Despite the enviable success of the new system formed after the abandonment of the gold standard, the British government and financial authorities had in effect developed a response to prevailing circumstances which, while being perceptive and in many ways technically brilliant, left their core beliefs completely intact. The autarkic potential of the Empire was to be exploited not as the foundation of political and economic hegemony, but as the basis for the restoration of worldwide free trade. Hopkins' memo to Chamberlain concluded with the hope that economic revival within the British economic orbit 'might, I think, communicate itself later, through reviving confidence, to the gold standard world'.[76]

Ralph Hawtrey, the head of the Treasury's Financial Inquiries Branch, wrote in a 1931 appendix to his earlier book on the subject that 'we should absolutely refuse to return to gold till there is some adequate safeguard against undue fluctuations in the purchasing power of gold'.[77] Hawtrey's job made him in effect a spokesman for the Treasury view, and his combination of apparent hostility to gold with the hope of an eventual return to it is reflected almost exactly in a statement made by Neville Chamberlain, before the Ottawa Conference of 1932 that 'we must make it clear that we have no intention of returning to the gold standard unless we can be thoroughly assured that a remedy has been found for the maladjustments which led to the breakdown of that standard last year'.[78]

The British government accepted that the post-war gold standard had been fatally flawed and would not, therefore, seek to re-establish the old system while a handful of nations sought to hoard the world's gold supply, but still they looked forward to a day when gold convertibility might be resumed. There was no suspicion that the correctly identified maladjustments that had wrecked the gold standard may have been expressive of a fundamental change in the relationship between economics and the state.

Shortly after the return to gold in 1925 Hawtrey had rejected without ceremony Keynes' ideas for the establishment of a sterling bloc as an alternative to gold: 'At the present time the logic of facts has disposed of Mr Keynes's proposals. Gold is *de facto* the international currency, and this country must do as others do and adhere to it.'[79] In 1931 he acknowledged that the government was responding to the departure from gold with 'precisely the plan advocated by Mr Keynes'.[80] This did not mean, however, that the sterling bloc as an end in itself should be accepted. Hawtrey stated that 'sterling might really become a rival standard to gold, as Mr Keynes hoped', but continued 'we cannot count on that'.[81] He went on to advocate an eventual return to gold in association with a suitably contrite United States.

As in 1918 the British felt able to reconstruct the international economy, this time on the basis of the sterling bloc, which had developed unexpectedly as a microcosm of the ideal world economy. A floating pound embodied all the advantages of the pre-war gold standard within the area, and it was the system rather than the metal itself which mattered to the British. Gold itself had been brought into disrepute and in 1932 a minority report of the League of Nations Gold Delegation advocated a return to gold only if certain preliminary measures were taken. In Britain: 'Treasury Officials remained skeptical about Britain's power to reflate the world economy either by effort or by example, but they took this list of preconditions to their hearts.'[82] Not least among these was the traditional British opinion that, in peacetime, 'gold mattered only as a way to settle international obligations, and it should be freed for this use'.

The experience of the 1920s had taught Britain that her commitment to gold and free trade was in no way appropriate to the circumstances of the post-war world. The lesson had been absorbed, however, that after the fall from the gold standard the sheer size of sterling holdings around the world and recovery in Britain would help to restore some of sterling's status as an equivalent to gold. The British had in fact begun unconsciously to exert their power, which was based on the size and natural wealth of the Empire, not the liberal system. The events of the 1930s would demonstrate, however, that although Britain's superb technical response to the world collapse left her relatively strong and financially well placed, the retained belief in the ultimate restoration of the gold standard provided a rallying point for British liberals.

There was an ambiguity in the concept of sterling as a replacement for gold in peacetime. Whilst protectionists might think that sterling's impressive solidity after the collapse of gold proved their point, liberals could imagine this to be a survival of the pre-war system when the two were synonymous. This would ultimately prove to be a fatal flaw in the seemingly complete triumph of protectionism and imperial preference in 1932. It was a weakness that would manifest itself to decisive and appalling effect in the defence and strategic spheres. This riposte would be based, paradoxically, on British recovery and facilitated by the influence of internationalists in government, their intellectual cohesion in public life, and perhaps most importantly, the help they would receive from the United States.

2

'On the Upgrade': Britain's Unwelcome Recovery, 1931–36

The fundamental restructuring of the world economy after 1931 restored London's leading role in international finance. This position was left vacant by the spectacular economic collapse of the United States, which had inadvertently undermined the gold-based financial structure essential to its domination of world markets. When this crashed down, 'leaving wreckage strewn across the world',[1] many outcomes became possible. If the new world of blocs promoted warlike political extremism, it was also true that more than ever in the harsh and anarchic new climate, material wealth and economic strength were essential ingredients of power. The British possessed both, and in the early 1930s they used these assets to impose their will on the international economy.

However, the parlous American position after 1931 remains understated as an ingredient of British power. American economic preponderance is assumed, even by revisionists who argue that 'economic determinists' overlook Britain's global presence and existing forces, and 'that the reality of British power was more important and more effective than was American potential'.[2] This is true but to express the scale of British power in terms of 'a superiority of two to one in cruisers over the United States'[3] in 1939 is to ignore the fact that the worldwide British presence was of great economic, as well as military, significance. The growth potential of the United States, though vast and concentrated, was by the same token confined within its own borders and, given its matching diplomatic and military introspection, the nation required a functioning global financial system to exert its influence across oceans. The trading significance of America's gold hoard diminished after sterling, the world's major reserve currency, went off gold. In economic as well as military terms, the isolationist, disarmed and

24

geographically remote USA was effectively a regional power without, in the 1930s, the physical power or financial leverage even to collect its foreign debts.

The impact of 1931 can be seen in Britain's dynamic economic performance and the recovery of the Empire before the outbreak of the Second World War. Not least amongst these gains were the possibilities created for imperial defence. Economic growth was of great strategic importance, as it increased war potential and facilitated British rearmament. It was imperative for British security, as well as British prosperity, that nothing should undermine the new international system. However, the United States realised with a clarity born of harsh experience that Britain's gain was its loss. Consequently, in the years between sterling's departure from gold and the outbreak of war the Americans sought to bring sterling back into a fixed relationship with the dollar, do away with the Ottawa system of preferences and the sterling bloc, and thereby regain economic hegemony.

In pursuit of these goals the United States was initially powerless, and could only appeal to Britain's liberal conscience. While memories of 1931 were fresh, such proposals were rejected scornfully, especially by the chancellor of the exchequer, Neville Chamberlain, who thought 'that we have the misfortune to be dealing with a nation of cads'.[4]

In 1934, the State Department's British Empire Committee sought ways of disrupting the new British system but found none in existing circumstances. By 1936 the American authorities were coming to realise that the British position could only be undermined from within, and Cordell Hull's propaganda offensive against the Ottawa system, which began in January of that year, was perfectly timed to assist those forces within the British establishment and public life which had never been reconciled to the new economic order of the 1930s. Their influential position in the machinery of British government then became of crucial importance, and Hull's campaign, along with the Tripartite Agreement of September 1936 to stabilise pound, dollar and franc, gave the necessary impetus for a drive against Ottawa.

2.1 The economic foundations of strategic strength

After the British economy's survival of the 1931 crisis, relief was followed by swift adaptation to changed circumstances. A new emphasis on stimulating the domestic economy was underpinned by a determination to provide consistently cheap credit. The maintenance of an interest rate of 2 per cent was facilitated in 1932 by the introduction of the Exchange Equalisation Account, which managed the floating pound through the manipulation of gold and foreign currency reserves.[5] This was the reverse of the gold standard mechanism which had maintained a stable currency by adjusting Bank Rate. The British economy was further reinforced in 1932 by the introduction of comprehensive protection for industry and agriculture in the Import Duties Act and the Horticultural Products Act, which introduced a global 10 per cent tariff on imports into the UK along with import quotas on agricultural products.

The moderate tariffs and quotas provided for in the Acts could be raised on application by interested parties to the Import Duties Advisory Commission, but the interests of the Empire and the emergent sterling bloc as essential components of the new system were safeguarded. Imports from the Empire were temporarily exempted from the Acts until the Ottawa Agreements of August 1932 formalised privileged access for Empire producers. Subsequent agreements with the other members of the sterling bloc, such as the Roca–Runciman agreement with Argentina in 1933, completed the new economic order of the British world.

These measures answered British and Empire needs perfectly, and the excellent economic performance which followed contrasted visibly with the catastrophe that had overtaken Britain's chief trading rival, the United States. Nevertheless, in the context of rearmament a continuing perception of Britain's inter-war 'weakness' in international trade has overshadowed the resurgence of Britain's economy after 1931, and the current account deficit provided a marvellous excuse for failure in rearmament.[6] In fact, it was a necessary component of British strength and the Treasury knew it.

The competitive benefits of sterling's 1931 devaluation were common to those substantial areas of the world economy which were linked to the currency, and were not limited to the United Kingdom. Similarly, the newly fragmented state of the world economy and the formulation of tariff walls against British goods, even within the Empire, were unquestionably harmful to British exports. With the exception of 1935, the current account of the balance of payments was consistently in deficit in the 1930s, as the demand for imports in the expanding British economy grew and international prices recovered. Before the Great War this might indeed have constituted an alarming state of affairs, but the British economy had changed.

In 1913 imports had accounted for 31.1 per cent of national income, but by 1929 this figure had declined to 26.7 per cent and in 1938 stood at only 17.6 per cent. In the same period exports declined from 23.2 to 9.8 per cent of national income.[7] Thus it can be seen that between 1913 and 1938 the gap between imports and exports expressed as a percentage of national income was virtually unchanged. This was because the decline of exports relative to imports took place within the context of a declining percentage share of both figures within national income.[8] In other words, the importance of the balance of payments to the United Kingdom was declining in relation to that of the domestic economy. This fact reveals a central truth of the inter-war years, that the British economy was experiencing transformation rather than decline.[9] Redirection of investment was hardly surprising in the troubled trading conditions of the inter-war years. In the 1920s, high rates of interest and official discouragement of foreign lending concomitant with the return to gold[10] attracted funds to London, and after 1931 it became safer to invest capital at home rather than abroad in a world of defaulting debtors.

The effects of the restructuring of the British economy visible in the balance of payments figures were also evident in the figures for capital formation and growth of national income, especially after 1931. Net domestic fixed capital formation, including investment of funds in British industry that might before the First World War have gone abroad, increased steadily in the inter-war years. In the 1920s this reflected the imposition of controls on foreign lending designed to prop up sterling, but after 1931 domestic investment was a central pillar of economic recovery. In the years 1934–38, net domestic fixed capital formation reached its highest levels of the inter-war years, and exceeded £200 million (at 1938 prices) in each of the years 1936–38.[11]

This level of investment made possible extremely impressive economic growth and, despite the deficit on the balance of payments current account, the decline in national income caused by the Depression was more than reversed by 1934. In that year the net national product (gross national product minus capital depreciation) grew by more than 7 per cent (at 1938 prices) before settling to an impressive average of 3.45 per cent growth between 1935 and 1939.[12] This was a virtuous circle as growth made possible further investment which made possible further growth, and British figures are still more impressive when contrasted with those of the United States, which ran a surplus on current account. Having 'cast off the gold standard', Britain 'enjoyed a rate of economic recovery that far surpassed that of the United States'.[13] Comparison of growth figures shows this to be no overstatement. Gross domestic product in Britain grew by an average 2.3 per cent per annum between 1929 and 1937, whereas that of the United States was no higher in 1938 than in 1929. Between 1929 and 1937, British industrial production grew by 3.4 per cent per annum compared to 0.4 per cent for the US economy in the same period.[14] On the basis of these figures[15] it has been justly asserted that: 'During the 1930s (1929–37) the tide ran strongly in Britain's favour', and that compared with 'different time spans . . . the interwar years and especially the 1930s were more favourable to this country than periods either before or after'.[16]

Strong growth helped Britain's financial position by increasing the attractiveness of sterling for foreign investors which, allied to the advantages of the sterling bloc, ensured that foreign currency and gold continued to flow into London. The seemingly paradoxical increase in the strength of sterling as Britain's trade gap widened demonstrated the fundamental strength of Britain's economic position in the 1930s. The British economy could afford to run a current account deficit at no risk to domestic economic stability, and in fact a current account deficit contributed to the steadiness of the economy by preventing demand-pull inflation. Germany, by contrast, lacking Britain's access to overseas supply was to experience severe 'overheating' of its economy by 1938, as demand outstripped productive capacity. In Britain, the fear of classical economists was that a balance of payments deficit would drain gold and foreign currency reserves and thus devalue the currency. The emergence of the sterling bloc and the system of tariffs introduced in early 1932 and at Ottawa prevented any such development.

Although short-term foreign capital entering Britain might well disappear in a crisis, if this were permitted by the British authorities, the reserves of sterling area economies were held predominantly in sterling in London. Sterling could not depreciate against currencies which were pegged to it, and a trade deficit with these economies, as the economist Hubert Henderson observed in 1932, would have the effect of increasing their London balances and strengthening the pound on the international exchanges.[17] The USA, furthermore, had made it clear in 1933 that it would use its reserves to prevent any significant decline of sterling relative to the dollar.

The move towards greater trade within the sterling area, as against the dollar-based economies, increased British financial strength. Although depression had reduced international trade after 1929, British imports from the Empire remained constant in value between 1929 and 1936, while imports from the rest of the world declined and imports from the United States more than halved. In the same period Britain's exports to non-Empire countries were more than halved in value, but exports to the Empire, which fell by less than a quarter, spared Britain from the full effects of the Depression.[18]

During the recovery an increasing proportion of the current account deficit was incurred with the sterling area in pounds, and the economic strength of the area as reflected in level of the sterling relative to such currencies as the dollar and the franc, continued to grow.[19] The new intra-imperial trading bloc based on British growth was, therefore, of mutual benefit to its members not only during the Depression but also during recovery. This was by no means an invisible phenomenon and it became increasingly obvious over time, embarrassingly so to economic liberals who reacted instinctively against the idea that the Ottawa system might prove permanently beneficial to Britain, despite its evident success. In a report to the Cabinet in 1936, the government's chief economic advisor, Sir Frederick Leith-Ross, acknowledged that the growth of the economy was the prime cause of the current account deficit and the strength of sterling and admitted that: 'in practice the effect of the balance of payments on the exchanges may for long periods be outweighed by the influence of more powerful factors'.[20]

The self-reinforcing economic strength of the sterling bloc has now been perceived by economic historians, but not its implications for Britain's great power status in the 1930s. As the balance of payments has overshadowed more relevant information in the rearmament debate, so economic historians have not fully considered the strategic implications of Britain's economic resurgence in the 1930s. It has been noted that British 'gentlemanly capitalists' encouraged tariff discrimination against British exporters within the sterling area so that local production could generate the revenues necessary to continue debt repayments to London.[21] The figures quoted above, however, demonstrate that British production was not sacrificed to benefit bankers, but redirected to the domestic market. This development was in the interests of rearmament, especially in industries at the 'cutting edge' of technology, but it was also beneficial for industrial development to occur in the Empire, increasing imperial strength.

Industrialisation outside the United Kingdom should be considered as a logical organic development of the imperial economy.[22] The notion that the metropolis should forever provide manufactures in exchange for the raw materials of the underdeveloped world was a most brutal and dated form of imperialism, associated at this time with the United States and expressed repeatedly in the free trade sermons of Cordell Hull, who complained to Sir Ronald Lindsay that British policy 'was every week rapidly driving all food and raw material producing nations to a policy of industrialization and that no matter how cruel this might be it was wholly and hopelessly uneconomic from everybody's standpoint'.[23] This view was effectively summarised by Leo Amery: 'Cordell Hull really represents mid-nineteenth century vision on economics, coupled no doubt with the desire to create an American export hegemony in the world.'[24] Amery shared with his mentor Lord Milner a belief 'in the "natural harmony" between the colonies and the metropole and refused to acknowledge that any conflict could arise because of development'. Amery stated plainly that 'we cannot develop them [the colonies] and help them without an over-spill of wealth and prosperity that would be an immense help to this country . . .'.[25] A desire 'to develop the Empire and break decisively with the prevailing orthodoxy of *laissez-faire*'[26] could therefore be seen from a moral as well as economic perspective. Churchill's free-trading principles were combined with a crudely derogatory attitude towards the coloured peoples of the Empire, which created friction with Amery when he became secretary of state for India.

It has also been argued, again in an echo of contemporary thinking, that the sterling bloc was sufficient to ensure the economic stability of the Empire but 'was simply not big enough or influential enough to offer a cure for an ailing world economy in the 1930s'.[27] Such an endeavour, though, was in no way relevant to Britain's task. This was to reconstruct its defences without wrecking its economy or sacrificing its international economic position to the United States. Sound foundations were laid after 1931, and by 1936 these had been built on with great success.

2.2   American problems

The United States was at the heart of the Depression and had no means of insulating itself from its effects. Despite the physical self-sufficiency of the United States economy, overcapacity in primary production actually made dependence on foreign markets, and the British Empire in particular, a fact of American political life in the 1930s. This situation was not new: Andrew Mellon, then secretary of the Treasury, had 'observed in 1923 that with a "balance" among industries, the United

States could do without exports. He admitted, however, that such a balance did not exist',[28] and when depression came it still did not exist. A balance did exist, though, in trade between the United States and the British Empire,[29] although the composition of this trade was unhelpful. The United Kingdom itself ran a continuous deficit on visible trade with the United States. Protected US manufacturers purchased raw materials from the British Empire and exported finished goods to the UK, which in turn exported its manufactures to parts of the Empire enjoying a trade surplus with the United States. This triangular pattern of trade enabled American manufacturers to maintain the value of their exports to Great Britain between 1929 and 1936, though this was no comfort to agriculture.

American farmers and primary producers had to export their surpluses to the United Kingdom, which in the mid-1930s imported 'more than a third of the world's exports of wool, motor spirit, iron and steel, wheat and maize; more than half of the world's exports of eggs and cheese; three-quarters of the beef exported; and very nearly all the mutton, bacon, ham and pork'.[30] The protection of the British market for such undifferentiated products, along with sterling devaluation, hit American exports hard at a time when the position of American primary producers was already desperate. The political consequences of this situation could not be overstated. After the election of Franklin D. Roosevelt, New Deal politicians saw the American Depression squarely in terms of a collapse in agricultural prices and sought the salvation of the farmer as the key to US recovery.

In 1933, however, the American economy was entirely incapable of absorbing its agricultural production and unrest was growing. On 9 May, Roosevelt was told by the governor of Minnesota that 'unless something were done at once farmers in his state would resist any attempts at foreclosures. In Iowa they already had.'[31] Henry Morgenthau Jr, then head of the Farm Credit Administration, recalled that 'the smell of revolution was in the air' and that 'we had to do something about farm prices . . . and we had to act fast'.[32] Practical solutions, however, were not easy to find and domestic measures did not permanently raise prices. To dispose of its farm surplus, the Roosevelt Administration was forced to address the fundamental realities of its trading position, namely 'the dominating commercial problem of the United States – our relations with the British Empire'.[33]

Roosevelt's task in finding agreement with the British was not helped by his early actions as president, when the domestic aspects of the New Deal took priority. In March and April 1933 the president executed a series of measures which temporarily removed the United States from the gold standard and devalued the dollar. His aims were to raise US prices, aid exports and thus end the agricultural Depression. Such considerations were not foremost in British minds, however, and when the export of US gold was prohibited on 19 April 1933, the prime minister and a team of senior civil servants were travelling to the United States to discuss currency stabilisation with Roosevelt prior to the World Economic Conference.

Sir Frederick Leith-Ross saw the American action as an attempt at 'a competitive depreciation of the dollar with the pound', and when asked by MacDonald how to respond recommended that 'our best course would be, on arrival in New York, to transship to the *Mauritania* (which was due to leave New York the same day) and go home, as the American action made nonsense of all the plans for the Conference'.[34] The visit went ahead, but Roosevelt's actions in 1933 angered all shades of British opinion, including liberal idealists whose support the USA would soon need. Though prepared to act ruthlessly and quickly to gain an advantage, he had already reached the limits of unilateral American action.

The sheer scale of US gold and currency reserves meant that the president could choose any pound–dollar rate he pleased, but could only really prevent competitive British devaluation. Forcing the pound down would simply damage American competitiveness. Pushing the pound above a certain level by devaluing again would, as the reaction of the internationalist Leith-Ross demonstrated, be regarded as a hostile act. Roosevelt had only to compare the moderate levels of existing British tariffs with those of his own country to know that considerable increases and extensions to imperial preference were possible. Given its desperate need to export, and its already prohibitive levels of protection, America was likely to lose any tariff war.

Within the Empire, the situation was clearly perceived as a struggle for supremacy between the pound and the dollar. Sir Ernest Oppenheimer, speaking in the South African Parliament, made the position clear: 'There is no such thing as financial independence, and there is no such thing as a natural currency system.'[35] He concluded that South Africa faced a stark choice 'between one managed currency – sterling – and another – the gold dollar'. There was very little that the Americans could do to influence such decisions except to ensure that the dollar was as competitive as it could be against the pound and to hope that the British would return to a system of fixed exchange rates and in some way modify the new tariff system.

The development of the world economic system after the British abandonment of gold exacerbated the American Depression, while reducing dramatically America's ability to influence international economic developments in her favour. Ultimately, economic concessions on the part of the British Empire were essential if the American economy were ever to recover. With no weapons to hand, the USA resorted to propaganda.

Roosevelt's secretary of state, Cordell Hull, had been marginalised and indeed scorned by his government as the American delegate to the World Economic Conference, but his rehabilitation after this point revealed Roosevelt's shift to a more internationally minded policy.[36] Having steered his Trade Agreements Act through Congress by June 1934, Hull was encouraged to take it to the world, and as an accord with Britain would be the most valuable of all possible trade agreements Hull became the spearhead of American attempts to negotiate a revision of British trading practices to American advantage.[37] In September 1934, preliminary studies of the issue were made in the State Department by a specially constituted British Empire Committee. Its language did not evoke the comity of nations.

The Committee speculated that in the long term 'if a successful attack can be made upon the Ottawa Agreements, the strategic point of attack would be Canada'.[38] In the short term a 'program for immediate action should explore the possibilities of bilateral treaties with the British Empire countries under the limitations imposed by the Ottawa Agreements'. To this end, it was thought best to 'contemplate bargaining item by item, with a minimum of national planning and a maximum of opportunism'.[39] Despite these aggressive intentions it was realised that overtly intimidating behaviour carried risks. The possibility of threatening Canada during negotiations was raised. This

method of attack would be to offer concessions, but to back these up with the threat that if the Ottawa agreements are not renounced in the interest of a satisfactory trade agreement with the United States, this country would enter upon a policy of counter-discrimination against Canada. It could be argued that the imperial preference system amounts in reality to unfair discrimination against foreign countries. It could be argued that the whole imperial preference system has no standing in international law, particularly in view of the fact that the Dominions have in recent years achieved a status in international law as independent nations. Thus, the Dominions are recognised as separate countries by the League of Nations and by the Statute of Westminster.[40]

Canada's special measures against the USA 'would appear to be a clear case of discrimination which might well justify retaliatory treatment'. In this case: 'The program of retaliation might be extended and include the United Kingdom. This would involve the denunciation of our treaty of 1815, requiring a year's notice. Action proposed against Canada might be applied against all the Empire countries.' However,

any threat of trade war on the British Empire would react unfavourably on the immediate program of domestic and world-wide recovery. The very denouncement [sic] of our treaty with England or the threat of a trade war with Canada would be likely to strengthen deflationary tendencies. In the third place it is more than questionable whether a threat of discrimination on our part would be adequate to bring results. Indeed, there is a danger that such a proposal would inflame and strengthen jingoistic and nationalistic and protectionistic [sic] sentiment in Canada and the various British Empire countries, thereby solidifying and increasing the British imperial system.[41]

The outlook for America in 1934 appeared to be bleak. The British Empire Committee had appraised the situation with complete accuracy. It wished to destroy the British imperial economic system, but Washington possessed no power of coercion and any attempt was likely to strengthen the Ottawa system. Negotiation also seemed unpromising as there was no obvious imperative for British concessions, and no prospect at all of American producers making such reciprocal gestures as would tempt even British liberals in the direction of a trade agreement. The Committee's impressions were reinforced by a conversation between Under-Secretary of State Phillips and future Washington ambassador Lord Lothian on one of the latter's many visits to the USA.

Lothian expressed himself, according to the evidence of Phillips' report, frankly.[42] MacDonald, as a result of Roosevelt's actions in 1933, 'was now the "laughing stock of the British public", wholly discredited. It was natural, therefore, that he should be sore and not well disposed to this country.' Baldwin, after his attempt to renegotiate Britain's American debt in 1923, 'had been tainted by failure ever since. He was, therefore, not well disposed towards this country.' Lothian characterised the most significant developing partnership in Cabinet in equally unflattering terms. 'Sir John Simon he characterised as a "fish"' who, despite not being 'so hopeless as he would appear on first impression . . . was not a man on whom cordial relations could rest.' The heir apparent, 'Chamberlain represented a purely local point of view; he was not internationally minded and, although a brilliant man, could not be counted upon to favor cooperation with the United States.'

Clearly, Lothian's reputation as a catalyst for improved Anglo-American relations was not earned by fostering respect for his government. Indeed, even at the political grass roots Lothian was not enamoured of his countrymen. 'Englishmen', though interested in the New Deal, 'were not convinced, however, of its ultimate success; they felt that the United States was still on the downward spiral, and that until the bottom was reached and the movement upwards begins, there was no disposition to join hands with the United States in any economic program'.

Lothian stated, almost regretfully, that 'present British policies towards international trade were still effective and conditions throughout the British Isles were still on the upgrade'. However, 'Lord Lothian thought that this upward movement would cease before many months and that thereupon and thereafter the British Government would be more favourably disposed to discuss ways and means with other countries to do away with barriers to international trade.' Unfortunately for Lothian, British conditions continued on the upgrade, with no end in sight.

American fortunes would change with the deteriorating diplomatic situation. Hitler's renunciation of Versailles and announcement of rearmament in 1935 provided an obvious British interest in friendly relations with the United States. Initially, however, this did not suggest the purchase of American goodwill with economic concessions. In 1936, on the contrary, the official British reason for treating American approaches with caution was that the deteriorating diplomatic position of the British Empire made it essential for Britain to strengthen the Ottawa system and reject any liberalisation of her international economic situation. From this position, the subsequent British volte-face was remarkable, and its causes can be found in the internal struggles of the British governmental machine.

2.3   Limiting factors in the perception and consolidation of British strength

In May 1931, the prime minister was shocked to discover that the League of Nations Agricultural Credit Scheme, which required a British financial contribution, had been approved by the Treasury and the Foreign Office together and the necessary credit arranged. Alerted to this development, MacDonald, in a strongly worded reply to a memorandum from Sir Robert Vansittart, expressed his surprise that the matter 'appears to have been under consideration for some time & has not been brought up to the Cabinet'. He 'knew nothing of this', and went on to describe how he had seen 'the Chancellor at once & heard that he had just approved though with hesitation, & had wired Geneva. Up to then I had seen no papers.' The prime minister then asserted that the matter was 'an issue of first class importance' which 'cannot be decided between Departments'[43] and must be addressed by the Cabinet.

Although the prime minister, on this occasion, exercised his authority, the incident revealed several themes which would be of importance in the course of finance and diplomacy in the 1930s. The difficulty of exercising political control over departmental ideology was particularly significant. As the Dominions secretary, J.H. Thomas, pointed out, the scheme so swiftly approved by the Foreign Office and the Treasury sought by creating a 'convenient geographical bloc' to 'range Europe economically against the rest of the world',[44] and that 'while as an individual State the United Kingdom is part of Europe, she is also, as a member of the British Commonwealth of Nations a part of the rest of the world'. Thomas asserted that for Britain to have adopted such a scheme would have been to 'lay us open to the charge of having thrown over the Empire in the interests of Europe just at the time when we profess ourselves as anxious to develop a scheme of Imperial economic co-operation'.[45]

The Treasury attitude to imperial unity was expressed in a letter sent by Sir Frederick Leith-Ross to the Foreign Office, before MacDonald got wind of the scheme. Speaking on behalf of the Lords Commissioners of the Treasury, Leith-Ross stated that:

> In their Lordships' view it would be better from every point of view that His Majesty's Government in the United Kingdom at the appropriate moment should take a definite decision, on the merits of the scheme as they affect the interests of this country and leave

the Dominion Governments to express any views which they may hold on the subject as independent members of the League of Nations.[46]

Unfortunately for their Lordships, 'every point of view' did not coincide with their own, and with the political mood of the country swinging so heavily in favour of imperial economics, such a brazen attempt to bypass Parliament and Cabinet on a prominent issue invited censure.

The issue was not, however, an isolated attempt by officials to drive policy: its singular features were the clumsiness of the manoeuvre, its openness and the effective opposition it provoked. The affair was illustrative of developments in the British system of government in the twentieth century and the effects that these had on the process of political decision making. The changing shape of the governmental machine, in conjunction with developments in party politics, gave rise to a situation between the wars in which the true power-political interests of the British Empire were inadequately recognised, and in which the lack of an effective political voice to define and defend these interests resulted in the success of a liberal view almost by default.

The pre-First World War Liberal reform programme and the enormous demands upon government caused by the war created an unprecedented administrative machine, uncomfortable to a professional Civil Service that had been schooled in the essentially legal functions of a state dedicated on 'laissez-faire' principles to 'three classic activities – the maintenance of internal law and order, the defence of the realm, and the conduct of external relations'.[47] This view was reasserted after the Great War when the 'back to 1914' movement swept away most of the administrative machinery created in the war. Ironically, that which survived was to prove of enormous assistance to civil servants in the assertion of their traditional opinions. Official attitudes were also preserved by the division of Civil Service into an elite administrative class, closely concerned with the formulation of policy, and a subordinate executive class, which dealt with the technical work of departments.

Much remained that could not be undone. Even the 1914 state had been far more complex than that of 1900, and many wartime innovations became permanent features of government. This was reflected in the survival of the Cabinet Secretariat, which had developed from the War Cabinet Secretariat, and was sustained by its secretary, Maurice Hankey, 'despite opposition in certain quarters – notably the Asquith liberal press – to the idea'.[48] The Secretariat constituted a response to the rapidly increasing volume of government business, and by delegating much of the policy-making process to a system of sub-committees it sought to ensure that the scale of work that reached Cabinet was manageable and to prevent 'Cabinet time being taken up by matters of minor importance'.[49] This rather begged the question of who precisely should decide what was, or was not, a matter of minor importance.

A consequence for ministers of the increased workload was that their departments could no longer be run like offices, a situation which caused them to depend increasingly upon the advice of their senior civil servants and on the information prepared by them. In 1937, for example, Frank Ashton-Gwatkin at the Foreign Office sent a draft to Sir Frederick Leith-Ross of a memorandum to be circulated under Foreign Secretary Anthony Eden's name calling for a wholesale revision of the Ottawa system.[50] Although this document was framed in the first person singular, Eden had not yet seen it.

Leith-Ross queried whether the request it contained for a Cabinet Committee to consider trade policy revision was intended to be composed of ministers or officials. Leith-Ross felt that only a ministerial committee would do. Later when Eden approached Chamberlain with the final memorandum he stressed that he wanted a ministerial committee to consider the issue. Upon considering a memorandum from Leith-Ross, Warren Fisher added in his own hand the opinion that a committee of officials should in fact precede that of the ministers in order to present the latter with a considered view of the technicalities of the matter. Shortly afterwards Chamberlain replied to Eden that he thought it best for a committee of officials to precede the ministerial committee. Thus an approach to a major question of policy, apparently decided in a ministerial exchange of views, was in fact the sole work of the chief economic adviser to HMG and the permanent head of the Civil Service, although the systematic normality of such practice was such that of all the parties involved, perhaps only Leith-Ross was aware of the fact.

Also, the proliferation of subcommittees reflected the fact that departments had to cooperate on complex issues such as in the foreign, economic and defence spheres, and most liaison of this nature on the policy level would take place between civil servants of the administrative class. Lord Bridges, a Treasury man who replaced Hankey as Cabinet secretary on his way to becoming head of the Civil Service, noted that the 'experience of anyone who has worked in Whitehall is that there is an early stage in any project when things are fluid; when, if you are in touch with those concerned and can get hold of the facts, it is fairly easy to influence decisions'.[51] The influence of politicians could be diminished if officials combined to shape policy before Cabinet had a chance to consider alternatives.

In Cabinet, if a politician found himself in accord with Civil Service opinion in the formulation and prosecution of policy, the active assistance of the administrative machine would greatly enhance his political influence. It was much easier to swim with the tide of 'expert' advice than against it. To carry their views against officials, politicians had to be vigilant, determined and united. These qualities were lacking in the field of imperial and defence economics for a variety of reasons, and with melancholy results.[52]

In the immediate aftermath of the war sufficient of the wartime spirit of imperial unity and national planning survived to dilute the pure concept of free trade. The introduction of some preferential duties for imperial produce and the Safeguarding Act of 1921, which provided a degree of protection for British industries struggling in the post-war climate, were, however, measures taken very much against the tide of national opinion, both popular and expert, and 'in 1921 and 1922 nobody had any doubt that the path of wisdom lay in promoting the return of gold, as recommended by the Cunliffe Committee'.[53]

The Labour Party, under the influence of Philip Snowden, was committed to a return to gold, and free trade was 'a powerful unifying factor' for the schismatic Liberals.[54] In this climate, the paralysing situation developed whereby 'Liberals realised that the classical precepts no longer applied to the home market but . . . insisted on their application to the international market', while the Tories 'realised that they no longer applied to the international market but insisted on applying them to the home market'.[55] Before 1931, therefore, there could be no coalition between the Conservative and Liberal parties, and any grouping between Labour and the Liberals would, as in 1924, commit the government to free trade.

A curious feature of the 1930s was that after the defeat of classical economics in 1931, the successful new system did not create a political constituency dedicated to its survival. Advocates of an imperial economic structure, such as the Empire Economic Union, were dissatisfied with the post-1931 state of affairs which they saw as being at best an anaemic step in the direction of imperial economic federation. Only a single imperial currency and a far more rigorous tariff structure than that introduced in 1932 could satisfy them, although such measures would have robbed the prevailing situation of much of its self-sustaining flexibility and alienated those parts of the sterling area that were not inside the Empire.

An appeal to the chancellor of the exchequer, Neville Chamberlain, by Leo Amery calling for a single imperial currency was rebuffed by reference to precisely these arguments. Chamberlain summarised the position shrewdly: 'The more I see of this difficult and complicated question the more I am convinced that it would be wrong to lay down rigid rules in conformity with theoretical considerations. There are too many factors in the case which do not lend themselves to theory.'[56] The political philosophy of other protectionist pressure groups, such as the Federation of British Industries, was not broad or deep and was satisfied with the new framework of protection. The Federation in particular could only be relied upon to resist specific attacks upon existing tariffs and quotas or to agitate for new additions. British opinion in the 1930s was to become trapped within an ironical paradox: ardent imperialists sought to realise their goals by impractical and inappropriate means, while the financial authorities were operating an extremely successful imperial economic policy for which they had little liking and which they would seek to abandon as soon as circumstances permitted.

In the context of the failure of protectionist ideology to coalesce, the political groupings which had grown out of Lord Milner's 'Kindergarten' were particularly important. This has been described as being 'for nearly forty years Toryism's only effective doctrinal body',[57] yet many of its most influential adherents were connected with the Liberal Party, for instance Lord Lothian, the future ambassador to Washington, who resigned from the National Government over the Ottawa Agreements.

Lothian, as a founder member of the 'Round Table' group, had a decisive influence on the economic philosophy of the former Kindergarten, which was entirely liberal, and he was reinforced by the activities of his friend Lionel Curtis, who founded the similarly internationalist Royal Institute of International Affairs and 'became the prophet of Chatham House'.[58] The economic views of Lothian and Curtis developed from an imperial vision which for the Kindergarten had been formed before the First World War, and has been described as being influenced by 'Joseph Chamberlain's imperial tariff movement and the movement for an imperial federation'.[59] This was not quite the case after the First World War, yet while the economic soul of the Kindergarten became liberal and left the Chamberlainite aspect of imperialism behind, the imperial political vision remained, and the two strands became fused together.

It was possible for ardent imperialists in the Conservative Party to be equally enthusiastic free traders in the manner of Winston Churchill, and after the debacle of 1923, and the return to gold in 1925, the Round Table and Chatham House incursions into Tory economic ideology were not obtrusive.[60] But as 1931 approached and the political inconsistency of such a position became increasingly clear, the liberal stranglehold on Conservative Party ideology, as opposed to policy, was not relinquished. The stifling of any coherent protectionist doctrine in Conservative economic thinking, and the obvious incompatibility of such views with the Labour and Liberal positions effectively precluded the adoption in the public life of the 1930s of advanced protectionist theory such as that existing in Germany. The views of Empire free traders strayed into a polemical wilderness, further and further from the contemporary mainstream of political action. The practical result of liberal domination of the Round Table group was explained in Lothian's 1933 pamphlet *Liberalism and the Modern World*: 'The great weakness of the Liberal Party and the great strength of Liberalism is that, thanks to their own work in the past, two-thirds of the Conservative Party and two-thirds of the Labour Party are in fundamentals still Liberally minded.'[61]

The formation of the National Government modified the political position, but consolidated its essentials. Conservative dominance and the catastrophic failure of classical economics made a return to gold and free trade inconceivable in the short term, and the introduction of protection and the Ottawa tariffs provoked a resignation of National Liberals. These policies, however, had been introduced as a technical response to the emergency rather than as a conscious application of ideology. Politicians and administrators were happy to see them remain as crisis measures, but the political advocates of imperial economics remained fragmented and lacked an intellectual driving force which might have enabled them to perceive the possibilities of the developing sterling bloc, and around which they might have coalesced as an effective grouping.

Nevertheless, the success of wartime planning had led to a feeling that some form of 'economic general staff' might be of use, and in 1929 Ramsay MacDonald instituted the Economic Advisory Council to be his 'eyes and ears on economic questions'.[62] The Council was a disappointment but after its effective demise in the 1931 crisis it produced an influential offshoot in the Committee on Economic Information, which produced reports on the national economy for consideration by the Cabinet. The Committee included leading Treasury officials such as Phillips, head of finance, and Hopkins and eminent economists like Keynes and Henderson.

It has been suggested that the Committee was largely responsible for the Treasury's increasing sympathy for the advanced economic thinking represented by Keynes,[63] but it was almost exclusively concerned with the domestic economy. Keynes and Henderson were closely associated in the late 1920s with the radical Liberal 'Yellow Book'.[64] Keynes' criticism of exchange rate policy in the 1920s was based on the damage caused by the return to gold on the domestic economy. Once the direct link between sterling and Bank Rate had been severed in 1931, his interest in international economics was like the Treasury's dedicated to creating conditions in which international free trade could be re-established or at least approached.

The differences between Keynes and his autarkic German admirers on this point are obvious. Keynes did not modify his internationalism until the eve of the Second World War. Thus it was that the most advanced British economic thinking gave no backing to a British development of the policies of economic nationalism practised openly by Germany and hypocritically by the United States. Conversely, the intellectual compass of liberal economic views in Great Britain at this time was impressive. The views of Keynes and Henderson were well represented in the press. Their Cambridge colleague Walter Layton, who was founder of the Liberal 'Next Five Years' group, edited *The Economist*.

At the core of the Round Table group's ideology, political as well as economic, was a belief inherited from the Kindergarten that Britain and the United States 'shared a common culture and a common purpose'.[65] This romantic view had accompanied appeasement of America in the diplomatic arena before the First World War, and in the 1930s similar acts in international finance would wreck the economic foundation of British rearmament. In 1936, the dated 'pan-Anglo-Saxonism' of the Kindergarten resonated with the new and determined efforts of Cordell Hull to undermine the imperial economic system, as a group centred around Lothian, and Gladwyn Jebb and Frank Ashton-Gwatkin of the Economic Section of the Foreign Office, discovered to their delight.

The complex system of government administration by subcommittee produced by the Great War had blurred the distinction between administrative and political issues and led to a situation where the influence of civil servants upon policy was very great. Even in 1931 Foreign Office and Treasury officials had on their own initiative attempted to direct the economic future of the Empire in flat contradiction of government policy. Although the grand scale of the infringement on that occasion provoked the prime minister's rage, it was true that in smaller ways politically important decisions could be taken behind the disguise of departmental routine.

To resist the arguments of officials required constant vigilance and the repeated exercise of political will. This state of affairs was in contrast to the Nazi and American systems, in which the growth of competing political and administrative empires, each seeking the favour of the head of state, precluded the development of a monolithic official machine with the capacity to direct political thought.

In the early months of 1936 Cordell Hull launched in earnest his campaign for a trade agreement with Great Britain, and the measure of his success was to be seen after concurrent but separate negotiations culminated in the Tripartite Agreement on exchange rate cooperation between Britain, the USA and France. From its conclusion liberal opinion in the British government began to gain ground and voices were raised in support of an Anglo-American trade agreement. The motives of those involved differed widely, yet the coalition of forces in favour of an accommodation with the United States became so powerful that it not only swept aside all opposition but gained sufficient momentum to triumph over the ultimate doubts of many of its supporters.[66] The process was aided by the swift appreciation in the United States government of the opportunity that was being presented to undermine the imperial economic system and regain the advantage that had been theirs before 1931. The State Department's skilful handling of this process was based on the solid groundwork of the 1934 British Empire Committee, and the sheer perseverance of Hull. American success was made possible by the peculiarities of the British political system, which magnified the influence of a handful of liberal economic thinkers against the express wishes of people and Parliament.

3

'The Destiny of Tomorrow':
a Transatlantic Alliance Forms
against Ottawa, 1936

In January 1936 Cordell Hull approached the British Embassy. 'Anxious for Anglo-American rapprochement, and somewhat unversed in economic matters',[1] the ambassador, Sir Ronald Lindsay, listened as Hull outlined his grandiose plan for the restoration of international free trade. Hull had utilised the powers he had gained under the Trade Agreements Act of 1934 to pursue a 'program' based on the negotiation of a number of bilateral trade agreements with foreign countries. He believed it was the only one 'that could either consistently or safely be considered, especially by important commercial nations like Great Britain and the United States',[2] and informed Lindsay of 'certain methods and practices in trade on the part of his Government which . . . were seriously handicapping the prosecution of our international trade recovery program'.[3]

His specific objection was that bilateral agreements negotiated by the British, such as that with Spain, had the effect of diverting the 'increased exchange' made available under the corresponding US agreement 'to Great Britain under her clearing arrangements and at the loss of the United States'.[4] In addition to the Spanish example, Hull complained, 'a number of similar clearing arrangements on the part of the British Government were understood to have like obstructive and handicapping effects upon the efforts of this Government to carry forward its broad program with the favored-nation policy underlying it'. Hull summed up with reference to a number of these examples that 'the British, by unusual and objectionable methods were forcing the bilateral trade practice at the expense of healthy triangular and multilateral trade'.[5]

Hull's actual goal was a trade agreement with Britain itself, by far the world's largest importer and in contrast to other nations increasing its imports to fuel a growing domestic economy. Britain, however, remained committed to protection of domestic industry and imperial preference. Empire producers were by 1936 gaining an increasing share of the British market and British policy was clear, successful and domestically popular. It held no special place for the United States, and Hull's prospects appeared to be bleak. The commercial logic of the situation demanded considerable American concessions to British exporters, if the British government were to be induced to reverse its policy and absorb the American surplus at the expense of its imperial trade. Anyone but Hull might have despaired of success, but none could have been better suited to the task and he discovered the means to achievement where none appeared to exist.

3.1   Opening shots

Hull's initial blustering reflected the weakness of the American position and his lack of effective bargaining counters. He 'stated that of course the British Government had a perfect right to take these shortsighted steps as we considered them, wherever practiced and by whom',[6] and later 'that of course the British Government could go along with the expectation of a more or less favorable development in their domestic economy, sitting behind tariff walls and Empire preference'.[7] His arguments for change were that Britain's resulting prosperity was in some unspecified way 'artificial' and 'temporary', and more importantly that the system as practised by Great Britain would be the direct and sole cause of war. Hull noted the 'astonishing development in world affairs' of 'a million heavily armed men on the march from Italy to Ethiopia', and that the 'British Government had felt obliged to prepare a huge budgetary increase of $1^1/_2$ to 2 billions of dollars for heavily increased armaments'.

At this stage Hull's arguments left the British unmoved. They felt no need to justify their actions to a country with America's record in international trade. Furthermore, Hull's tone was insulting. In a further meeting with Hull on 5 February, even the sympathetic Lindsay had to warn the secretary of state that his method of approach might be counter-productive. He reported to Eden that 'I dared say that there might be some features in British policy which were displeasing to him – some British rats which were eating his corn; but if in his contemplated communication he began to throw rats at us, we might answer by throwing back hippopotamuses at him, and the only progress we should make would be along the path of recrimination.' Such a development was 'something to be avoided above all things, and was my reason for speaking to him as I did'.[8]

Despite the surrealism of Lindsay's metaphors, Hull comprehended his message and switched to a warmer, personal approach. He told Ray Atherton, the chargé at the US Embassy in London, that he did 'not think it desirable at the present stage to address a note on this subject to His Majesty's Government' but to 'ascertain first whether Mr. Eden and Mr. Runciman [president of the Board of Trade] were aware of the divergent trend of policies of the two Governments'.[9] Hull instructed Atherton to approach Eden first and 'endeavor to obtain his interest and support without, however, burdening him with the technical details'.[10] Atherton interpreted Hull's instructions by refraining, on his own initiative, from handing Eden a copy of Hull's memo, 'to avoid its passing into the hands of the Foreign Office experts who would merely write a technical appraisement'.[11]

Eden was thus forced to take 'extensive notes' and form initially a purely personal impression of the situation from American information. He was 'obviously unaware of the extent that British practice had deviated' from the American conception of fair trade practice, and upon making the point that 'in determining the British course of action in this matter there were many other allied considerations for discussion with the United States' he was told that 'the essential first and foremost was that the two countries as the two great trading nations should agree in principle to work for the abolition of trade barriers'. This produced no objection and 'Eden said he agreed with this and felt it was vital for the economic welfare of the world we should endeavor to accord our two views'. Eden expressed his appreciation of Hull's personal approach and told Atherton 'that from the notes he had made he would at once proceed to take the matter up with the Foreign Office experts' and 'discuss the matter with Runciman'.

The Foreign Office, though, had already been in contact with the Board of Trade, which on 14 February had received Lindsay's report to Eden on his January meeting with Hull.[12] Despite his warning to Hull, Lindsay revealed himself to be in accord with the secretary of state's sentiments. After noting the increase of US interest in cooperation with Britain, and criticising the 'characteristic fashion' in which the Americans, having made 'fervent appeals' in this area 'offer no concrete proposals and are aggrieved when they receive none', Lindsay argued that:

> If the other questions are treated as incidental and the real issue on which Mr. Hull wishes to elicit the views of His Majesty's

Government is 'the wider measure of economic cooperation between the two countries', I should like to suggest that the events of the past year have largely eliminated the obstacles to any such discussions which were pointed out in Sir Robert Vansittart's letter and enclosures of 23rd July last, viz:

Stabilisation
Imperial Preference
War Debts
Trade Agreement.[13]

Lindsay's advocacy did not embody any fervent espousal of free trade, but in line with the tradition of British officials who were not professionally concerned with economics he assumed it to be a good and natural thing. There was no thought of the preferential system as a fundamental support of British power in times of crisis, and the four items listed in the ambassador's memorandum were seen solely as inconvenient impediments to American support in a deteriorating political environment.

Lindsay argued that it was 'very clear that the political situation in Europe is far more involved and perilous than it was a year ago',[14] he stated that if the promised memorandum from Hull 'turns out to be a plea for closer cooperation, Mr. Hull's initiative may partly be accounted for by the greater imminence of European War which, in his view, is so largely due to economic causes. What I fail to find any convincing reason for is the seeming fact that he should desire Anglo-American cooperation more keenly than His Majesty's Government.'

Lindsay's frustration reflected the fact that the voice of the Foreign Office was not dominant in the formulation of the British government's policy. To capture the foreign secretary and his officials was by no means to win the war. The 'economic' departments of the British government bristled at criticism of the technical aspects of British commercial policy. The encouraging tone adopted by Eden was balanced almost immediately in a speech by Walter Runciman, the president of the Board of Trade, to the Bradford Chambers of Commerce on 27 February, in which he affirmed British commercial policy and criticised American practice, doubting the ability of 'the United States to throw down her tariff barriers so long as she maintains her present fiscal system'.[15]

He continued that it was 'not for me to teach the Americans how to do their business but I have no hesitation in saying that the rapidity and volume of their trade would be vastly increased if the United States would release some of her stores of gold and if her attitude towards the borrowing nations was a little more adventurous as her own home policy'. Atherton, reporting to Hull, added that the 'best available press report of Runciman's references to his trade agreements' was that: 'We hope to get into foreign markets by reason of these agreements and I intend to pursue this policy as long as I am where I am.' The speech provoked an immediate telegram from the secretary of state, asking Atherton whether he thought Eden had talked to Runciman before it was made. Hull described himself as 'very anxious to have any information which might become available to you relating to this subject'.[16]

Atherton discovered that the Foreign Office 'had communicated with the Board of Trade' concerning Hull's approaches, but that Eden had not contacted Runciman personally or known of his comments and 'he was obviously somewhat taken back when they were first brought to his attention'.[17] This passage of exchanges suggested the most profitable line of approach to the British. Any attempt to argue against the technical details of British commercial policy would be rebuffed, as the Treasury and the Board of Trade did not take kindly to attacks upon their professional expertise and held that of their American counterparts in particularly low esteem. Conversely, Eden's response had shown that the British government was not wholly united behind its policy. A general appeal to liberal sentiment might divide it further.

3.2   A different tack

Hull had a chance to consider these points while the German reoccupation of the Rhineland preoccupied the British Cabinet, and when he finally handed the British ambassador his original memorandum, another was attached which struck a much more moderate tone. It specifically retracted his previous appeal on technical details, stating that he regretted 'to learn that the British Government construed my proposal, which was in the nature of an inquiry, to embrace minor and other subordinate questions of a controversial nature. This was entirely foreign to my purpose.'[18] He simply wanted to know whether the British 'Government could see its way clear to pursue virtually the identical course the United States Government has pursued under the Trade Agreement Act of 1934'.

Hull then aimed for the moral high ground, stating that the 'mere announcement by the British Government' of such an intention would have a considerable 'moral effect' throughout the world. Hull's message was amplified by his special assistant, James Clement Dunn, when the memoranda were handed to Lindsay, who 'called the Ambassador's attention' to Hull's 'particular wish' that his initiative should 'not become involved in technical discussions as to the exact methods of its execution' and that a declaration of the type Hull sought 'would not obligate the British Government to any immediate or specific steps, but would have the effect of giving assurance generally that it was the intention of the British Government to carry out such a program'.[19] This shift of emphasis proved to be a masterstroke. Hull's appeal to a liberal spirit in trade and his association of increasing international tension with its absence appealed to a broad spectrum of British opinion, including those with no economic interest who simply sought allies against Hitler.

Hull was also sending his message through the line of least resistance. Upon receipt of Hull's second memorandum, Lindsay expressed relief at Hull's new moderation and told Dunn that 'he would make every effort to explain the matter again to his Government particularly along the lines of the Secretary's new memorandum and hoped that from the policy viewpoint it could be accepted and put into effect by his Government'.[20] On 1 April, the ambassador remarked to Hull that his memorandum had 'lifted all the problems relating to international economic affairs to a higher and clearer level'.[21] This level, free of wrangling over tariffs and quotas, was clearly more congenial to the Diplomatic Service and the Foreign Office. Eden, upon receiving the memorandum himself hinted why: he told the American ambassador, Bingham, that 'while he was not an expert on the technical side of this subject, he was fully aware of its importance and its political implications and that it was his intention to make every effort to avoid a conflict of trade policy between Great Britain and the United States'.[22] Eden, like Lindsay, saw no reason why economic matters he did not understand should be allowed to constitute an obstacle to Anglo-American harmony.

Despite his enthusiasm for Hull's views, Lindsay had felt it necessary to warn him that 'it might seem to the British Government more or less difficult to reverse its present definite course and attitude' and that 'their country was moving forward fairly well in the present situation and the disposition might be to so continue'.[23] Other sources emphasised this note of caution. On 7 April Bingham reported to Hull that he had in fact dined the previous day with the 'permanent Assistant Secretary to the Board of Trade' who described Runciman as 'far more liberal in his views and policies than any successor was likely to be' and characterised him as 'a good man struggling against an adverse tide of events'.[24] This rather unpromising information was reinforced when Bingham talked with a 'high Treasury official', and 'he too stressed the urgency of European political situation as the primary factor dominating British policy in all fields which compelled, reluctant as they were to admit it, a policy of expediency in economic and financial international questions'.

These British responses indicated that the policies of protection and imperial preference were the natural responses to new dangers. Hull, though, had received enough encouragement to continue and could now rely on the foreign secretary to promote his views within the British governmental machine. Although Hull thought the British attitude 'disappointing',[25] he saw 'a chance that fuller consideration may produce a change in their present judgment, and induce them to undertake the step I have suggested'. To this end he would 'continue the effort here to secure full consideration from them for the wisdom of some such step. I desire to do likewise in London.' Hull instructed Bingham to 'take advantage of all opportunities to present these views to the British Government' and, upon 'a suitable and propitious opportunity', to 'talk again with Eden and Runciman, and leave with them an informal memorandum in summary of your remarks', which Hull had thoughtfully provided.

Eden received the latest memorandum on 28 April, and provided an official response, asking Bingham to tell Hull that 'his Government has taken great satisfaction in the views you have expressed in your communications and is giving them active sympathetic consideration'.[26] Furthermore, the British government was preparing a memorandum for Hull, which Eden hoped would 'show that the aims and methods of his Government are substantially similar to those of our own'. This promised little, but after months of effort Hull was on the verge of establishing a dialogue with the British government. He pressed on, and having gained Eden's support attempted to establish a direct line of communication with Runciman. At a lunch appointment, Bingham handed the new memorandum to Runciman and was asked to convey the latter's 'acknowledgement' of the message which Hull had conveyed to Runciman 'through his son'.[27]

Although Runciman defended his policy along familiar lines, his 'attitude did not remind' Bingham 'in any way of his remarks' to the Bradford Chambers of Commerce, and he felt that Runciman was 'at pains to give me the palatable interpretation of British commercial policy within the limits of what they conceived to be their greatest self interest'. Runciman told Bingham 'that in his speech before the [A]ssociation of British Chambers of Commerce' on the following day 'he would make occasion to set forth anew the Government's viewpoint'. The tone of this speech, though, was far from warm. Bingham reported that Runciman 'referred to the fact that I was present and added: "The American Ambassador is the representative of a Government which has again and again stated that it wished to see a much freer flow of international trade. In so far as it lends itself to that ambition, they will find us ready to cooperate."'[28]

Runciman's cool tone reflected the mood of his business audience. On 30 April, Hull had received a telegram from the American Consulate in Birmingham explaining the attitude prevalent in Britain's industrial heartland.[29] The consul, James R. Wilkinson, had

> heard a discussion being carried on by a group of important businessmen in this City. . . . There seemed to be among these men a general agreement that by and large the British business public is extremely hostile toward any move involving the lowering of British customs duties on American goods or involving the loosening up of any measures now restricting their introduction into this country. . . . This attitude, it was stated, is attributable to a widespread belief that, in no circumstances and despite the declarations of our Federal Administration to the contrary, will the United States ever give any substantial quid pro quo in exchange for British tariff favours.

British industrialists were probably more aware than their government that, as Runciman said in a rhetorical flourish concluding his speech: 'The turn which economic issues take today in large part spells the destiny of tomorrow.'[30]

On 26 May, Bingham was given the British government's memorandum to Hull, which asserted British liberal credentials, regretted necessary deviations and expressed willingness to reaffirm its attitude along the lines suggested by Hull.[31] He would have derived more encouragement from a report by Atherton, summarising 'a luncheon conversation with senior officials of the Board of Trade and Treasury regarding certain economic and financial questions'.[32]

The sentiments of these officials differed sharply from those of the businessmen overheard by Wilkinson. They doubted the practicality of a trade agreement, but asserted their liking for freer trade:

> As regards the general question of a more liberal and enlightened commercial policy, both the Board of Trade and Treasury official [*sic*] emphasized the pressure which the departments concerned and the Government came under from Members of Parliament and special interests, and took the line that since the disease of protection had come on this country when it was advanced in age it was all the more violent in its initial stages. They both felt that the present House of Commons was essentially a protectionist body, which saw the immediate objects of attainment, especially as regards specific products, and tended to disregard the eventual results and the broader national interests. Furthermore, 'the war mentality' arising out of the international situation was playing its part. In the circumstances those ministers who had a liberal trade outlook, as well as permanent officials of the same conviction, had to content themselves with attempting to check the excessive zeal of the protectionists until such time as opinion began to move in the opposite direction, which would then give them the opportunity for a frontal attack.

An example of the prevailing climate was provided:

> Captain Wallace, Parliamentary Undersecretary at the Board of Trade, who was sufficiently new at his job to consider himself more a member of the Conservative party than a Government official, stated in private only yesterday that he would just as soon have the Argentine negotiations fail, for such a failure, far from reacting adversely on the Government, would be popular in the House of Commons.

In addition to the British government memorandum, contacts were under way at the official level with regard to the negotiation of a trade agreement. Sir Frederick Leith-Ross, the chief economic adviser to the British government, and Oscar Ryder, a member of the US Tariff

Commission, met in London and agreed that the Americans should produce a list, both of the concessions they sought from the British and those that they were willing to give in turn.[33]

Shortly afterwards, H.O. Chalkley, the commercial counsellor of the British Embassy, was called to the State Department's Division of Trade Agreements, ostensibly 'for the purpose of discussing the progress of the exploratory studies of trade relations between the United States and the United Kingdom',[34] but in fact to receive American demands. Chalkley was told that the Americans 'believed that a comprehensive trade agreement of great value to both countries could be consummated provided the British Government would be prepared to consider modifications of imperial preferences affecting a very substantial portion of our export trade with the United Kingdom'. In the absence of such modifications 'it was pointed out that only a very limited agreement, if indeed any agreement at all, could be negotiated'.

Although Chalkley 'was assured that this did not mean that we would request the abolition of imperial preference', American aspirations had leapt from a desire for revised British commercial practice in third markets to a demand for the wholesale revision of the Ottawa system. The Americans made it known 'frankly' that they were 'somewhat concerned about the preliminary negotiations' between Britain and the Dominions concerning measures to replace the Ottawa agreements, which were to expire in August 1937. It would be 'unfortunate' if any new agreements should 'preclude the possibility of a really worthwhile agreement with the United States'. Chalkley 'did not show much enthusiasm in regard to these suggestions', and doubted the basis for an agreement.

Chalkley's lack of enthusiasm continued at the next meeting. He presented the Americans with a short list of British requests for tariff reductions which, he said, was 'one year old, unofficial and subject to revision',[35] and which was sufficiently modest to include golf balls as a separate category. In return he stated that the United States could expect 'very little indeed, in the way of reductions in duties', and argued 'to the effect that there was very little proof that imperial preferences are of themselves effective in diverting American trade'. He was 'emphatic in suggesting that the words "abolition of preferences" be not used in negotiations', and even stated 'that effective argument against them was difficult except in very exceptional circumstances'. Far from considering concessions, Chalkley 'stressed the value to the United States of securing stability of the *status quo* both with respect to import duties and to preferences while pointing out the necessity for the increase in some of the existing import duties'.

In Britain, Atherton gained the impression in conversation with Chamberlain and Runciman, that the attitude of both men 'was based on Cabinet consultation and decision to play for time'.[36] There remained Eden, who on receipt of another Hull memorandum 'said he wished to continue to handle this matter personally',[37] but the political response from London was frankly discouraging. Hull's achievement in cultivating Eden and persuading the British to even talk had been impressive, but his only real bargaining counter was the worsening diplomatic situation, regarding which current British commercial policy was still deemed appropriate. Hull could only persevere.

Another memorandum expressing regret at the delay in the promised British declaration was followed by a visit from Lindsay, bearing an extract of a speech by Runciman in the House of Commons on 15 July. This was obviously designed to convince the Americans that Great Britain had no dark motives. Runciman's speech had pointed out Britain's tremendous and unexploited power to influence world trade in its favour. In fact: 'The British import market, which is by far the largest import market in the world, has been kept open for the goods of all nations on fair and equal terms.'[38] The clearing arrangements entered into by the British government abroad were the minimum required for 'self-defence', given that: 'Upon certain countries and for a certain period we could no doubt force the greater quantity of United Kingdom goods.' Despite this, the British had 'used the power of our huge import market with great caution to promote the sales of our goods abroad rather than to compel artificially changed purchases'.

Hull had cause to be grateful for British restraint in its trading practice, but he could take this for granted. He needed concessions, and told Lindsay that 'in the abstract' Runciman's statement was 'excellent and encouraging'[39] and that he wished to 'express . . . appreciation of the tone of Mr Runciman's remarks, especially as viewed from the abstract standpoint', but he 'would not be quite frank if I did not express a little disappointment in the failure of Mr Runciman to indicate a single step or act or utterance' in favour of 'a liberal commercial policy'. Hull went on to say that 'unfortunately the inert or static attitude of the British government in this respect was pointed to both at home and by most of the capitals of Europe', and that 'the British Government was not moving one fraction of an inch in the direction of either carrying forward any kind of a program or furnishing any kind of leadership'.

Hull also mentioned 'the desultory conversations between the British Government and the United States Treasury Department' and wondered 'why it would not be possible'[40] for the two governments, in addition to their announcement of common purpose, to 'undertake to keep the pound and the dollar within certain ranges'. Summing up, Hull elucidated his latest bargaining position that 'the British Government was almost absolutely static with reference to its economic and commercial policy; that it was seemingly settling and falling back to a two-fold major objective of large armaments and Empire preference; that it was in these unfortunate circumstances that I was finding it difficult to induce other countries in Europe to move forward in support of the liberal economic program'.

Hull's tirade did not provoke a retort. Perceiving that Lindsay 'seemed much interested and entirely sympathetic with these inquiries in the nature of suggestions', Hull proposed 'a purely oral conversation for the benefit of our respective Governments which he could carry home with him' in the event of there arising 'such facts or developments as would afford an occasion and a basis for such oral conversation'.

Despite his comments, Runciman's speech had encouraged Hull and he instructed Bingham not to hand on his previous critical memorandum until it had been revised.[41] Also, Eden informed Bingham that the speech would have gone further towards the American position but for time pressure.[42] If Hull had hoped for some immediate move in the British position, however, he was to be disappointed. There followed a period of apparent calm, and after a month of delay, he sent a further memorandum bemoaning a lack of progress, which Bingham was to use in meetings he was instructed to arrange with Eden and Runciman.[43]

Eden defended himself by reference to his recent and impeccably internationalist speech at Geneva, and complained that the difficult political situation was holding up the sort of movement that the Americans desired. He said that Lindsay had 'strongly presented the view of the American Government on the general subject' to him and 'expressed his deep interest, in which I have no doubt he is sincere, in doing everything possible to maintain the best relations with the United

States and said that he would give this matter more time and effort and would take it up with Runciman and Neville Chamberlain'.[44]

In keeping with the current American pessimism, however, Bingham thought of Eden that he must 'doubt his ability to influence his colleagues sufficiently to modify their views'. Also, while Bingham was talking to Eden, Under-Secretary of State William Phillips, on a visit to Britain, took the opportunity to talk to the foreign secretary's principal officials, Vansittart and Cadogan. Phillips explained the Hull Program to the latter, but: 'At this point Mr Cadogan admitted his ignorance in regard to the entire subject.' He 'had evidently not given much consideration to this whole question. Again and again he pleaded ignorance', but

> stated that for forty years the British Government had taken up the cudgels in favour of the lowering of tariff barriers but that the world had not followed them in this respect. He also reminded me that the United States had been one of the principal champions of the high tariff policy and that in present circumstances the British public had come to believe that their interests were best protected by the present commercial policy of the Government. Politically, therefore, it would be very difficult for the British Government now, to seem to go back to its former freer trade policy and, in fact, this could not be done without serious political complications. Commercially, the British were doing well under the present system of specialised agreements. They had the approval of the British public.

Phillips summarised:

> In brief, while it was apparent that Mr Cadogan was not responsible for, or particularly in touch with the new British trade agreements, he was in entire sympathy with them and was not particularly concerned with the fact that the continuation of the present British policy might lead the British and American Governments in opposite directions.

Talking to Vansittart, Phillips 'had very much the same impression that Sir Robert was not particularly interested in or concerned with commercial matters'. Phillips concluded that 'after my conversations with both Vansittart and Cadogan I feel that, unless the approach can be made through higher channels, these two men in the Foreign Office at least will not go out of their way at the present time to meet our desires'.

This time appeared to be the low point of American attempts to engage British interest in an agreement, but appearances were deceptive. Cadogan's financial ignorance would prove a two-edged sword, as would Vansittart's lack of interest, and despite Eden's disappointing display a variety of information would be presented to Washington towards the end of 1936 to suggest that opinion in the British political establishment was moving the American way. When Chalkley was summoned to the State Department for discussions on 21 September, the Americans gained the impression that he was under instructions to broach the subject of trade negotiations in such a way as to stress the urgency of the matter.[45] Forces had been at work to reward Hull's efforts.

3.3   Morgenthau tips the scales

Hull had referred to the 'desultory conversations' taking place between the British and US Treasuries concerning currency stabilisation. The occasion for these talks was the impending devaluation of the French franc and the general desire that this should not cause chaos on the exchanges. While Hull had been pursuing his trade agreements programme Morgenthau, in the traditionally disjointed manner of American policy making, had on his own account been pressing hard for a currency stabilisation agreement between the franc, the dollar and the pound, with the active support of Roosevelt. His motives were complex and in part rooted in his fierce anti-Nazi convictions. On the other hand, if this produced the long hoped for pegging of sterling to the gold dollar so much the better.

In 1935, with the memory of Roosevelt's behaviour concerning the World Economic Conference still fresh, Morgenthau's efforts were greeted 'with derision by the British authorities'.[46] A year later, however, after the election of Blum's Popular Front and the subsequent flight of capital from Paris, it became evident that the franc was about to be driven from its gold parity, along with the other currencies in the European gold bloc. The British then became interested in some form of cooperation to manage the situation and after much haggling an accord to manage the French devaluation was reached. However, there seemed at first little cause for specifically American jubilation. The Tripartite Agreement was a fig leaf disguising the French devaluation as part of a general international rearrangement of currencies.

The now traditional American attempt to peg sterling to the dollar at a high parity – on Roosevelt's insistence Morgenthau advanced the figure of $5 – met with the traditional rebuff, the British simply promising to avoid competitive devaluation. This response did not surprise the American authorities. John H. Williams, the vice-president of the Federal Reserve Bank of New York, told Morgenthau that 'the British are not planning to play with us in this matter at all . . .' and that 'it would clarify the situation if we would recognize that we have no real power over them at this stage. . .'.[47]

Morgenthau's excitement during the negotiating of the Agreement was largely confined to the effect he imagined it would have on the dictators,[48] and the main concern of the British was to ensure that the French did not come entirely off gold as the ability to exchange francs for gold greatly facilitated the operations of the EEA. The compromise agreement creating the '24 hour gold standard' allowed the British to sell francs for gold at a price to be renegotiated each day, and Morgenthau found himself forced to accord similar facilities to the British, as he was unable to prevent any devaluation of sterling. So: 'Without discussion, he dropped his request for an explicit commitment by Britain on the sterling–dollar rate'[49] as a precondition for convertibility facilities.

This was a major concession, as the US had previously only sold gold for currencies that were on a full gold standard. If Morgenthau tried to buy gold with pounds in the international market, rather than from a central bank, he only raised the price of gold and depreciated sterling still further against the gold dollar. Morgenthau found that 'I am buying sterling and I can't convert the damn stuff.' Believing that: 'No country wants to sit and hold paper',[50] he agreed '[i]n the spirit of the Tripartite Agreement' to sell gold to the British at $35 an ounce, an arrangement that was eminently satisfactory to London.

Hull's interest in the Tripartite Agreement would have been greater had he known of its effect within the British government. In the closing months of 1936 the movement for a modification of the Ottawa system was becoming firmly rooted. Hull's propaganda offensive had provided support and encouragement to like-minded elements within the British establishment, the most prominent of whom were in the Economic Section of the Foreign Office.[51]

Frank Ashton-Gwatkin and Gladwyn Jebb, candid enemies of the Ottawa system, planned for the economic appeasement of Germany through concessions designed to draw the Reich back into the international financial system. They moved in June 1936 after a dinner party organised by the economic adviser at Australia House, at which a number of economic liberals were present, including Jebb and Leeper of the Foreign Office. Discussions resulted in Professor Noel Hall of London University being prevailed upon to write a memorandum detailing a scheme for economic appeasement.

The idea of making unreciprocated concessions to Germany never excited much enthusiasm outside the small circle of its proponents and when, before the memorandum had 'taken final shape', Jebb 'presented the substance of it privately to Mr. Waley of the Treasury [head of foreign finance] and Mr. Brown of the Board of Trade, neither were very encouraging'.[52] When the memorandum was finally prepared, however, Germany was not its only focus, and it made the specific point that: 'It should be noted that the policies which are advocated here fit closely with those which Mr. Cordell Hull has been following under the Democratic Tariff Legislation'; and further: 'A development of British Empire Policy that is compatible with more generous international policy in the United States has much to commend it.'[53] Hull had thus become, unknown to himself, a player in the debate within the British governmental system on the course of economic policy. Jebb maintained that 'neither Mr. Leeper nor myself take any responsibility for the Hall memorandum, but . . . we are both impressed by the desirability of its being subjected to the most sympathetic consideration by the experts of His Majesty's Government'.[54]

Despite the introduction of an American dimension, the Hall scheme could not gloss over the undesirability of unilateral concessions to Germany. As Vansittart noted in conversation with Ashton-Gwatkin, the scheme 'certainly had attractive features', but if it caused 'unemployment in this country, the chances of getting Ministers to agree to it were the reverse of bright'. Ashton-Gwatkin replied that any unemployment resulting from the scheme would 'most likely be temporary' and intriguingly 'that there were great possibilities of camouflaging the scheme by representing it as primarily designed to encourage trade within the Empire'.[55]

Little came of the Hall scheme's main aim of the economic appeasement of Germany. The obvious costs defeated any attempt to make the scheme appear beneficial to the Empire, although Eden became and remained enthusiastic about it. Such failures to carry the whole package of economic appeasement measures have been taken as evidence that the 'economic' departments within the British government which had constructed the post-1931 system would always defend it successfully against the schemes of liberal idealists.[56] If one takes a departmental view, the Treasury and the Board of Trade certainly resented Foreign Office encroachment on their territory, partly for political reasons but chiefly because, as Hull had discovered, they were extremely sensitive to any attempt to denigrate their professional expertise. Sir William Brown at the Board of Trade summed up this attitude when considering an early draft of Runciman's July speech to the House of Commons aimed at Hull: 'I attach a draft which was originally prepared by the Foreign Office, but has been modified here in order to reconcile it with some actual features of our commercial policy.'[57]

Such asperity did not mean, however, that the Treasury or the Board of Trade were immune to a liberal message, in terms either of departmental ideology or as individual civil servants. The 1931 economic changes had never been presented in either department as anything other than crisis measures, and after a period of recovery it was inevitable that they would be called into question. For the Ottawa system to be undermined it was not necessary for a full-blown scheme of economic appeasement to succeed, merely for aspects of such thinking to be accepted in the government. Indeed, the more stridently the whole package was promoted, the more moderate its individual aspects would seem.

3.4   A decisive shift

The effects of the changing climate of British opinion promoted by Hull became manifest toward the end of 1936, when various papers were presented to the Cabinet preaching the liberal gospel in the wake of the Tripartite Agreement. On 28 October 1936, the Cabinet considered a memorandum from the Board of Trade[58] prepared after a meeting 'under the Chairmanship of the Financial Secretary to the Treasury, at which Sir F. Leith-Ross and officials of the Treasury, Board of Trade and Foreign Office were present'. This stressed that the governments involved in concluding the Tripartite Agreement 'attach the greatest importance to action being taken without delay to relax progressively the present systems of quotas and exchange controls with a view to their abolition'.[59]

This policy was 'strongly' endorsed by the League of Nations Assembly in a resolution calling for 'all States to organise, without any delay, determined and continuous action to ensure its application'.[60] Having established the credentials of a liberal programme, the memorandum noted the difficulties involved but concluded that 'the present seems the "psychological moment" for attempting some action in the international sphere, and it is felt that the possibility of a multilateral agreement ought to be explored'. Indeed some work had been undertaken already. Leith-Ross had already met M. Rueff, the financial attaché at the French Embassy, and the good offices of the Belgian government were being sought to take soundings for a move in the European context concerning which the 'United States Government would need to be kept informed at all stages and given the opportunity of participating should they desire to do so'.

In this paper, liberal civil servants appeared to be making an effort to feel their way round the flank of Cabinet opposition, and hustle through a change in the government's policy under the cover of a concerted international move towards freer trade. The unpopular idea of German economic appeasement was dropped, along with the politically charged question of agricultural preference. Instead it was mentioned that Leith-Ross had supposedly been told by Rueff 'that some agreement might be reached between the "free currency" countries to abolish their *industrial* quotas as *between themselves*'.[61] The paper then attempted to generate a sense of urgency. It noted that Rueff would shortly return from Paris, and 'it is desirable that before then H.M. Government's attitude in the matter should be settled as far as possible'. In fact, the whole impression of international movement for change, culminating in the Van Zeeland Mission, was generated by Leith-Ross through his extensive network of international financial contacts.[62] Nor had he been idle on other fronts.

Shortly afterwards, Leith-Ross presented a report to the Cabinet on the balance of payments[63] which suggested reasons and remedies for the existing deficit on current account. He attributed the primary cause of the deficit to the fact that 'greater industrial activity and purchasing power in this country has led to a greater volume of imports of foodstuffs, raw materials and manufactured goods, the principal value of which lies in their raw material content'.[64] For the same reason, goods had been diverted from export to the domestic market. The demands of rearmament were also mentioned, along with a rise in import prices. Leith-Ross expressed no alarm at the deficit and pointed out that a run on the pound and a rise in interest rates were unlikely to follow from it. In fact, British money rates were 'lower than those of any European country', and attempts to 'discourage the investment of British capital abroad by the control of new capital issues', allied to a general 'absence of credit-worthy foreign borrowers', created conditions which 'have tended to increase the plethora of funds seeking investment at home, and thus to give an additional stimulus to domestic trade production, while, at the same time, strengthening the value of sterling'.[65]

He listed a number of ways in which the deficit might be eliminated, rejecting import control and deciding that: 'The preferable course seems to be to meet the adverse balance of payments by other means, and, in particular, by allowing the exchange to adjust itself as it may be expected to do, to a slightly lower level.'[66] This 'has the advantage of operating on a very wide field, Viz., the trade of the whole sterling area; so that a relatively small deviation in the balance of payments can be corrected by a small change in the level of the exchanges'.[67] Seemingly as an afterthought Leith-Ross then stated that '[f]or the rest' some means might be found of stimulating exports and at this point the tone of his paper changed radically.

The whole second part of the report amounted to a thinly veiled attack on imperial preference. The success of post-1931 policy was turned against it: 'Recovery has by now reached a high level within the sterling area, and the scope for further expansion of trade is consequently greatest in the countries outside the sterling area.'[68] He argued that Britain's 'policy, by establishing a preferential or favourable position for our exports to the Empire and to the countries with which we have negotiated Trade Agreements, has accentuated the competition which we have to face in other countries, particularly in South America and the Far East, where the scope for expansion of trade is now most marked'.[69]

Leith-Ross reinforced these questionable assumptions by quoting 'an interesting article'[70] in the Liberal publication *Political and Economic Planning,* which in November 1935 claimed that its June issue of that year 'showed that the primary producing interests of the overseas Empire must inevitably be far wider than the British market, and that the industrial and commercial interests of Great Britain are far wider than the market provided by the overseas Empire'. It also appealed to the consciences of its readers: 'We expressed fears concerning the ultimate wisdom of a policy which, in face of the traditional British conception of imperial trusteeship has sought to exclude from the Crown Colonies cheap manufactured articles which the United

Kingdom cannot supply on competitive terms and which, by reason of their low standard of life, Colonial populations urgently desire.' A copy of this publication was also placed in the Foreign Office records, with a note by Jebb that it 'may be used in connection with the Hall memo'.[71]

Leith-Ross's paper was an elegant exposition of the developing liberal arm of the movement towards accommodation with the United States. Instead of denigrating the post-1931 system, it simply argued that a policy designed as a crisis expedient had succeeded, could no longer be justified and should now be supplanted. The argument in favour of freer trade was based on supposition, but played, like Hull, on fears of possible stagnation and economic aggression. There was also a calculated appeal to the conscience of the Cabinet with the assertion that imperial preference was morally as well as economically flawed.

In December, the Twenty-First Report of the CEI concurred: 'The recovery which has taken place both in the United Kingdom and in the Empire as a whole has involved a considerable dislocation of trade with the rest of the world. It is gradually becoming clear that full recovery, both in the Empire and in the rest of the world, cannot be expected without some resumption of trade along its old channels.' The conclusion was reached that 'changes in British policy since 1931 have probably caused the main alterations in the channels of trade, and therefore it rests largely with us now to do what is possible to restore the situation'. To this end, 'in our opinion the objective of policy should now be to seek to expand trade, wherever possible, between the United Kingdom and the Empire, on the one hand, and the rest of the world, on the other'.[72]

By the end of 1936 the policy of imperial preference was under concerted attack within the British establishment. In the Cabinet, Runciman was increasingly well disposed to a US trade agreement, but the most powerful backing came at the official level. Leith-Ross had made his opinion clear and the presence of Hopkins and Phillips in the CEI indicated their compliance. That Keynes and Henderson were on the Committee was also an indication that the views of professional economists were in line with more liberal trading practice. Such thinking reflected the influence of Hull's constantly reiterated message: that world crisis was based on protection, and that Great Britain was responsible and presented the main obstacle to a solution.

For those influenced by this argument the motives of the United

States in presenting it were immaterial, as was any question of the sincerity of the professed American desire for mutual concessions. The Ottawa system seemed unassailable, but its opponents were coordinating their efforts and had direct access to the Cabinet, the principal policy-making body of the Empire. The year 1937 would begin promisingly for them with Runciman's visit to the United States, during which he would meet Hull and Roosevelt.

4
The Devil in the Detail: a Necessary Case for Economic Danger and the Formulation of the Fourth Arm Policy, 1937–38

Runciman visited the United States in January 1937, having first 'had a talk with Anthony [Eden] and with Leith-Ross', by whom he was 'appraised of the worst rocks, which I hope to have the good fortune to avoid'.[1] Neither Eden nor the ubiquitous Leith-Ross could have objected to the impression made by Runciman's less famous mission. In conversation with Hull he defended his record as a liberal in difficult times, which compared favourably, he noted, with that of the secretary of state.[2] He did not, furthermore, rule out some adjustment of the Ottawa system, as 'the details were always capable of discussion and readjustment',[3] a message he repeated in Parliament on his return, and more strongly in a letter to Baldwin. He told the prime minister that he had defended British policy but noted: 'On the other hand, a certain degree of elasticity in the tariff undertakings which we gave at Ottawa would undoubtedly have facilitated negotiations with the United States of America.'[4] He also suggested a direct link between imperial defence and the economic appeasement of the Americans: 'If we are able to reach a trade agreement with the present Administration, there is no doubt that it will make much easier their co-operation with us in case of trouble in Europe.'

A memorandum prepared for Roosevelt[5] by Hull prior to their meetings with Runciman described him as 'an old time Liberal and free trader', who was 'at present extremely nationalistic, as has been evidenced by his promotion of and subscription to policies calculated to gain unfair advantage over American interests in many parts of the world'. In return, Runciman traduced Hull who 'appeared to ignore our agreements, being so proud of his own 13 that he scarcely listened to the fact that we had made 23'.[6] Runciman, though, belied Hull's caricature and revealed possibilities for the United States. He suggested to Hull that it would be desirable to 'draft expressions of principle to which the United Kingdom, as well as the United States of America, adhere'. Then, 'we could both put ourselves in a position to instruct our officials'.[7]

Runciman's manner, shifting between firmness and conciliation, suggested a transitional stage in British policy. Complaining of the recent Neutrality Act, he told Roosevelt

> that the natural result would be to make countries like the U.K. turn away from the U.S.A. to other sources of supply, because we could not run the risk of finding ourselves choked off some day, perhaps in our time of greatest need. As a simple business precaution we would deal now with countries which would be our supplier in the future and we would avoid countries which might cut off our supplies at the behest of the Senator Nyes of the day.[8]

These remarks might be considered the high water mark of imperial self-sufficiency in the defence sphere. Thereafter, the argument that American support must be bought with economic concessions became dominant. Roosevelt asked Runciman if he felt his trip had been worthwhile, to which he 'replied that one did not cross the North Atlantic in the winter merely for a holiday'.[9] The British liberal resurgence would now take hold of policy.

4.1   Breaches in the dam

In early 1937 London was blessed with an abundance of American sermons on the economic and political benefits of free trade. In January, Hull renewed his propaganda offensive against the Ottawa system with a lengthy memorandum reiterating his arguments of 1936.[10] In February Morgenthau, following up the Tripartite Agreement, delivered a similar message to Chamberlain through the British Embassy.[11] This stated that the burden of armaments was bringing the world to financial ruin and the risk of war. He told T.K. Bewley, the financial adviser at the British Embassy, that 'if Mr. Morgenthau could do anything to help to prevent such a war he would (in his own phrase) die happy: he was inclined to think that the situation might be saved by a bold initiative by the United States and Great Britain'.[12]

The message echoed Hull's argument that protection, by denying universal access to resources, made war to gain them more likely. Rearmament could be taken to represent an advanced stage of this process and

Morgenthau's argument stressed not only the desirability of an Anglo-American attempt to liberalise trade but also its urgency. To this end he raised the possibility of sending Bewley to England immediately on an American destroyer. Chamberlain's eventual reply, however, consisted of carefully phrased platitudes, and the correspondence was passed over to Hull, who simply continued his campaign.[13] From this point, negotiations were conducted solely with the State Department, and there followed a series of seemingly negative exchanges which disguised the fact that the Americans now had a foot firmly in the British door. Not for the first time or the last, the wholly ingenuous British approach betrayed them. Washington's tone was intransigent, but the British response was one of disappointment rather than irritation and based its objections on points of practicality rather than principle. The Americans began to sense profit in their endeavours.

In mid-1937, the State Department presented the British with an extensive list of demands to be conceded before negotiations for a trade agreement could be announced. Once again a blunt attempt at coercion did not receive the brisk rejection it merited, for by this stage liberals in government were pushing hard for American appeasement. In March, Eden, in a memorandum originally drafted by Ashton-Gwatkin,[14] 'asked Chamberlain for a ministerial committee on tariff policy'.[15] This request, which crystallised the accumulated wisdom of the higher Civil Service, asserted that as it was not possible to 'be certain of peace in our time' it should be seen whether 'the policy of 1931 now should be modified in the circumstances of 1937'.[16] The momentum generated at the end of 1936 was consciously maintained with specific references to the Leith-Ross paper on the balance of payments, and the Twenty-First Report of the CEI, along with a general assertion that 'many authoritative and independent persons have suggested for quite different reasons that the time has come to call a halt to, and if possible to moderate, both the development of the Ottawa principle and the progressive protection obtained by British industries in the U.K.'.

Liberal activists, such as Ashton-Gwatkin and Jebb, could now push American appeasement with confidence. It appealed to those in the Foreign Office who mistrusted the Hall scheme, and the deteriorating diplomatic situation of the mid to late 1930s lent urgency to the belief of 'anti-appeasers' such as Vansittart that closer ties with Washington could only enhance British strength against potential aggressors, despite the wall of neutrality legislation then being built. Vansittart, anticipating in 1933 the need for American support against Germany, had asked: 'How would that square with a sterling bloc? Ill, I should say.'[17]

Vansittart's position was shared by other important officials, like his successor Cadogan, who 'freely admitted his ignorance of finance',[18] and had little conception of the dangers of tampering with the Ottawa system. Thus, in March 1937 Lindsay replied to a suggestion from Eden as to 'how the attitude of America can be most favourably predisposed towards us for the contingency of a European war', with a letter saying he had actually been about to make 'the strongest plea I possibly could', advocating 'a trade agreement with America on the broadest possible basis'. Although claiming that he had always been in favour of such a move for economic reasons, Lindsay now thought that 'on *political* grounds I have come to the conclusion that a trade agreement is the only important active measure that we can take to predispose America favourably in the manner we desire'.[19]

The Foreign Office drive towards a trade agreement gained surprising impetus when Chamberlain became prime minister and his policy agenda proved amenable to cooperation with Eden and his officials. At meetings of the Cabinet's Foreign Policy Committee in 1937, held concurrently with the Imperial Conference, Chamberlain's enthusiasm for the economic and colonial appeasement of Germany was not contagious. The chances of enticing Hitler into a liberal system with bribes seemed absurdly slim, yet the idea of employing similar tactics to win the support of the United States proved more successful, as cause and effect of a formidable consensus between Chamberlain and the leadership of the Civil Service.

The Interdepartmental Committee on Trade Policy, which Eden and the Civil Service had called into being, reported, unsurprisingly, in favour of more liberal British trading practice. When a prospective statement on the report was discussed in the FPC, debate centred round Section IV, calling for an 'open door' in the colonies. Eden advocated 'acceptance of the recommendations in principle because this would contribute to the improvement of our relations with the United States, the Oslo group of countries and Japan'.[20] In response, the new president of the Board of Trade, Oliver Stanley, warned of a 'widespread suspicion, both at home and overseas, that the Government might be contemplating a general abandonment of the whole system of Imperial preference'.[21] Yet supporters of the imperial economic system had already been outmanoeuvred. The lord chancellor, Viscount Hailsham, complained that he had expected that the matter under discussion would be limited to the German issue: 'He had never thought that the Enquiry would be extended to questions such as the abolition or relaxation of imperial preference in the Colonies.'[22]

At the next meeting, however, which considered the text of a statement on the report, Eden said that he 'would like to see some reference to economic and political appeasement included in the first sentence of the statement'.[23] The new prime minister clearly supported this sentiment and later told the meeting that he 'hoped that the Committee would not forget that this question had become a much wider one than the return to Germany of her former colonies. There was no doubt that the United States would greatly value a gesture.'[24] This comment conflicted with Chamberlain's reputation for hostility to the United States, yet his unwillingness to tolerate American interference in the diplomatic sphere, as during his later break with Eden, did not preclude attempts to draw the USA closer to Britain to strengthen his own position.

Equally surprising, considering Chamberlain's role in constructing the Ottawa system, was his willingness to sacrifice it to gain American support. However, as Hankey shrewdly noted: 'The truth is that Chamberlain, while at the Treasury, absorbed many of the ideas of that Department.'[25] A former chancellor could approve of any concession which liberalised trade, and to which 'the United States would attach importance . . . out of all proportion to its real significance'.[26] In the context of the prime minister's dream of a general European settlement, the economic cost of American appeasement seemed well worth paying. His grave underestimate of this cost served only to facilitate the effective bonding, through the Treasury and Foreign Office, of the domestic and international wings of liberal orthodoxy in rearmament. As prime minister, Chamberlain was able to neutralise the professional jealousies of the two departments in the sphere of economic policy and unify their efforts, to increasing effect.

Sir Frederick Leith-Ross followed up his subtle advocacy of 1936 by stating baldly in 1937: 'The time seems to me to have come when we ought to reconsider our general attitude towards stabilisation and work for a general agreement.'[27] This, he explained, meant a return to gold. His thinking was entirely consistent with his earlier view of 1933 that future prosperity depended on 'securing international agreement for the relaxation of tariffs, the adoption of more liberal monetary policies, and the abrogation of exchange controls, and so on'.[28] This view chimed with Vansittart's opinion of 1933, despite the latter's implacable hostility to Germany and his advocacy of great armaments, and it is thus possible to see why, after 1936, British international financial policy began to move away from the economic imperatives of imperial defence identified in the First World War, rather than towards a strengthening of the Ottawa system as the logic of a deteriorating international system suggested.

Chamberlain's arrival as prime minister was the pivotal event in the disastrous course of British defence finance. The move against Ottawa was conducted with his support and he pushed the Dominions hard towards acceptance of a reduction in their preferences, in pursuit of a quick settlement with the United States.[29] This, though, was no easy task, as the secretary of state for the Dominions, Malcolm MacDonald drily revealed, to the FPC: 'The discussions with the Dominion Delegates [to the Imperial Conference] had been as helpful as we had expected, though perhaps not as helpful as we had hoped.'[30] There was also powerful opposition in Britain to any relaxation of the Ottawa system, and tortuous wrangling with the Americans ensured that more than a year was to pass before the trade agreement was successfully concluded.

The important fact, though, was that the issue was now above the counter in Cabinet and the official object of policy. This meant that despite the British government's statements of 1936 that it must rely on imperial resources and guaranteed lines of supply in a dangerous world, rearmament based on imperial resources was now endangered.

4.2 The home front

The Foreign Office view that war could best be avoided by securing some form of diplomatic commitment from the United States, rather than embarking on the undiplomatic task of developing British war potential, held obvious attractions for the Treasury in its goal of maintaining a balanced budget at low levels of taxation. In 1936, under Chamberlain, the Department had found itself at odds with the political pressure for increased defence expenditure, and helped only by Baldwin's instinct to recoil from rearmament.

Far from public opinion in 1936 constituting a brake on rearmament, the domestic political situation demanded a minimal level of spending which was from the outset distasteful to the government.[31] The Defence

Policy and Requirements Sub-Committee of the CID, in its report to the Cabinet on the Third DRC Report of October 1935,[32] considered the financial implications of rearmament with some trepidation. Lord Weir, at the Committee's first meeting, briefly and bluntly encapsulated the economic implications of rearmament:

> There were bottle-necks at the moment and if expansion was commenced these bottle-necks must unavoidably get worse. He was, therefore, bound to state that the programme recommended could not be carried out in the period envisaged unless a definite turn-over to a semi-war organisation was undertaken. The scheme was unrealisable in the time considered necessary unless this semi-war organisation was introduced or, alternatively, a reduction was effected in normal civil activity and our export trade.[33]

Weir's last sentence explicitly raised the possibility that given the correct thoroughness of effort, rearmament would not damage the civilian economy and that more disruption would occur if the rearmament programme were to be carried out in competition with the normal peacetime activity. Hankey added his support and 'said how glad he was that Lord Weir had raised this aspect of the problem'. He added: 'The position in Germany was different; she had already gone to semi-war conditions.'[34]

None of this was satisfactory to Chamberlain, who pinned a superficially authoritative Weir down to details. He 'referred to a statement made by Lord Weir that the programme envisaged in the Defence Requirements Report could not be carried on except by adopting semi-war conditions and asked what these conditions were'. Weir attempted to elucidate and

> said that although he had had experience of production under war conditions, he had never considered the question of semi-war conditions in relation to this country. It was well known that these conditions existed in countries such as Germany and Russia where there was central control. He did not consider such a system, i.e., peace production with a war type of control could ever be carried out in this country.[35]

Weir then retreated from his earlier implication that economic controls would ease the burden of rearmament on the civilian economy and said that he 'considered that semi-war conditions would necessitate interference with existing civil and export trade'. Baldwin, seeing that Weir had retreated under Chamberlain's fire, followed the logic of the revised position. He 'referred to the question of estimating the time necessary to carry out the programme without semi war conditions which Lord Weir had stated could not be effected without interfering with private industry'. Weir 'said this was a very difficult question and the estimate would depend on the quantitative character of the programme'. Baldwin persisted in a fruitless search for facts and 'asked whether Lord Weir, on the material in the papers already submitted to the Committee, could calculate the productive capacity of the country – a matter on which the Committee had little knowledge. It was a matter of vital importance to ascertain what could be produced and in what period of time.'[36]

These exchanges implied a fluid situation in which knowledge was slight and a variety of policy options available. The views of Chamberlain and the Treasury, though as usual forcefully expressed, represented only one such option. Characteristically, Baldwin seemed unwilling to impose an opinion, and the Committee's Report in February 1936 incorporated Weir's view, as the government's most respected outside expert, in the context of the existing fiscal orthodoxy represented by Chamberlain. The main text of the report quoted[37] a statement on financial control made by Lord Weir, in a memorandum included as Annexe C, that

> the conditions are in some measure akin to War conditions. The word of the man responsible for Supply must carry, and the spirit and enthusiasm which he has evoked in the contractor's mind must not be chilled by delays of approvals, caused by financial control. I do not mean that any loose disregard should prevail on the financial side, but the keynote must be that 'the job must go ahead'.[38]

Despite the note of restraint adopted at the end of this statement, its repetition in the main report showed that it was nevertheless controversial to the Committee, which noted emphatically that:

> We are at one with Lord Weir in agreeing to the urgency of the matter, but it would of course be impossible to adopt any unconstitutional methods of financing whereby the Treasury loses control over expenditure. We have no reason to believe that Treasury control,

adapted to meet the particular circumstances, is incompatible with rapidity; the machinery lies to hand in the existing Inter-Service Treasury Committee which has proved most effective during the crisis caused by the Italo-Abyssinian dispute.[39]

It was further stated that 'under Lord Weir's proposals, the supplies called for in the 3–5 years' programmes are to be secured without interference with or reduction of production for civil and export trade'.[40]

These conclusions are revealing of the state of British thinking at a crucial juncture. In the field of defence finance, the course of development since the First World War was reiterated. There was to be no interference with the peacetime economy and peacetime fiscal probity, though the dividing line between peace and war was becoming indistinct. However, in worsening diplomatic circumstances the struggle to impose a budgetary limit on rearmament was to be every bit as tough as negotiating a trade agreement with the Americans, and, in contrast to the shadowy world of economic diplomacy, the consent of Cabinet and Parliament would be required. Great skill and perseverance would also be required, but Chamberlain possessed these qualities in abundance.

4.3   Manoeuvres

The attempt to contain rearmament within a balanced budget, and without disruption of the civilian economy, supported liberal internationalists in their assault on the Ottawa system, and added weight to Chamberlain's policy of appeasement. If defence expenditure broke its chains then the necessary changes in Britain's international financial policy would sweep away the American negotiations along with cherished liberal freedoms, especially free movement of capital.

During 1937 Chamberlain, as prime minister, was better able than before to act on his belief that the cost of rearmament would overstrain and thus undermine the economic strength of the nation. It has been observed that 'Chamberlain upheld normal trade with reasoning that gave his doctrine the powers of both admonition and salvation' and that he 'acted upon these principles with a tenacious consistency that could only be inspired by faith – that war would not come to pass'.[41]

However, his case had to be made. The powerful voices which had coalesced around Hull's drive for a trade agreement would not all support limitation of rearmament expenditure. Vansittart, for example, would certainly rebel. Chamberlain could rely on his chancellor, Simon, and Treasury civil servants, who shared his concerns and were guided in Sir Richard Hopkins' words, by the 'assumption that we shall not, and cannot afford to, allow ourselves to slip quietly into American or French budgetary methods but shall strive, at any rate till disaster over-whelms us, to keep within the limits of decent finance'.[42]

To ensure success, a doctrine would have to be formulated for the rationing of defence expenditure which could be used as an effective political weapon. Consequently, throughout 1937 the Treasury devised means of quantifying and then controlling the cost of the rearmament programme. At the end of the year Sir Thomas Inskip, minister for the coordination of defence, presented the new doctrine and by February 1938 the concept of the fourth arm was firmly established as government policy. This success, however, was hard won.

In January 1937, during a meeting of the Cabinet, 'a request was made that in this critical year the Cabinet might be given information at rather shorter intervals as to progress with the armaments programme'.[43] The result in February was Inskip's paper 'Progress in Defence Requirements', which revealed delays resulting from inadequate capacity. Bottlenecks of this type were inevitable in an economy undergoing rearmament and were a feature of German and later American experience. However, commenting on Inskip's account of shortcomings in the provision of machine tools and anti-aircraft equipment for the Navy, Chamberlain 'wished the Cabinet to realise that these two instances showed that even the present programmes were placing a heavy strain on our resources. Any additional strain might put our present programmes in jeopardy.'[44]

In fact, bottlenecks in production were simply evidence of the inadequacy of existing plant in the defence industries. The test of resources would be whether or not new plant could be created and maintained. This was as yet unknown, but the artificial correlation of existing productive capacity and the totality of national resources prefigured more sophisticated Treasury alarmism concerning threats to the general 'balance' of the economy. It was an argument likely to impress the uninformed with the apparent evidence of their own eyes while remaining usefully vague about numbers. This was particularly important, as the Treasury's calculations rested on the guesswork of a single official.

Also in January, Sir Richard Hopkins, now second secretary at the Treasury, concocted a maximum figure for defence expenditure which the Department was prepared to finance from taxation, of £1100 millions, and realising this to be politically inadequate, he decided to sanction a loan to boost the total to £1500 millions, which might be acceptable to Cabinet but which nevertheless came down firmly in favour of 'business as usual'. Early in February, therefore, Chamberlain informed his colleagues that 'as the Cabinet must long have realised, it was not possible to finance the whole of our Defence Requirements Programmes from revenue',[45] and he thus requested authorisation to seek borrowing powers from Parliament before the Budget. This may have given the Cabinet the impression that the money would be found for the programmes they had agreed. In fact this measure simply authorised spending up to the Treasury's then secret ceiling, and in the ensuing months a plan was prepared to enforce this limit.

A convincing argument that a determined rearmament drive would destroy the economy was not easily drawn together from the various strands of Treasury thinking. An attempt at such a synthesis was presented to the Cabinet at the end of June in Sir John Simon's paper 'Defence Expenditure'. In the preamble Simon humbly acknowledged that the work was largely Chamberlain's, but the report was actually prepared by Hopkins. His long initial draft had defeated Chamberlain's attempt to work through it in the small hours, and he ordered it shortened for ministerial consumption.[46] The streamlined report put before the Cabinet stressed the exponential growth of 'capital' expenditure, that intended to remedy deficiencies, on defence between the first and third DRC reports and the figures revealed during the Treasury's work in January on the defence loan. The report stated that:

> Figures such as these indicate the pace at which the cost to be met continues to grow and show that there is at present no trace of finality. We are running the gravest risks if we do not resolutely insist on correlating the rising total burden of Defence liabilities to the whole of our available resources. Indeed, the means of correlation is, under existing practice, rapidly breaking down.[47]

The report introduced the Cabinet to the maximum figure of £1500 millions to be spent on defence in the five years 1937–42, which 'must be regarded as a maximum' and stressed that in the event of 'a set-back in trade – indeed, if prosperity does not increase – the sum available is likely to be less and even very substantially less'.[48] Perhaps anticipating trouble in enforcing this figure, which was after all 'based on a general examination by the Treasury of the cost of the programme as revealed in January 1937',[49] and took no account of international dangers, the authors of the report shrewdly stressed in conclusion the basis of their argument in external finance.

In a domestic context there were too many counters to Treasury reasoning, ranging from a Ministry of Supply, with compulsion of labour and capital, to increased taxation. It could not be argued that resources were stretched to the limit until such measures had been employed. The external position, however, provided a logical answer to this problem as no precedent for its control by formal machinery existed from the previous war, and no political constituency existed which would press for such control. This state of affairs would endure. In January 1939, with war a daily threat, *The Economist* launched a severe attack on the government's unpreparedness. It noted that:

> There is an important point of principle involved. The Prime Minister has told us that he will not introduce a war-time regime until an emergency actually arises: there can be, for instance, no Ministry of Supply and no compulsory register until war is actually in sight. And on Tuesday Sir Auckland Geddes [adviser to the Lord Privy Seal] revealed that, although a Ministry of National Service already existed in skeleton form, with a 'young and active man' already earmarked to be a Minister, neither would be produced until the day of disaster dawned. Perhaps the best comment on the doctrinaire position which the Government have taken up in this matter was made by Sir Auckland himself:-
> As an island nation (he said) we have been accustomed to wars which allowed us a period to make the necessary arrangements after the beginning of the war. That position is now past.
> That is precisely why, in Mr Eden's words, 'The nation would welcome the greatest possible national effort in every sphere of defence' – even in peace-time.[50]

The Economist's argument left untouched the basis of fourth arm policy in the threat of rearmament to the pound. Indeed, in its previous issue the journal had warmly approved of the government's action in transferring the gold in the Bank of England's Issue Department into the EEA to be squandered in support of sterling. The contrast is telling. Simon's report to Cabinet concluded with a statement, redrafted by Sir Warren Fisher to read more emphatically,[51] that:

While in this note I have confined myself to a brief exposition of the relation of the programmes to our Exchequer resources available out of taxation or loans, this is only one aspect of the problem. Ultimately our resources have to be measured in terms of man power, productive capacity, and the maintenance of the balance of our general trade, without which our imports of essential raw materials and food could not be obtained. These matters cannot be excluded from any review of the problem.[52]

Simon's paper, which called for a review of Service programmes to fit the new financial ceiling, was approved by the Cabinet. Service ministers, however, were rightly concerned that commitments already agreed in Cabinet would be reneged upon. Simon drew a distinction between programmes agreed by both Cabinet and the Treasury Inter-Services Committee and those simply agreed by Cabinet which could be reviewed. The home secretary, Samuel Hoare, objected. He 'pointed out that if the figures of Defence expenditure had increased rapidly, this had been by deliberate decision of the Cabinet on a review of the whole international situation'.[53]

This rebuke from such a senior political figure reflected the fact that the Cabinet could not be trifled with and might turn. The 'balance of our general trade' in the narrow sense of the balance of payments would not suffice to scare ministers, as it was impossible to thread a needle from trade gap to currency collapse. Trade was already evidently in deficit and had been for some time, yet the chief difficulty experienced with sterling was actually to keep it below an exchange rate of $5. Foreigners continued to compete for access to the British market, and essential imports showed no signs of drying up. The Cabinet could, however, be outmanoeuvred and Simon set his mind to a more surreptitious way of advancing policy.

After the Services' estimates had been duly despatched to the Treasury, and a new Treasury paper prepared, Simon wrote to the prime minister concerning the best method of translating the exercise into policy.[54] He considered that a 'slightly varied' DRC Committee would be appropriate, although the effect of the variations would be anything but slight. He stated that 'I do not think the Foreign Office need be represented, and it would be well that in addition to Sir Warren Fisher, who was an original member, Sir Richard Hopkins and Sir Horace Wilson should be added.' This body, newly packed with the Treasury architects of the rationing concept and cleansed of their rivals from the Foreign Office, 'would then, in the light of these documents, consider the comparative claims upon the resources of the country in the widest terms, including the necessities of overseas trade, manpower, etc., with a view to making a report to the Cabinet as soon as may be'.

This committee's conclusions would reach the Cabinet with the authority of a Cabinet Committee rather the Treasury alone, and would thus be harder to resist. Or as Simon put it, 'it seems to me that it is likely to be a quicker and more effective way of getting to a definite result than the alternative method of the Treasury coming forward now with a maximum global figure which will at once set everybody disputing'.

The Committee so constituted duly assembled, but even without Vansittart, the idea of rationing was by no means universally welcomed. The Treasury's figures still did not reflect complete national mobilisation for defence. The simple concept of rationing could not answer fears for national survival. Hopkins conceded that his total for rearmament of £1500 millions was by no means the maximum that could be raised. He revealed that: 'Generally, in regard to our financial capacity, he felt that looking only at the period 1937–41 we should be able to obtain £1500m. *or rather more from revenue and borrowing without a great increase of taxation* [italics added].'[55]

His justification for rationing was that 'looking beyond 1941 the expenditure of £1500m. would lead to a higher cost of maintenance than we can afford without a great increase of taxation'. Nevertheless, at a previous meeting Hopkins had seemed unworried by the prospect of an increase in taxation. Inskip had asked whether

> the Treasury had made an estimate, possibly an arbitrary figure, of the amount which it is within our capacity to provide for defence in the next 3–4 years. He felt that without guidance on this point the Cabinet could scarcely reach a decision on the programmes. He invited discussion on his suggestion that we should not look too far ahead. If measures deemed necessary for security can be taken presently, should we be deterred by doubts as to what we may be able to maintain in five years time?[56]

Hopkins stated his view that, considering future costs, £1500 millions was the maximum available without an increase in taxation but added curiously: 'The purely economic effect of a rise might not be too serious.

The danger is rather psychological.' Ministers would thus be invited to constrain defence policy within a global budgetary figure specified according to rule of thumb by Hopkins, though even he felt that more could be raised without taxation and that taxation itself could safely be raised. Inskip was torn between his own instinct to press ahead and his respect for the Treasury view, to which he succumbed. Criticism of Hopkins' reasoning came from Hankey, who 'suggested that if, to give security and avert war, the needs of defence were predominant in the next four years, some heroic measures would be justified on grounds of defence analogous to those taken in 1931 on grounds of economic stability'.

Hopkins took this to be a plea to sacrifice social spending for defence within the global limit. He stated that: 'A major consideration was expenditure on unemployment assistance which, in contrast to a figure of £20m. in 1929, does not now fall below the level of £65–55m. at best owing to the block of permanently unemployed. It is capable of rising to £100m.' He did not explain how, according to his hypothesis, unemployment could rise steeply in an economy straining every sinew to produce weapons.

It was clear that given the doubts expressed by Hankey and Inskip, not obvious rebels, the Treasury could not hope to sell rationing to the Cabinet on the grounds either of current or future strain on productive capacity or the tax system. This was reflected in the tone of two papers written by Inskip and Hankey and circulated with proof copies of the former's 'Interim Report' to Cabinet. Inskip expressed himself in a forceful yet contradictory manner, reflecting his personal uncertainty. He believed that 'expenditure on re-armament for the next four years ought to depend on what we need now to make us secure and on what we can afford now and not what we can afford in five to ten years time'.[57] On the other hand: 'The husbanding of our financial resources is almost as much a matter of defence as the provision of material and personnel. I suggest that this should never be forgotten.' For Inskip, therefore, defence finance was a balancing act: 'I suggest that expenditure should not be contemplated on a scale which is likely to exhaust our financial resources. The question is how we are to reconcile the two desiderata, first to be safe, secondly to be solvent.'

4.4   Tying the knot

The provisional nature of the estimates provided by the Service Departments meant that Inskip was compelled to produce an 'Interim Report' to the Cabinet in December 1937 which, in the absence of hard figures, 'was less a detailed examination of actual and prospective Service programmes than a statement of the general principles upon which such programmes should be based'.[58] However, the paper, largely drafted by Treasury civil servants, managed finally to knit the various themes that the Treasury had pressed upon the Cabinet into a winning political formula, or as Simon put it: 'A classic statement of the elements that make up our strength for national defence.'

The report was named 'Defence Expenditure in Future Years', and it recapitulated to Cabinet the Treasury's line that rearmament was upsetting the balance of normal trade. Incremental demands for the funding of agreed programmes were beginning to outstrip the existing defence budget, and the likely cost of major new programmes was threatening to exceed that which could be provided within the context of a balanced budget and the existing defence loan of £400 million. The levels of expenditure envisaged by the Services were now described as a threat, not to any one economic indicator, but to the general 'stability' of the entire economy. The concept of stability gave the argument its internal logic, and made possible the famous assertion that:

> Seen in its true perspective, the maintenance of our economic stability would more accurately be described as an essential element in our defensive strength: one which can properly be regarded as a fourth arm in defence, alongside the three defence services, without which purely military effort would be of no avail.[59]

This argument was a triumph of logical manipulation, and the basis of the Treasury's attempt to 'justify' limited rearmament 'as a positive force in the emergent rearmament policy',[60] for it removed the rock on which earlier Treasury appeals for economy had foundered, that defence and fiscal economy were in opposition. It asserted that defence costs must be curbed to strengthen the economy for war.

Threats to economic stability replaced current account deficit as the most likely cause of a fatal sterling collapse, developing the earlier concept of dangers to 'the balance of our general trade'. The phrase was repeated four times in Inskip's report, in a passage reproduced almost verbatim from a Treasury memorandum prepared by Bridges,[61] being transmuted in a series of logical steps in consecutive paragraphs to the new term, 'economic stability'. The idea had been developed to the point where the definition of 'balance' as the result of matching debit against credit was replaced by the sense of balance as if on a high wire.

Which minister would care to be held responsible for tipping the economy over the edge?

However, for the argument to function, the horrors of instability had to be credible to the Cabinet. The successful amendment was to link the idea of an overstrained economy with a threat to the external value of the currency. If the Cabinet was discussing expenditure, an unbalanced budget would be the agent of doom; if the balance of payments, then deficit would suffice; if industrial capacity, then inflation would hasten the end. The need to assert a consecutive causal chain of disaster from unbalanced budget to currency collapse had been broken and now any one of these factors could pose a fatal threat to economic stability. The political utility of the fourth arm argument lay in the fact that it was vague as to causes but absolutely emphatic as to effects, a device made possible by its theoretical basis in the external position.

The domestic and international aspects of the 1937 drive for liberalism in policy, had, through Chamberlain, achieved effective mutual support. The Treasury's success in constraining defence expenditure made possible a liberal stance in economic diplomacy, while in turn the supposed threat of rearmament to the external position made feasible the same limitation of the Service programmes. Thus: 'The amount of money which we can borrow without inflation is mainly dependent upon two factors: the savings of the country as a whole which are available for investment, and the maintenance of confidence in our financial stability.' Britain should 'avoid at all costs any action at the present time which would affect our stability. Nothing operates more strongly to deter a potential aggressor from attacking this country than our stability.' Obvious military weakness, it was acknowledged, might tempt an aggressor despite Britain's stability, and Inskip tendered to his colleagues the revised formula that: 'The problem before the Cabinet is, therefore, to strike a proper balance between these factors' and provide adequate armaments 'without making demands on our resources which would impair our stability, and our staying power in peace and war'.[62]

The defence of the Empire, like its economic well-being, was to be subordinated to the survival of the international financial system and Britain's position within it. The argument was familiar enough to appeal to the disproportionate number of National Liberals in the Cabinet and unanswerable by the rest, to whom the intricacies of international finance were a closed book. The political effect of the fourth arm argument was confirmed when Inskip presented hard figures for future expenditure in his February 1938 Further Report, and was able to impose them without difficulty on the Cabinet.

Inskip's 'Further Report' imposed a limit of £1650 million on defence expenditure over five years, or £1570 million for the Services when ARP and interest on the defence loan were subtracted. Inskip appeared to offer a compromise to the defence Departments by agreeing to spend as much immediately as he believed industry could cope with, to ensure the full utilisation of existing plant in 1938 and 1939. This was not a mighty sum.

The Services' inflated estimates for 1938–39 amounted to slightly less than £2000 millions over five years. Inskip's rejection of this figure as certain 'to definitely impair that economic stability which is an essential part of our defensive armour', reveals that his idea of the full employment of industry did not differ markedly from that of the Treasury. He noted that even the approved sum would 'involve maintenance costs on the conclusion of the programme of no less than £255 millions a year. The Treasury cannot see any prospect of any sum approaching this figure being made available on the basis of existing taxation and £400 millions of borrowed money.' Inskip's hope was that 'before this point is reached the position may have changed, and the need for great armaments disappeared'. Moreover, his statement that defence expenditure for 1938 at £345 million would match existing productive capacity referred only to the current organisation of the economy. In the event that 'heavy excess expenditure over such a figure were contemplated, it would appear that we must envisage war measures of compulsion on industry and labour, not only most difficult politically, but threatening the maintenance of that stability which it is an essential defence interest to preserve'.[63]

This was a much more powerful and aggressive political argument than had yet been deployed in favour of orthodoxy. It covered dissent like a blanket and permitted continuous attack on the government's critics, especially Conservatives who could be warned that precipitate rearmament courted revolutionary upheaval. In this context it has been argued, for example, that: 'Inflation's adverse effect on Britain's international credit position, and consequently on trade, was but one element of the Treasury's concern.'[64] This was true but to the Treasury all routes to revolution were economic. Social unrest would be a secondary effect of any breakdown in the fourth arm policy.

Thus, 'the problem of balancing Britain's security against her international solvency'[65] was in fact the answer to the government's policy dilemma. The plausible contention that Britain's international solvency was threatened by rearmament was the one essential component of the fourth arm policy, without which demands for greater and more rapid improvements in British security could not be resisted and a case against massive expenditure sustained in Cabinet.

4.5   Available 'weapons from the authoritarian armoury'

The extremism of the move towards a purely liberal policy in defence finance can be judged by the sharply contrasting advice given to the CEI by the economist P.K. Debenham in October 1937.[66] His paper summarised the British position fairly from a liberal perspective, with the same classical assumptions as those informing political policy makers. His policy conclusions, however, bore little resemblance to those of the Treasury, even though he did not take account of the growing economy and assumed that the rearmament budget would have to be extracted from a fixed resource base.

Resources would come from existing spare capacity, enforced saving and some rationing. Even from these restricted sources, Debenham felt that: 'Given time and organisation the additional expenditure at present prices, which could be incurred by the full utilisation of all three sources is extremely large', and could be reckoned at 'between £400 and £500 million at present prices'. Further, 'the exact limit set to expenditure by our material resources is of no great significance, for it is probably well in excess of any proposal for increased armaments expenditure likely to be made'. Nor was the balance of payments likely to be a constraint on total possible expenditure as long as the EEA was able to cover deficits with its reserves. Debenham felt that: 'Provided therefore, that the exchange account is in a position to part with resources, there is much to be said in the interests of rearmament alone, for the policy of acquiescing in an adverse balance of payments during the period when British industry is readapting itself to changes in demand necessitated by the rearmament programme.'

Debenham foresaw pressure on the exchanges to come, as incipient US depression would draw reserves in that direction according to the classical balance of payments mechanism. In fact Nazi aggression would be the catalyst, but Debenham's predictions of necessary action are illuminating and prescient. He realised that: 'Just as the pace of rearmament in its first stages is limited by the technical organisation of industry, so, as the necessary adjustments are made and the rate of expenditure increases, a second limiting factor is encountered, namely the threat to the stability of the exchanges. The effect of the American depression has been to advance the date when this second limitation comes into play.'

Noting that the bulk of the gold reserve had come from 'the inflow of refugee funds' he went on to say that:

> If it became impossible to finance a moderate increase in the adverse balance of payments by drawing upon the gold accumulated in this country through the inflow of short term funds – and this would be the case as soon as the adverse balance reached a point at which through mistrust of sterling these funds began to be reconverted into gold or other foreign currencies – and if the adverse balance could not be diminished by any of the more orthodox expedients (e.g. the exclusion of competitive foreign imports, or the reduction of British costs through a moderate depreciation of the exchange or other means) then the choice would lie between confining armaments expenditure within the limits set by the necessity of maintaining the balance of payments in equilibrium, and of adopting less orthodox measures to improve our receipts from exports, and to reduce our imports.

Debenham was hinting at exchange control, and looking abroad he noted that 'comparison of German with French methods surely suggests that even judged by the effects on the standard of living the German methods are to be preferred; and they certainly have the advantage of having produced the armaments'. Debenham then went into a detailed analysis of the Schachtian methods of exchange control practised in Germany and soon to be necessary in Britain. This must have been painful for an economist of Debenham's stamp, and in conclusion he allowed himself the expression of a personal view, stating that:

> the great harm done by an accentuation of rearmament is not so much in the field of physical resources as in the field of economic organisation. It involves a progressive increase in Government control over economic activity. In particular it involves profound modifications in the organisation of international economic relationships, which, since they are likely to spread not only among the nations directly interested in rearmament, but also, in self-defence,

throughout the rest of the world, are likely to remain long after the hysteria which brings them into being has died down. With all its faults the comparatively liberal system of international trade, whose final interment we shall soon witness, did allow the choice of consumers to influence the course of trade. The system which seems likely to emerge will pay little regard to that.

Debenham saw the inevitable use of 'weapons from the authoritarian armoury' in the near future. Then,

> the first steps which will have to be considered are exchange control, and the limitation of dividends on ordinary shares. The second step would be measures to improve the balance of payments, 'aski pounds', differential exchange rates, export monopolies, and import boards for raw materials. Finally would come measures of price control and the control of the new issue market.

The fourth arm policy dictated that expenditure would be kept within such limits as to preclude exceptional measures. Debenham's prescription would then have contained rearmament within balance of payments equilibrium. However, as the current account of the balance of payments had not been in equilibrium for several prosperous years, the measure used would be the value of sterling in relation to the dollar. This had a residual mystique as an indicator of national solvency. As Debenham's gloomy analysis had concluded, the maintenance of 'balance', whether of payments or budget, was not really a practical option, even for a liberal economist. The British government, therefore, was determined to play Canute. When the consequences of this course became apparent, Debenham's paper was dusted off and discussed uneasily within the Treasury, before being finally rejected and interred.

4.6   The starting gun

The newly formulated fourth arm doctrine was tested immediately when, in the spring of 1938, the *Anschluss* began a panic flight from sterling. No similar crisis had been experienced in peacetime, and in the First World War financial orthodoxy had been maintained at the expense of extravagant borrowing in America to fund the support of sterling. Also, in 1914 sterling had not come under pressure until some time after war broke out.[67] From the moment of Hitler's move against

Austria, however, the British government would be faced with what amounted to a year and a half of undeclared war. This was perceived at once. On 14 March 1938, immediately following a Cabinet meeting called to discuss the *Anschluss*, the minister for war, Leslie Hore-Belisha, made the point to Basil Liddell-Hart, the military correspondent of *The Times*, who noted in his diary that 'H.B. said that he had read [passages from] *Mein Kampf* to the Cabinet at this morning's meeting. He remarked that people, even in the Cabinet, did not realise that 'we *are* at war' already – such is the new technique. I agreed.'[68] The Cabinet meeting was an immediate sign that the international situation had changed. Chamberlain faced demands: 'As surely as the night follows the day'[69] for the reconsideration of Service schemes, 'which the Treasury had hoped had been heard of for the last time', most notably from the secretary of state for air, Lord Swinton, who requested approval of a new scheme, 'K', for the Royal Air Force.

Swinton presented this scheme as an irreducible minimum for British security, but its approval would demolish the newly agreed fourth arm policy. Simon immediately 'pointed out that this was a very grave matter from many points of view'.[70] The chancellor's 'own view was that if the Cabinet were to adopt substantially scheme "K", it meant an end to the plan of fixing a total sum for Defence Expenditure. By no conceivable means would it then be possible to adhere to the Cabinet's decision of 16th February.' He then went on to elucidate fourth arm policy in all its vagueness and contradiction, arguing that:

There was a fundamental difference in our position from that of other nations. If we became involved in war, we could adopt unorthodox measures such as excessive borrowing, inflation of currency and so forth. At the present moment, however, we were in the position of a runner in a race who wanted to reserve his spurt for the right time but did not know where the finishing tape was. The danger was that we might knock our finances to pieces prematurely.[71]

From Hore-Belisha's perspective, Simon's problem was the location not of the finishing tape but of the starting blocks.

Inskip came to Simon's aid and 'confirmed the view of the Chancellor of the Exchequer that the adoption of Scheme "K" would wreck the armament programme recently adopted by the Cabinet'.[72] If the scheme were adopted 'it would be necessary to approach the Trade Unions with a view to dilution. Such approaches were likely to be badly received.'[73] Inskip 'was satisfied that what the Secretary of State for Air required to be done quickly would not be practicable without dilution of labour, which meant the exercise of strong persuasion – perhaps with compulsion in the background'. Chamberlain, perhaps sensing that such arguments were not sufficient for the new mood, called for further investigation of the matter. It would not rest, however, and the chancellor of the Duchy of Lancaster, Earl Winterton, attending his first Cabinet, brought in some of the cold outside air. He:

> urged that it was important for the Cabinet to consider the view of the 'Right' as well as of the 'Left' in Parliament. He himself had had exceptional opportunities for knowing Mr. Winston Churchill's views. Since joining the Cabinet and having access to Cabinet documents, he was deeply concerned at our inability to fulfil the pledges of the late Prime Minister. He could see the reason for the difficulties, but the Government were going to be faced with a strong demand. Even the News Chronicle urged that we should press on with rearmament. If the Government were to announce that the matter sas [*sic*] 'under consideration', they would be told that that was what they always replied and that the circumstances needed action.[74]

Winterton's forthright comments heralded Hore-Belisha's cutting intervention. Though he 'agreed with the Prime Minister that it would be inappropriate to adopt any particular scheme without further enquiry', he felt:

> It was necessary, however, to face the fact that the Cabinet's present decisions contemplated a re-armament programme spread over five years. It would be said that it had been embarked upon in order to meet a situation which was rapidly becoming imminent. He recalled that the Chancellor of the Exchequer had spoken of what we could do financially if engaged in a war. As a matter of fact, we were at this moment entering on war. The new method of war was for one country to fall on the other in the night.[75]

He then quoted the extracts from *Mein Kampf* mentioned to Liddell-Hart, which gave a more extensive definition of Germany's desired frontiers than Hitler would admit to in 1938. He concluded:

At present we were trying to carry through our Programme without any interference with trade against a Power that was concentrating every effort on armaments. We ought, therefore, to consider a great intensification of our effort. It was all very well to have a five years' programme, but we should not have five years for it. It was clear that Germany meant business.[76]

The tone of Cabinet debate was transformed by the *Anschluss*. In response to these demands for action, the new foreign secretary, Halifax, could only assert rather lamely that 'the events of the last few days had not changed his own opinion as to the German attitude towards this country. He did not think it could be claimed that a new situation had arisen.' Chamberlain had heard enough and concluded the meeting in a terse manner, irritated by Cabinet uncertainty. Had 'the Cabinet had been able to take decisions in time, it would have been possible to make an announcement on the morrow'.[77]

Chamberlain's discomfiture did not indicate impending retreat, despite the buffeting the government's position had received. Voices such as Hore-Belisha's, though increasingly numerous, were isolated from each other and lacked an ideological context. His access to Liddell-Hart was no path to the formation of a constituency as the latter's articles were being subjected to increasingly heavy censorship by Chamberlain's supporters at *The Times*, Dawson and Barrington-Ward.[78]

Hore-Belisha's intervention in Cabinet, though, had found the heart of the fourth arm debate. He had identified the origin of fourth arm policy in the earlier experience of the Great War, and the retained belief in a clean division between peace and war, before which normal financial machinery could be maintained. He simultaneously revealed the absurdity of this conviction in prevailing international conditions and the extraordinary difficulty of pressing this perception on the machinery of government.

Much has been made of the lack of support Hore-Belisha received from the Army Council, and the way in which this hampered his effectiveness in Cabinet.[79] However, even with their full support he would have lacked a doctrinal counter to the fourth arm policy and his acute intuition was not an adequate weapon. There was no military expertise on this matter, as war finance was not considered a military problem. The CID could not express an authoritative opinion on this issue. Swinton's apparent success in pushing Scheme 'K' led merely to a marginal increase in RAF funding, and the Army would pay for even this gain. Chamberlain's belief in continued peace meant rejecting measures of structural economic organisation necessary for war, and this position remained secure.

The pressure for increased Service funding was not the only financial consequence of the *Anschluss*. The flight of capital across the Atlantic began immediately, and in contrast to the government's determined resistance to higher defence estimates, this development would be met with vast expenditure. Here was revealed the absurdity of the fourth arm policy. The government would attempt to limit rearmament in the name of husbanding resources and maintaining Britain's international credit position. However, maintaining this position with peacetime free markets when, in a financial sense, war had already begun resulted in the stupendous expenditure of British resources across the foreign exchanges, dwarfing the extra funding required by the Services' 'impossible' demands of 1937–38.

In March 1938 a turning point had been reached. Peacetime conditions had ended and now was the time for Britain to look to her resources, economic and imperial, to weather the storm, to hold what she had and develop the financial machinery required for the physical outbreak of hostilities. Fourth arm policy, however, dictated the opposite course through the maintenance of 'business as usual'. A war-winning policy would have been an independent policy, and the effect of Hull's intervention in changing the course of British political debate in 1936–37 was enduring. The hope of reaching an understanding with America precluded the self-sufficient British attitude necessary to her development as a world military and economic power.

The position of economic strength built up by the British on the basis of the sterling area was solid, sustainable and invulnerable to US interference. The rise of the dictators, however, made it seem desirable for the British government, of its own free will, to barter economic power for political allies. The impetus for this view was provided by the Foreign Office and then pushed forward by Chamberlain, who by linking this movement with the financial basis of his defence policy was able to coordinate the Foreign Office with the Treasury on the issue, and assert his policy with such success that by the beginning of 1938 opposition had been overcome. The disastrous drain of reserves that began in March 1938 demonstrated the physical consequences of this policy. The flood of British gold about to inundate the New York markets simply revealed the fact that, behind the closed doors of the British government, the State Department's efforts to destabilise the Ottawa system had succeeded beyond its wildest dreams, for the fourth arm policy was in effect a ringing affirmation of liberal internationalism.

5
Between Hitler and Wall Street: Undeclared War versus Business as Usual, March–October 1938

Hitler's annexation of Austria created a tangible fear of war, evoked by *The Economist* before the reopening of Parliament in January 1939: 'Events in Austria, Czechoslovakia and Spain have brought the angel of death, whose companionship is the price of failure to be strong and wise in diplomacy, out into the open.' It observed that: 'Once again the resumption of business in a New Year finds British politics overhung by problems of foreign policy, defence and finance; and the skies are darker rather than brighter for last September's contact with the grimmest of realities.'[1]

Sterling came under immediate pressure after the *Anschluss*, as it was clear that Great Britain would bear the financial brunt of any war for democracy. The British authorities, however, were not helpless and possessed considerable assets which, had they chosen to exploit them, could have transformed the situation. Instead, free financial markets would be maintained during undeclared war, a policy fatal to British war potential and at once a suicidal act of charity to the struggling United States.

5.1 Ideological constraints on policy

The new crisis was exacerbated by the government's unwavering re-inforcement of failure in support of sterling. This can be understood in terms of the fundamental importance of external finance as the basis of the fourth arm policy. The genius of the Treasury's argument had been to multiply the direct routes to perdition through the collapse of the pound, often expressed as the destruction of Britain's 'credit' or 'credit facilities'. Such language slyly presented an image of Britain's relation-ship to the world analogous to that of powerless debtor to bank manager. A truer image would have placed Britain in the role of the bank's major shareholder, but Inskip's 'Interim Report', the 'classic statement' of fourth arm policy, had made no mention of Britain's ability to impose exchange controls, or of the availability of deferred payment for imports in the captive sterling bloc market.

Such concepts were dangerous: the fourth arm argument worked only if sterling was seen to be at the mercy of international capital flows, so that any fiscal excess would tip it into oblivion. As long as this seemed plausible, the ideological commitment to sound finance could be maintained even after strict budgetary balance had been relinquished. The spectre of sterling collapse enforced the rule that rearmament expenditure must be financed out of revenue and borrowing at peacetime levels of taxation, with future expenditure and loan repayment to be financed entirely out of taxation after the completion of rearmament.

Germany demonstrated daily that government action could manage the currency problems of rearmament, but free exchanges possessed remarkable credibility in the British political arena. The controversy provoked by the proposed Ministry of Supply was not repeated over exchange control. The First World War had introduced no precedent for the control of the currency in international markets, nor manifested any public evidence of an exchange crisis. It remained plausible to contend that the stability of sterling in war had been based in sound domestic finance.

Currency stability was the battleground of the financially orthodox, and the cornerstone of their credibility. To forestall the threat to fourth arm policy posed by alternative methods of economic preparation for war, the sterling–dollar exchange rate had to be maintained by conventional means in order to sustain the notional threat to economic stability. In practice the fourth arm argument would function not as an extra Service for defence but as parasite, sapping defensive potential to maintain the existing financial system.

It has been argued that the structures of defence and foreign policy in the rearmament period were shaped and limited by the need of the National Government to form a domestic political consensus.[2] In fact, the fourth arm policy scorned Parliament in its formation and execution and deliberately precluded socialist participation in rearmament. During 1938 and 1939, as the policy was wrecked by circumstance,

Chamberlain's government found that it had isolated itself at home. There remained the United States.

5.2 A sea change

The beginning of sterling's slide in the spring of 1938 was not merely a British problem. As the year progressed and crisis deepened, the scale of the issue would also ask fundamental questions of the United States. The point of contact between the economic conjuncture of Hitler, the British world and America was the US Treasury Department under Morgenthau. Unlike the State Department, the Treasury had no 'program' or premeditated economic attitude towards the British Empire outside the framework of the Tripartite Agreement, and was inclined to manage economic problems and formulate policy on a day-to-day basis, dealing first with the most pressing problems. Also unlike the State Department, the Treasury had a domestic economic agenda to which currency management was extremely sensitive.

By March 1938, with the United States firmly in the grip of the 'Roosevelt recession', Morgenthau was expected to produce fiscal remedies for this new and alarming crisis. The implications of pressure on sterling and the franc would pull the US Treasury in different directions. On the one hand, the attempts of the European monetary authorities to support their currencies flooded New York with gold. On the other hand, declining European currencies meant tougher conditions for US exporters and, as importantly, further depression of commodity prices.

There was no precedent to guide the Treasury Department in dealing with this situation, and, initially, no obvious indication whether or not the situation worked in America's favour. The result was a policy paralysis, wherein possibilities were continually discussed but action prevented by a mixture of bewilderment and fear. Inaction was justified by the hope that things might improve, and a dawning realisation that while sterling's decline was moderated by the sheer volume of gold the British were willing to expend, America was gaining on balance. This favourable situation was produced by British policy, but it was neither dictated by American pressure nor applied in the manner recommended by the American authorities. In fact, the interaction between Morgenthau's Treasury and the British between the *Anschluss* and the outbreak of war demonstrated the essential autonomy of British policy.

Before the Czechoslovakian crisis the attention of a harassed Morgenthau and his advisors became fixed on the plight of the French franc, which overshadowed the initially more gradual fall of sterling. This phase of US attempts to manage the Tripartite Agreement casts a new light on the Treasury's later dealings with the British, and on the supposed success of American attempts to 'bully' the British into supporting sterling with everything they had. The French, supposedly the weakest of the three parties to the Agreement, failed repeatedly to conform to its terms or inform Morgenthau of their actions, and treated his repeated communications in a sardonic and contemptuous manner.

The American prescription for French action was based on the imposition of exchange control as a preferable alternative to the devaluation of the franc. Analysis of this episode, and of the subsequent British crisis, shows quite clearly that had the British given up the fight to maintain peacetime financial practice sooner than they did, Morgenthau and his advisors would have acquiesced in the imposition of British exchange controls as the least of many possible evils. This would have been the most suitable development for British interests as war approached, but was the one outcome that the British themselves were determined to avoid.

5.3 The sterling crisis begins

The economic effects of the *Anschluss* were felt immediately, and their importance for the faltering economy of the United States was indicated by the speed with which the movement in the exchanges was picked up by American opinion. On Sunday 13 March, the *New York Times* front page gave equal prominence to a story detailing Hitler's 'triumphal parade' into Austria and another with the headline 'FOREIGN EXCHANGE TUMBLES IN CRISIS' which correctly linked the two events with the subheading 'Chief World Currencies Break Sharply in the Flight of Capital to Safer Centers'. It noted that: 'Conditions bordering on near panic swept the money markets of the world yesterday as Europeans rushed to purchase American dollars and gold after Germany's conquest of Austria.' In these circumstances, 'heavy demand for dollars in London found ready reflection in the fall of the dollar value of London gold at price-fixing time, and presaged an early return of heavy engagements of gold in Europe for shipment to New York'.[3]

In other words, it would soon be profitable to buy gold in London, and ship it for sale in the New York market. Already, the price of gold in London was 'within about 4 cents of the level at which it will be profitable to resume the movement from London to New York'.[4] Morgenthau did not share such excitement. He was warned in March that a decline in sterling would have the effect of 'reducing the purchasing power of the countries of the sterling area for products from this country, while making it easier for them to undersell us in the export market'.[5] The problem was not pressing in March, however, and the secretary was preoccupied by the likely devaluation of the French franc.

Morgenthau, as the architect of the Tripartite Agreement, was alarmed by the possibility of its breakdown. The prospect of unilateral French devaluation thus produced emotion and consternation but no threats. Morgenthau and his officials instead attempted to persuade the French to implement exchange controls rather than devalue.

Morgenthau said as early as 14 March that in France's position 'I would slap on complete exchange control and grant commercial permits.'[6] At the same meeting he raised the matter by phone with Roosevelt and Hull, the latter because exchange control would have implications for the recently concluded Franco-American Trade Agreement. Later that day he told his officials that:

> If I am willing to stretch this Tripartite Agreement twice as far as she was ever supposed to and have it include exchange control, the State Department can stretch their thing and say 'We will close our eye on this thing' and give these fellows a chance because when they first put on exchange control it has to be on everything because how are they going to distinguish, the first week, what is merchandise shipment and what is capital flight?[7]

The offer of US acquiescence to French exchange controls was made secretly and in person to Blum through H. Merle Cochran, the financial secretary at the Paris Embassy, but was politely declined.[8] The French were unwilling to take such action which was not feasible, to say the least, in the context of domestic politics, and indeed Harry Dexter White[9] had pointed out to Morgenthau that the issue divided left and right in France.[10] Thus, the United States would be left with little alternative but to accommodate the impending devaluation along with the third partner, Britain.

The British, despite their own developing plight, abhorred any form of exchange control. William W. Butterworth, the second secretary and financial secretary at the US Embassy in London, was told that: 'A breakup of the Tripartite arrangement would be hailed everywhere by advocates of autocracy as a disaster for liberal ideas in international finance and business.'[11] Joseph Kennedy, the new London ambassador, told Morgenthau that Chamberlain 'said that exchange control was a great – was a very serious thing because it was the beginning of the end and it was against all the policies that we've been trying to advocate'.[12] The secrecy of the approach to Blum was at least in part the result of unease at the likely British reaction had they been told of the move. White had told Morgenthau that 'I would be extremely surprised if Chamberlain would acquiesce'.[13] Archibald Lochhead, the US Treasury official who administered the Tripartite Agreement, thought this unreasonable and asked 'if you are wanting to take a great amount of capital out of Great Britain, do you think you can do that?'[14] The answer to this rhetorical question was soon to prove an emphatic 'yes', and Morgenthau anticipated trouble if the British were consulted: 'The answer would be no. And I have discussed that with the President. He said inform the British, but he did not say ask them.'[15]

Morgenthau found it increasingly difficult even to contact French Treasury officials, and remarked that, 'when it gets so that neither the British nor the United States Government can talk to anybody for two days in the French Treasury, it isn't very good, is it? Huh?' The secretary described himself at this stage as 'very calm'.[16] However, when in May the French announced their intention to devalue to 175 francs to the pound and raised the possibility that the devaluation might eventually go as low as 200, his calm evaporated. He said in a telephone conversation with Cochran: 'Well, as far as I'm concerned, as I say, I can't be too emphatic in my disgust and – ah – as far as I'm concerned it's the last time I take their word on anything financial.' He went on: 'Now I should think that the friendship of the United States would be worth something to them and they keep coming in here and making pretty statements and all that but they don't keep their word.'[17]

The franc having declined beyond the 175 figure mentioned by the French, Morgenthau told Cochran to warn them that 'they'd better

tonight bring that down to one seventy-five if they know what's good
for them', failing which 'I consider they've absolutely broken their
word'.[18] When Cochran passed on Morgenthau's sentiments however,
the French seemed unrepentant. Cochran reported back that there
was some confusion over translation of the original French message:
'And Rueff said, "Well, we must get some British academician to translate – to interpret"', prompting Morgenthau's reaction that 'Rueff's
getting a little bit too sarcastic and too funny.' Cochran concurred:
'I said that absolutely, I said, "We don't want any Britisher to translate
that or anything else!"'[19] Continuing French insolence was hard for
Morgenthau to bear. He told Butterworth that 'I can't tell you how much
I am upset over – to think that a whole French Government would
act the way they act. I mean to me it's just unbelievable in international
history.'[20]

Finally, the French ambassador was called in to hear the worst, but
he retreated deftly behind the language barrier. Morgenthau told him
in the presence of Herbert Feis, the State Department's adviser on international economic affairs, that: 'the French Treasury had "chiseled" on
their agreement ever since the recent negotiations had started and that
he was disgusted with their conduct and practically at the end of his
patience'.[21] The direct approach backfired. Mistranslating the American
vernacular, 'The French Ambassador showed great distress', despite Morgenthau's assurance 'that this was not a personal matter between the
secretary of the Treasury and the French Ambassador, but in the relations between the two Treasuries'. The secretary, nevertheless, 'in order
to appease the Ambassador voluntarily offered to destroy the steno-
graphic record of his conversation and carried out this offer by burning
the notebook in the fireplace in his office'.

5.4   The 'Roosevelt recession' and the 'billion-four'

Whilst Morgenthau was wrestling with the French, his Department
faced pressure to stimulate the domestic economy. The Roosevelt recession had wiped out the gains made since the beginning of the New Deal
and resulted in a situation in which 'in the year of the Munich crisis,
the U.S. share of world manufacturing output was lower than at any
time since around 1910'.[22]

American national income had contracted to $65 billion, though
$80 billion was thought to be required for full employment. The
Treasury's task, therefore, was to raise national income by all means
available. Fortunately, the Treasury controlled a huge reservoir of

sterilised gold, growing daily as the European currency crisis took hold. This reserve had obvious potential as a tool for recovery and was burdened with a controversial history that made its liquidation all the more attractive.

In the relatively buoyant economic circumstances of 1936, the US economic authorities feared inflation and had taken steps to restrict credit. The Inactive Fund was created, in which the existing gold reserve and additional gold imports were sterilised to prevent their use as a basis for expanded bank loans. By early 1938 such measures were blamed for renewed recession. On 13 March, amidst fresh reports of depressed American production, a leading article in the *New York Times*, under the heading 'Financial Anemia', drew attention to a speech by Leonard Ayres, the vice-president of the Cleveland Trust Company, which

> diagnoses the economic malady from which the country is now suf-fering. The capitalistic system, he points out, requires a continuous flow of new capital; and because that flow has been checked, busi-ness stagnation has resulted. He points out, as others have, how we have finally managed to check the flow of capital from all the principal sources.[23]

Ayres was not alone in this view. On the same day, in a meeting at the Treasury, William O. Douglas, chairman of the Securities and Exchange Commission,

> said that he had told the President that as we have been going along for the last four years with consuming power falling off and without any sufficient backlog of capital expenditures, we have reached the place where there is no longer any capital market. While he thinks it is necessary to spend to increase the consumers' purchasing power, he feels very definitely we can never pull out of the depression by that method. The key is the opening up of the capital markets and getting a regular flow of funds back into industry. We are very foolish if we sit back and hope that business will 'catch' as it has in the past.[24]

Morgenthau was keenly aware of the problem, and extremely sensitive to press criticism. He believed in balanced budgets, however, and did not share the Keynesian enthusiasms of his younger advisers. Nevertheless, he saw a way out of his dilemma, suggesting that 'we could take $100 million gold from the Federal Reserve and use it as capital for the regional banks and "go places"'.[25] This idea presented possibilities for pump priming without deficit financing, and further investigation took place. As the idea took root, it soon became apparent that the amount of sterilised gold available with which to 'go places' was massively in excess of $100 million. In an internal memorandum it was revealed that: 'As of March 31, 1938 the Treasury held gold in the inactive account in the amount of $1,183,000,000 and free gold in the working balance of $210,000,000, or total gold available for creating credits with the Federal reserve banks thereby increasing our cash balance, if the Secretary deems it wise, in the amount of $1,393,000,000.'[26]

On the same day, in a paper prepared by his advisers, Morgenthau was strongly advised to desterilise gold as the best means of increasing bank reserves, a move which, quite apart from its technical benefits,

> will be a spectacular pronouncement of a Government policy which the public would interpret as expansionist, and therefore contribute toward the development of a psychology favorable to expansion. It would strengthen the expectation of rising prices because it would be evidence that the Administration proposes to take aggressive steps to reverse the present deflationary trend.[27]

This recommendation was accepted, and on 14 April 1938 the US Treasurer was instructed to liquidate the Inactive Fund and distribute what was to become known as the 'billion-four' to the 12 Federal Reserve banks, thereby ensuring that the reflationary effect of the move would be felt throughout the United States.

The excitement displayed by the American press as gold poured in from abroad was, therefore, understandable. As far as public opinion was concerned, new gold fought the Depression. The British, however, disapproved of Morgenthau's action, as was revealed in a telephone conversation between the secretary and George Harrison, the governor of the Federal Reserve Bank of New York, who enquired about foreign reaction. Morgenthau replied that he 'thought the British were a little bit childish about it. They said they had seen this and that and the other paper, didn't understand it. In the first place, they've got an Embassy with forty or fifty people in it; if they can't read our newspapers and send the cables over, I don't know. . . .'[28]

White was similarly sceptical, noting that 'I venture to predict that when next week's "Economist" comes to us, there will be a very excellent analysis of what desterilization meant and accomplishes, which was probably written 24 or 48 hours after the event. No difficulty in understanding it.' He was right about *The Economist's* grasp of the matter. It was to observe that: 'The increase in the deposits of the member banks in recent months is one of the outstanding economic phenomena of the period.'[29] Harrison perceptively observed that, 'I think the amount is probably what made them think it was not routine.'[30]

The British had little justification for open hostility: classical gold standard theory called for the monetisation of inflowing gold. However, the British knew that Morgenthau's intent was reflation, not resurrection of the gold standard. His action implied a level of state intervention in the workings of the domestic economy that was quite alien to official British thinking. Chamberlain told Daladier in August that

> I have seen various plans and suggestions urging us to expand credit further, but these have always seemed to me to miss the point. Our trouble has been not at all to expand credit on the basis of our gold stocks but to persuade people to use the credit which has been created in some abundance. If I ask what is the reason on the one hand for the renewed demand for gold and on the other for the failure of international business and commerce to expand, I come back immediately to the conclusion that it is due to fear of the international political situation.[31]

Characteristically, Chamberlain perceived basic truths but refused to draw pertinent conclusions. He never spoke of such ample unexploited capital in Cabinet rearmament debates. Moreover, his knowledge that the gold drain was politically motivated makes more damning his government's toleration of it on ideological grounds.

5.5 Morgenthau's gold dilemma

The simultaneous struggles with the Depression and the French established the character of the US Treasury's responses to the British crisis. The French episode had demonstrated America's inability to respond effectively to any sterling devaluation. However, the British were evidently determined to support the pound with their reserves, and the decline of sterling was thus initially gradual while New York's gold influx accelerated. The sheer scale of it presented severe technical problems for the US Treasury, which could only process so much at a time and was fully occupied getting the original 'billion-four' into the system. Morgenthau was in danger of building up a new gold reserve so large as to make it appear that he had in some underhand way reverted to sterilisation. It began to seem that the continued gold inflow might be too much of a good thing.

Roosevelt, in conversation with Morgenthau, had wondered aloud as early as 16 March: 'What would be the effect of our declining to receive all gold? I wish you would make a study of it for me.'[32] Morgenthau was immediately sceptical, fearing that 'it would upset everything terribly in this country' and that furthermore: 'The gold would go to England. All my reactions are against it.' He agreed on the study anyway, and produced a discouraging memorandum on 23 March. Such a move would cause 'wild and chaotic fluctuations in foreign exchange rates throughout the world' and that as America held half of the world's gold it would be obviously unwise to create a situation whereby: 'The world would be encouraged to attempt to do without gold, leaving us (and England) holding the bag.'[33]

Thwarting Roosevelt's inane idea, however, simply made the point that the Treasury's hands were tied. To safeguard its own economic position and secure the full value of its immense gold stocks, the United States would have to play the international financial game to the extent of receiving all the gold that was coming. Morgenthau's problem in the short term was what to do with it. On 29 August 1938, George Harrison wrote to Morgenthau that: 'Over the past several months comment has appeared in the newspapers that the Treasury has been sterilizing gold since the desterilization of April 14, 1938. In the last few days and, in fact, several weeks ago, we received a number of telephone calls from people in New York, asking whether it is true that the Treasury is sterilizing gold.' This was because of the 'constantly rising amount of gold held in the Treasury General Fund, which has been increasing ever since April as the result of gold imports and other gold acquisitions by the Treasury which have not been utilized by making transfers to the Gold Certificate Fund of the Federal Reserve System'. Harrison warned 'I think that you would want to be informed of the interpretation placed by some persons upon the current treatment of gold.'[34]

Over the summer, the intensifying Czechoslovakian crisis accelerated the influx. After the crisis, *The Economist* noted that: 'In July gold imports were relatively small; in August they rose rapidly; and in September the net influx was about $600 millions.'[35] Even as Harrison wrote, matters were coming to a head.

By early September, American public opinion was becoming ever more excited by the arriving gold. The *New York Times*, as if in a war report, trumpeted 'POUND OFF AGAIN: MORE GOLD TAKEN',[36] and told its readers that the $6,100,000 of gold 'engaged' on 2 September 'Makes Total Taken in England for Import Here $83,400,000 Since July 26'.[37] The actual movement of the metal was deemed to be of interest and it was reported that the 'Holland America liner Nieuw Amsterdam arrived here last night from the Channel ports with $12,225,000 gold, shipped at Southampton and consigned to the First National Bank and the Bank of Manhattan Company here. The metal will be landed this morning at Fifth Street, Hoboken.'[38]

Gold pushed itself to the top of the Treasury's list of problems. On 21 September, the issue was discussed at a long meeting.[39] Because of gold inflows the Treasury's general fund had grown to $800 million, and in line with Harrison's earlier warning it was feared that if it topped $1000 million the Treasury would be accused of recommencing sterilisation. At this meeting it was decided that all new gold acquisitions would be pumped into the Federal Reserve system with additions to make round numbers from the General Fund, which would then function as a very sizeable reservoir of gold, slowly emptying. In this way the European gold drain and the reflation of the American economy became linked on a daily basis.

5.6 Morgenthau's sterling dilemma

The September crisis ensured that creating a mechanism to integrate the gold influx would not of itself be an effective American response to sterling's weakness. When war seemed imminent, no amount of support from the British reserves could prevent a sharp deterioration in the value of the pound. This situation caused general confusion in the United States. On 4 September 1938, the *New York Times* argued that sterling's fall was being engineered deliberately because 'the advantages of a lower pound to help stimulate domestic recovery outweigh any remaining advantages of a higher pound to help the rearmament program'.[40] A day later, however, under the headline 'LONDON JUSTIFIES

FALL OF STERLING', the paper whilst maintaining that: 'Recently, official support for sterling has been almost entirely withdrawn' contradicted itself with the observation that 'support is by no means entirely lacking', as the 'British exchange fund continues, for instance, to supply gold as freely as possible for shipment to the United States and is purposely maintaining that London price of gold at a level that encourages such shipments'.[41]

This uncertainty was fully reflected in the deliberations of the US Treasury. There seemed, however, to be no possibility for action where the benefits obviously outweighed the costs or where the likely consequences were clear. The Treasury was determined to act in American interests, if it could only be discovered where they lay. In a Treasury meeting at Morgenthau's home, called to discuss possible American policy in the event of war, Russell Leffingwell[42] remarked that 'it might be wise to find out what it is the British want us to do with respect to sterling and then we could cooperate with them', to which Morgenthau 'responded that the important question was not what the British wanted us to do but rather what was good for the United States to do'. Leffingwell stood his ground and said: 'Of course, but you can't fix the price of sterling. England will have to do that. The important question is are you willing to continue to take gold freely at the present price?'[43]

Meanwhile American warships sailed to Portsmouth, on Morgenthau's initiative, to remove US-owned gold before the fighting started. However, on a strictly practical level, if he accepted that the British were doing their utmost to hold sterling and yet failing, then the implications were worrying. It has been suggested that Morgenthau coerced Britain into a full-blooded support of sterling, a position based on the attitude and prolific memoranda output of Harry Dexter White, Morgenthau's most hawkish adviser on Anglo-American affairs. This assertion is beside the point, as the British monetary authorities were already fully committed to the defence of sterling. However, even if the opposite had been true, as White believed, American options were few.

White prepared a memorandum for Morgenthau outlining what have been described as 'methods of bullying the British into holding sterling at $4.80'.[44] He returned frequently to the ideas contained in this paper,[45] bringing them up again and again at meetings as sterling's plight worsened, but their impracticality was obvious at the time and would become more so, repetition and elaboration doing nothing to alter the case.

The first of White's suggestions was to announce a violation of the Tripartite Agreement of 1936, to shame the British. This, of course, would also destroy Morgenthau's proudest creation. The second possibility was to reopen negotiations on the Anglo-American Trade Agreement, then approaching fruition. However, the detrimental effects of such a move would be felt more at home than in London. Roosevelt, moreover, was keen to see the Agreement enacted, and Morgenthau would not compromise Hull's pet project. Both measures would also have sent to the world a message of disarray in the democracies that neither Washington nor London wished to transmit.

White's third option was to devalue the dollar against gold and restore the pre-existing sterling–dollar parity. This would certainly have been effective, and was the one possibility that the British consistently took seriously, fearing its likely effect on the world economy. As the 1933 precedent showed, this was an area in which Roosevelt might act by executive fiat to override his Treasury's wishes. However, potential effectiveness did not equal practicality. Morgenthau and the British were united in their belief that such an action would finish the Tripartite Agreement.

This was unfortunate for the British, because in terms of their war potential in 1938 dollar devaluation against gold would have been beneficial. Sterling's plight would have been eased and the dollar value of British gold stocks would have increased, enhancing Britain's ability to wage war. As will be seen, though, Morgenthau was moving away from such a solution. The fourth possible action listed by White, the conversion of US sterling balances into gold, was an unrepeated oddity.

An indication of the low salience of White's views at this time was that his memorandum was not produced at the meeting for which it was prepared, as this was preoccupied with the plight of China. When White mentioned his paper Morgenthau told him that: 'If this Chinese thing doesn't take too long, maybe we can do a little sterling afterwards.'[46] The occasion did not arise, and indeed White himself seemed to acknowledge the weakness of his specific prescriptions in concluding his memorandum with the observation that: 'The chief and decisive weapon in our arsenal is that England needs our good will much more than we need hers at the present time.'[47] This statement, which remains a commonplace of diplomatic histories, is debatable to say the least in the economic and financial arena. In terms of national interest, sterling's slide was also America's problem. However, Morgenthau was beginning to perceive that if the British were indeed sacrificing their financial strength to hold sterling, a negative policy of inactivity might reap dividends for the United States.

At the 21 September group meeting at the Treasury Department, after the scheme to deal with incoming gold had been formulated, the economist Jacob Viner, a visiting consultant and former Department employee, asked Morgenthau about the Treasury view on the 'drop in sterling . . . speaking as an outsider'. Morgenthau replied that 'I can answer that fairly simply, as an insider. I don't think that until this war situation clears up there is anything that we can do about it, and if anybody in this room knows anything that we can do about it, I wish they'd tell me.'[48] The meeting was uncomfortably aware of American vulnerability on the issue and their dependence on the good faith of the British authorities. It was feared that this might be undermined by the agitation of the British press in favour of devaluation.

An obvious possibility was for the Treasury to use its Stabilisation Fund, a broad copy of the British EEA, to buy sterling. The use of the Stabilisation Fund for this purpose was never seriously contemplated, however, as it meant a politically unacceptable gold drain. The Treasury regarded the stabilisation fund as a contingency reserve to deal with unforeseen crisis rather than a tool of day-to-day currency management. America therefore absented itself from the currency market and was utterly dependent upon British action to change the situation.

This curious and important effect of the gold inflow was also acknowledged when John H. Williams[49] pointed out that 'we seem to be moving back toward – to the orthodox position in international currency matters, giving up gold sterilization and so on; and the question is whether that's the best position to be in. I don't know whether it is or not. It does open up the possibility of England's operating on us.' This could be 'the best solution' but only 'if we could trust them to be wholly unselfish and to take into account not only their interests but ours'.[50]

These comments were an accurate reflection of the situation facing the United States, which still needed a functioning international, or perhaps more accurately trans-imperial, financial system to drag its economy out of the mire and exert global influence within which Britain remained at least an equal partner. As liberal internationalism became less and less appropriate to Britain's circumstances, its importance increased for the United States. Consequently, it was important to avoid any action which might drive the British towards autarky.

Throughout the various crises Morgenthau was helped in keeping his nerve and maintaining a passive policy by intelligence from London. The Treasury's information on the sterling market was excellent. It received daily reports from L.W. Knoke, a vice-president of the Federal Reserve Bank of New York, who spoke daily on the telephone with George Bolton, principal of the Foreign Exchange Section of the Chief Cashier's Office at the Bank of England, and from Butterworth who worked with the British Treasury. The irony of this situation was that Morgenthau was better informed of the operations of British markets than the British Cabinet, which had to make do with infrequent and partial statements from Simon. Even more importantly, Bolton's habitual frankness meant that Morgenthau knew at least as much of the Bank of England's thinking and dealings as did the British Treasury. Morgenthau could, therefore, judge the candour of Treasury comments against the information he received through Knoke.

5.7   Morgenthau sees his way clear

The passing of the Munich crisis lifted the sterling problem temporarily from Morgenthau's shoulders, and the reports from London concerning the attitude of the British authorities were heartening. The pound, which had touched a low of $4.61, rose more than 10 cents before the Munich euphoria wore off and the pervasive sense of crisis returned to drag sterling down once more. The unruffled British reaction to the loss of gold during the crisis contrasted sharply with American excitement at receiving it. While the American press was sufficiently excited by gold receipts to keep score by the day, British fears were calmed by the belief that when the crisis ended the gold would return.

Even as sterling pressure began to build again in October, Henry Clay, economic adviser to the Bank of England, exhibited a complacent front to the Americans. He was fully aware of the political cause of sterling's difficulties, and 'in the course of a short conversation' with Butterworth he 'remarked on the diminution in the pressure on sterling but added that "these spasms temporarily spend themselves but the movement will be resumed" because the Munich settlement is being increasingly regarded as a truce not a peace'.[51] Clay's surprising calmness in the face of this grim prospect gave Washington a false impression of Britain's ability to meet renewed pressure.

The roots of Clay's equanimity were ideological rather than empirical, as he revealed when he 'went on to say that the United Kingdom could lose a lot of foreign funds without serious domestic repercussions; that after all the gold reserve had been built up against the contingency of foreign withdrawals and therefor [sic] there was no reason why it should not be so employed'. The essence of this view was expressed in the CEI's advice to the Cabinet of October 1937 that 'large scale gold movements should be looked upon as a normal element in the preservation of financial equilibrium, and that the stocks of gold in monetary use should be widely distributed'.[52]

British gold was certainly being distributed, but not widely, and Morgenthau was gaining a shrewd perception of how to proceed. He realised that America could do nothing to coerce the British in a crisis, but he knew also that the British monetary authorities could be relied on to do their utmost to maintain the pound for their own reasons, and that a mechanism now existed to manage the gold inflow which was thoroughly advantageous to American interests. In the relative calm between specific crises, therefore, he was relaxed and confident, knowing that a gradual fall in the sterling exchange would not rock the boat and being secretly comfortable with any level above $4.50. Indeed, resistible pressure on sterling was desirable because British expenditure of reserves maintained the gold flow whilst mitigating the pound's decline and the consequent loss of US competitiveness.

Morgenthau told a meeting early in October that: 'I may be all wrong, but I am going to do what I do very rarely – make a little forecast: I've decided that if I was in Europe and I had any money, at best I'd want to invest it in American property, using the all inclusive word, and I am just thinking that money is going to keep right on coming over here, because it's the only place for it.'[53] He continued: 'I mean, if I had any money and I was a European, after what's happened, this is the place I'd want to invest it, and, therefore, I think gold will continue to move this way.'

Morgenthau's spirits thus moved up and down with the exchanges and consequently with Britain's diplomatic distress. Unfortunately for his peace of mind politically inspired currency crises now came in quick succession. Burdened by other business, happy with the immediate situation and lulled by British complacency, he did not immediately perceive the signs of renewed crisis after the brief financial honeymoon of the Munich Agreement. They were there, nevertheless.

5.8 'Business as usual' tested to the limit

Butterworth told the Treasury on 4 October that 'for the moment the belief appears to be growing that the pound is not yet a buy'.[54] Bolton, at the Bank of England, told Knoke on 6 October that 'The market was a peculiar one at the moment. Nobody quite knew which way the cat was going to jump.'[55] However: 'As regards sterling, the feeling in London was that it would go weaker and there was talk of $4.50 or even $4.35 to the pound.' In contrast to Clay's calm assurance, *The Economist* observed uneasily that 'normal conditions are yet to be re-established. This is an unexpected phenomenon which will take some explaining.'[56]

Hitler's Saarbrücken speech of 10 October, in which he asserted that Germany no longer required the tutelage of British governesses, then opened a new phase in financial events. The speech, which in Knoke's description of Bolton's opinion, 'seemed to put an end to the so-called peace that they believed they had secured at Munich',[57] began an assault on sterling sufficient to dispel any complacency. Bolton told Knoke that, 'the rate had opened today at 4.75^{1}/_{2}$ and in less than 5 minutes he had sold about $6,000,000. In addition he had put £750,000 gold into the market at a price to enable its being shipped to New York and thus furnishing more dollars.'[58] When Knoke contacted him at 11.10 a.m. 'total sales so far had been $11,000,000. How long this present movement against sterling would last he didn't know but it very obviously had its origins in the bitter disappointment over Hitler's speech.'

The Economist became anxious at the implications of sterling's failure to rebound after Munich. Stark facts were explored such as that: 'At a rough approximation, three-quarters of America's enormous gold acquisitions reached her from or through London', and that: 'The United States took from us the prodigious sum of £126.7 millions', while: 'Arrivals of new gold from South Africa gradually dwindled away.'[59] The journal went on to make the uncomfortable calculation that the EEA's 'reserves of £297.8 millions on March 31st last, must by now have become sadly depleted'.[60] And as if these losses were not bad enough: 'The dominating factor in the money market is that so far none of the funds which left London during the crisis have shown the slightest signs of returning. On the contrary, the departure of the hot money is now being followed by the transfer to New York of what hitherto had been regarded as permanent balances in London.'[61] Such were the mechanics of undeclared war.

At a meeting of the US Treasury held on 21 October[62] to discuss the deteriorating sterling situation, the lack of American policy options was again made painfully clear. Harry Dexter White encapsulated the position by stating that: 'It is clear that at present any alteration in the rate is practically British-determined. They can determine the rate and we can't, except indirectly.'[63] This indirect method was, as Jacob Viner[64] guessed, '[b]y changing the price of gold' to which he added that 'we're the passive agents'.[65] US Treasury officials felt a sense of powerlessness and frustration appropriate to an earlier time, a feeling that had been encapsulated by Haas in his weekly business report of 12 September, which wondered whether the 'present decline in sterling might not have the same effect upon our economy as England's abandonment of gold had in 1931'.[66]

Later, as sterling seemed likely to be overwhelmed, Morgenthau would echo these sentiments, telling a Treasury meeting that 'I don't want to be in this chair and see us go through another '31 and '32 . . . I wonder how many people realise what was happening to us in '31 and '32.'[67] However, he remained as convinced of British good faith as he had been a month earlier, when he said:

> I want to say this for the English operation of their funds: that they've gone the absolute limit to cooperate with us to keep the thing – nobody could go further than they have. I mean they've gone the absolute limit. I mean I wouldn't have dreamt of suggesting to them that they go as far as they have. I mean they've just thrown everything into it. So as far as day-to-day operations are concerned, nobody could have gone further than they have.[68]

Morgenthau appeared to be suggesting that no action should be taken, and at a later meeting he confirmed that this was the case and explained why, when White reintroduced the idea of increasing the dollar selling price of gold to check speculation. Rejecting the notion, the secretary said that 'I have announced and the papers have carried and I get great satisfaction out of it "Morgenthau says business as usual".

I sounded that keynote. Told it to the President and it's gone through everywhere. Everybody has picked it up. I think it's most important.' White's suggestion 'would not be "business as usual"'. Morgenthau noted that 'the President read this article in the [New York] Times yesterday, somebody, about raising the whole question of gold and the President said, "Remember, I raised the question of what's going to happen when we get 80% or 90% of all the gold," and I said "Mr President so what! Who has a better suggestion?"'

Morgenthau further explained his reasoning: 'I don't want to do anything, as of today, to cast any doubt in anybody's mind as to the fact that we have grown up; we are the monetary center; we are conducting business as usual, and there is nothing in the world which makes me believe I have to worry.'[69] The phrase around which the British attitude to approaching war was based had crossed the Atlantic, but Morgenthau's 'business as usual' policy depended upon that of the British. If they continued to meet undeclared war with peacetime measures, then the economic balance of power could only tilt the American way. In February 1937, Bewley had described Morgenthau as 'a rather ignorant but an absolutely sincere and direct man'.[70] Alone, however, amongst American and British policy makers the 'ignorant' Morgenthau had perceived the logic of the situation, to the lasting benefit of his country.

The prize was so great that only a complete collapse of sterling, or one sufficient to force the secretary's hand domestically, would be sufficient to alter US policy. Morgenthau meanwhile had to encourage and support British policy, forestalling any move towards an imperial war economy. This meant luring the British ship of state on to the rocks. Sterling pressure could not be rectified by economic means and barring a swift and unexpected diplomatic success, there was no prospect of the drain ceasing before all reserves were exhausted.

Liberal repugnance for a world of economic blocs was not universal in British public opinion. Officials in the US Treasury deplored the tone of much of the British press, *The Economist* constituting an honourable exception. Many British writers believed sterling to be considerably overvalued, and Harry Dexter White kept a close eye on British opinion.

On 20 October, the Paris Embassy reported on a 'special article reviewing Britain's foreign trade policy in the FINANCIAL TIMES' which asserted that:

Needless to say the entire policy of reciprocity, subsidies and tariff bargaining is in general repugnant to the liberal economic traditions upon which British trade has been built. Nevertheless circumstances are now exceptional and international trade will not revive of its own accord. The greater necessity, then, is to secure for British exports a more reasonable share of the world's markets by expedients which shall be short termed without being short sighted.

This was compared with an editorial in *The Times* which stated that 'perhaps the chief lesson for this country is that it might be well for us to review very carefully our own traditional methods and to seeing whether, without sacrificing anything of value, we can modify them in a way which will enable us to compete more effectively with the new methods of the totalitarians'.[71]

White took these two examples, along with an illiberal letter to *The Times* from Keynes, as the possible 'harbinger of an altered commercial policy in recognition of the weakened British economic status as a consequence of the Munich episode. The item of October 13 introduces for the first time a note of hopelessness in Britain's monetary position in the near future.'

5.9   Paralysis in Washington

Two long meetings were held at the US Treasury on 21 October to which outside experts were invited. All were free to express an opinion, and though many of these were initially strongly held the position at the end of the day was one of bafflement and deadlock.

The first meeting was based around a paper prepared by Harry Dexter White, which reiterated his usual themes and which, owing to a shortage of copies, Morgenthau made him read out loud.[72] Of White's five points the first three analysed aspects of sterling's decline. The fourth asked 'what can we do about it' and the fifth 'Should we do anything about it?' On this occasion the use of the Trade Agreement provision attracted the most comment. White argued that

We could use the proposed United States–United Kingdom trade agreement as a lever to prevent substantial depreciation of sterling by insisting that a general provision be included which would terminate the agreement if the sterling rate declined by more than a stated percentage (possibly 5 per cent) from the rate pertaining on April 22nd 1938, the date on which the active negotiations began.

This idea provoked numerous objections. The setting of a floor at $4.50 would give the British 'a free ride'[73] down to that level and indeed the Americans had rebuffed earlier British requests for them to reveal such a rate for this reason. In any case, Morgenthau reiterated that he was not unhappy with the efforts made to date by the British authorities: 'if Sir John Simon should walk in here tomorrow and say, "are you dissatisfied?" I couldn't put my finger on anything to say where they had not done everything within reason to maintain the present rates, and when they spend 60 million dollars in one day I think that they've gone as far as they could within reason'.[74]

John H. Williams introduced another perspective when he said that depreciation might be in US interests, if it stimulated trade. He also added that with war approaching,

> I can see that the English in some ways would dislike a depreciation of the pound in so far as their thinking about the cost of armament, for example, the necessity of imports. They may be very desirous of preventing a drop in the pound. It is somewhat the same problem that arises for them in war. When they have purchases abroad to make, they're interested in supporting the pound. So it's a very mixed question.[75]

In view of these considerations, Williams thought that abrogation of the Trade Agreement 'would seem to me unwise'.

Williams' views carried the meeting. After lengthy discussion of the possible use of the Trade Agreement to bring the British to heel it was decided that the existing Tripartite Agreement would be preferable. This brought the meeting back to square one. White argued the case that the British were seeking competitive advantage, while Robert Warren[76] guessed that sterling was being blown about by great forces beyond British control. Others dithered between the two positions, but none suggested a policy.

A synthesis emerged, as Williams reiterated his view:

> The real point I'm trying to make is that we may be making a mistake in thinking about this thing as much as we have been accustomed to do in the past in terms of competitive trade advantage, because it is very difficult to say where our advantage lies there. . . . And it might well be that we should allow England a certain amount of advantage in our own interests.[77]

This was the rub. Even White agreed: 'That's quite possible. In other words, the larger situation has to be examined, and that's what I take it we're going to do here.' It remained difficult to act ruthlessly in American interests if these were not known. White noted that it was possible 'to get all sorts of hypothetical cases'. Williams suggested 'that what we're trying – really trying to do is find a basis for consultation that will come into play more or less promptly and effectively'.

Ultimately, Morgenthau asked Feis what the State Department attitude would be if 'I should invite a representative of the British Treasury to come over at once to discuss with them the trend of the sterling–dollar rate'.[78] He would 'discuss the tripartite agreement with them, not discuss the Trade Treaty at all. "This trend has been going on; I'm bothered about it. I want somebody to talk to about it." ' Feis responded for his department that: 'We'd regard it as a most natural action.' This conciliatory tone was matched by the meeting's working assumption of an acceptable lower limit for sterling of $4.50, some 20c below the rate then prevailing.

The meeting adjourned for the Department's officials and invited experts to come up with reasoned recommendations. Morgenthau reopened proceedings: 'Well, gentlemen, I suppose you've got everything solved, sterling is up ten cents, the world looks rosy? Who's going to report?'[79] White, as spokesman, confirmed the earlier meeting's general conclusion and rejected any 'floor or ceiling' for sterling in the impending trade agreement, and Randolph Burgess[80] added that the group agreed instead that: 'Our feeling was that the same result might be better achieved by trying to implement the tripartite a little further by seeking to get better consultative arrangements.'[81] According to Herman Oliphant,[82] talking to the British about the exchange rate in connection to the Trade Agreement 'pretty near brings trade agreements over into the Treasury' and Morgenthau replied: 'I don't want to do that. That's what I don't want to do.'[83]

The secretary was uncomfortably aware that the Trade Agreement was 'the apple of the eye of Mr Hull'. He would be happy 'if I can find some way of keeping out of their bailiwick so that I don't have to take a clause in there and tell them that "your trade treaty is through" – now that's what I don't want to do'. On the other hand 'I have no hesitancy in sending for Bewley on Monday and simply saying "I'm bothered about the trend and I'd like the best Treasury man to come over here and talk things over." ' Morgenthau added: 'Why should I interpret a State Department treaty for them? We can give them the facts.' He believed that 'I don't need anything more than I've got. All I've got to do is send for Bewley and say "Mr. Bewley I want to consult." That's all that's necessary.'

This was a suitably flexible and anodyne formula. Ambassador Kennedy argued that 'the tripartite agreement means a great deal more to the British Government than the trade treaty does', in which case, 'using the trade treaty as an excuse wouldn't bring them here any quicker. Frankly it might keep them away.' Indeed Oliphant raised 'the likelihood of the British postponing the signing of the trade agreement if this question were raised at this time'. Finally, Morgenthau concluded the group discussion with a summary: 'I think I've got what you people have in mind: in other words that we do this thing through the tripartite and not try to do it through the trade treaty. Isn't that right', to which Walter Stewart[84] replied on behalf of the group: 'That's right.'

The all-day meeting on 21 October was covered in the press. Bewley reported to Waley at the Treasury in London that:

> As a special Treasury conference reported to have dealt specifically with the sterling situation has been front page news in many of the papers here I asked Taylor [Assistant Secretary of the Treasury] whether he felt inclined to tell me what it was all about. He said that it was largely a routine meeting and that the report in the 'New York Times' (which I enclose) was pretty good. He subsequently added, however, that he expected he might shortly have something to communicate to me.[85]

Bewley was not unduly concerned. He noted that:

> I cannot imagine that any of the authorities here are much concerned with a fall in the pound to its present level of $4.76, and while Washington is profoundly disabused about the benefits to be obtained from monetary manipulation, I suspect that what the authorities here are afraid of is that if the pound fell much further – say to $4.50 or even $4.60 there would be strong pressure from the farm bloc in Congress for a corresponding cut in the dollar.

Bewley even thought that: 'Another possibility is that the Administration may calculate that to allow some slight fear of the stability of the dollar to get about may be helpful to sterling, as discouraging capital movements into the dollar.' He noted correctly that the US Treasury 'are, I think, definitely opposed to any ideas of dollar manipulation, so long as they are satisfied that the pound is not being deliberately driven, or held, down for competitive reasons'. In this respect: 'The danger is that if political pressure were strong enough the President *might* again take matters in to his own hands.'

Bewley's letter though, was 'a very advance warning. I don't think there can at the moment be any danger whatever of action of this sort, and it remains to be seen what sort of backing there may be in Congress for this sort of idea.' Later, Bewley met Walter Stewart, who described the meeting.[86] He was more expansive than Taylor, and mentioned Morgenthau's comment that 'a little birdie' had told him that the British might let sterling go after the Trade Agreement was signed. Bewley noted parenthetically that 'I shouldn't pay too much attention to that last remark: it is just the sort of thing that Morgenthau would say without meaning anything by it'.

Bewley was more appreciative of Stewart's view that the USA needed more information such as that concerning the holdings of the EEA. Bewley at first 'said that we refused to give this information to our MPs and that in the circumstances I didn't see how we could be expected to give it to America'. Stewart, however, made the pertinent point that 'before the funds were set up Central Banks exchanged information that was not given to Parliaments and that now central banks had to some extent been superseded by Treasuries he thought the same thing should be possible'. Bewley was surprised to learn that there was a faction in the US Treasury which felt Britain's defence of sterling to be half-hearted, 'as the gold exports seemed to make any such attitude really incomprehensible'.

Bewley concluded that 'if there are two parties in the Treasury, as I expect is the case, and if Stewart is right that the Treasury are likely shortly to approach us, we should do what we can to provide ammunition for the more sympathetic party'. Initial British receptiveness to the idea of providing information to Morgenthau was, therefore, born from a desire to cultivate support in Washington, and buttress what was seen to be Morgenthau's sympathetic position rather than as a response to US pressure, which scarcely existed.

Since the *Anschluss*, the Treasury Department under Morgenthau had been privileged spectators behind the stage on which the fourth arm policy was played out. With a view denied to the British audience, they knew the prohibitive cost of the production. As far as the British authorities were concerned, however, the show had to go on. There was method in London's madness. It would not have been possible to cut losses and anchor sterling with exchange controls, without admitting the bankruptcy of the fourth arm policy at home and unravelling the political coalition that had worked so hard to construct it. It was possible to maintain the facade of policy at the cost of pouring gold across the exchanges to prop up sterling. Also, the longer the farce was maintained, the more damaging would be the political consequences of revealing its failure. The tendency, therefore, was not to draw back but to go on, whatever the cost, in the hope that diplomatic salvation would arrive before perdition. To this end the liberal trend in policy was reinforced after the Munich Agreement, when negotiations with the State Department were finally concluded and the Anglo-American Trade Agreement signed. In this outcome there were two winners: the United States and Hitler.

6
'It Seems like Insanity': the Anglo-American Trade Agreement of 1938 and the Point of No Return

It was becoming apparent, outside the British government, that the international situation would not permit the normal conduct of financial affairs. Nevertheless, there would be no talk in Cabinet of a 'war chest' of gold and foreign currency reserves until 1939, and before *Kristallnacht*, the government could point to Munich and contend that the policy of appeasement was a success, with normal business of all types shortly to be resumed. It was, though, necessary to believe that the unwelcome economic effects of the September crisis were specific to it and would pass, and that efforts to gain American goodwill had in some way been effective. The signing of the Anglo-American Trade Agreement in November 1938 was, therefore, hailed as a 'landmark in the commercial intercourse between the two countries',[1] from which Britain could take comfort, despite the huge gains it afforded to the United States at the direct expense of Britain and the Empire.

The significance of the Agreement is still debated, and some historians, mired in its complexity, claim that Britain either gained from the exchange or was not seriously damaged in either a political or an economic sense. The general view is that 'the Anglo-American Agreement was a "balanced" one in the rather negative sense that neither side won significant concessions of real substance',[2] and consequently: 'By no one's standards could the trade agreement be classified as a success.'[3] This retrospective assessment regrets that the treaty was neither a large step towards the liberalisation of trade, nor of much significance for solidarity against the dictators. If, however, the Agreement is considered in the context of the economic viability of the sterling bloc and its implications for Britain's ability to sustain total war, it takes on a weightier aspect appreciated at the time.

6.1 The trade agreement: an invisible assassin

The *Journal of the National Union of Manufacturers* of February 1938, was quoted in the fiercely imperialist *National Review* arguing that the aim of the prospective agreement, 'to bind the two great democracies together in view of the growing menace of dictatorship', was unlikely to succeed as 'the dictators will view with equanimity an arrangement which, if it is concluded, will weaken England and the Empire, "just at a time when economic strength is most needed"'.[4] This view, buried by history, reflected the very real situation that in time of war the British economy should receive the greatest possible percentage of its imports from the sterling bloc, payment for which would be deposited in blocked accounts in London, to be released after the end of hostilities. Such a course of action would be counter-inflationary, would not threaten Britain's wartime solvency and would create a captive reservoir of purchasing power for British exports after victory.

The Anglo-American Trade Agreement threatened this reassuring prospect in many ways. In remaining peacetime it would disrupt the trading structure of the sterling bloc, and as the bloc's gold and foreign currency transactions were handled in London, any increase in American penetration of Empire markets would fuel the gold drain resulting from German action in Europe. These facts were belatedly recognised by the British authorities when the Agreement was suspended upon the outbreak of war. This, however, was yet another manifestation of the official belief that the financial and economic war effort could be switched on like a light bulb.

The Agreement, as its wartime abandonment reveals, specifically prevented any illiberal moves that might have been undertaken by the British government to increase imperial preparedness for war. It strengthened the fourth arm policy, confronting critics with the claim that any movement towards exchange control and the autarkic organisation of imperial resources would violate an international agreement freely concluded by His Majesty's government, as well as jeopardising the possibility of assistance from the United States in time of war. To dispute the many technical details of the Agreement is to lose sight of the fact that it represented a tripwire, set to trigger outraged complaint from Washington.

Considering the Agreement in crude terms of national advantage can be frowned upon. One of the few studies devoted to the subject, argues that: 'Economists certainly do not discuss trade negotiations in these terms and historians ought not to.'[5] This involves suppression of the historical record, such as the opinion expressed in the *National Review* of March 1938 that: 'This anti-Imperial trade policy which was designed, by its real authors, to weaken the British people and to disintegrate their Empire, is part of the great push brought against us since the war, and which has, owing to the moral weakness of successive governments, and the fatigue of those who fought, been partly successful in obtaining its object.'[6]

Even when historians overcome their scruples and look at the matter in terms of national advantage the issues are not always clear. It has been claimed that: 'While neither side made any great sacrifices in the trade talks, the United Kingdom, nevertheless, did get the better of the deal.'[7] This statement is based on Oliver Stanley's postdated attempt to put a gloss on the Agreement as a former 'consistent critic of the discussions', who 'once the treaty was signed . . . became its staunchest supporter'. Stanley claimed that the British 'would gain between £5,000,000 and £10,000,000 during the first year of the agreement' and 'expected these figures to increase substantially because of the devaluation of sterling'.[8] These figures are questionable to say the least, and even if accurate, a gain of £10 million represents miserable consolation for the hundreds of millions of pounds lost fighting this devaluation. It was understandable that the president of the Board of Trade should talk up an Agreement that his Department had negotiated,[9] and there are indications that the Board of Trade took a narrow technical view of the treaty as it related to Great Britain but refrained from taking the broader imperial outlook, which it thought less important.

In the weeks before the conclusion of the Agreement, Stanley and his officials had taken a less optimistic view of cooperation with the United States. Indeed, during preparations for a climactic meeting of the Cabinet's Trade and Agriculture Committee, which would recommend to the Cabinet a view to be taken on the continuance of the negotiations, the Foreign Office had found its position diametrically opposed to that of the Board of Trade. In an internal memorandum, Mr Balfour at the Foreign Office summarised the 'attitude' of the Board of Trade.[10] They were inclined to 'regard the agreement in the terms now proposed as highly unsatisfactory from the point of view of British foreign trade and of our inter-imperial commercial relations'. Furthermore,

As they see it there is an element of bluff in the United States attitude, and they are inclined to think that if we stand firm on some at any rate of the major points now at issue we can induce the United States to withdraw from their extreme position. Even if this assumption is wrong, they are disposed to discount the adverse criticism of Great Britain which a breakdown would arouse in the United States of America and to believe that world opinion will rightly recognise that we have rightly resisted an attempt to exploit our political difficulties for the purpose of inducing us to accede to excessive demands.

The Board of Trade had other concerns too. It was 'also apprehensive at the prospect of violent opposition from vested interests in this country as a result of an agreement from which they will suffer'. However, Balfour noted that: 'In general the Board of Trade view the negotiations mainly as a commercial proposition and maintain the view that the attitude of His Majesty's Government towards its conclusion should be determined on this basis.' The Board had been angered by the peremptory American technique in negotiation. It was certainly determined to resist fatal damage to British protection, and a Conservative-led government could only support this stance. Imperial preference was another matter.

Sir Arnold Overton, the head of the British delegation in Washington, recalled in 1939 that:

In the trade discussions last year we really had much more difficulty with Mr Hull over empire preferences than over our protective duties, and the root reason for this is his sincere conviction that measures aimed at diverting the channels of trade are harmful to all concerned. I know that this attitude is a trifle pedantic and illogical, but it must be reckoned with as a fact of prime importance.[11]

If the Board of Trade was not prepared to defend the imperial system, imperialists in Cabinet would have little chance against the combined forces of liberal internationalism ranged against them.

Liberal contemporaries, unlike Overton, saw the logic of Hull's arguments all too clearly and formed a more accurate impression of the likely consequences of the Agreement. In particular, the important distinction between the tariff protection of the British economy and the wider system of imperial preference within the sterling bloc was understood. Although the structure of strictly British protection was merely dented, the most important fact was the blow that was dealt to imperial preference as a practical concept. This was realised at a time when the issue between protectionists and liberal internationalists was still live. A writer sympathetic to the Agreement wrote approvingly that it 'represents not only a material but also an ideological inroad on the Ottawa system'.[12] The *National Review* concurred (and was quoted at length in the *New York Times*), noting that:

> It is true that the Anglo-American Trade Treaty does not altogether destroy the policy of Imperial preference, but it greatly compromises it by removing certain preferences thus giving our whole policy a tilt away from the Empire and towards Free Trade and internationalism, which the lessons of history show to be destructive to us.[13]

It added for good measure that it was 'the fatuous idea of the British authors of this plan that it will "please the Americans"'.[14]

The material inroad into the Ottawa system was bad enough. In a letter to Lord Lothian, the 'influential industrialist' and director of the Federation of British Industries, Mr Locock,

> stressed that the Agreement had really minimized [i.e. disguised] the adverse position of Britain's exports to the United States, because those from the Empire had been included in the calculations. As most of these exports were raw materials, British industrialists gained nothing from their sale. In fact they actually suffered, because the primary goods were then used in the manufacture of rival American products.[15]

The Economist calculated that concessions to the United States detailed in Schedule I of the Agreement when applied to actual figures for 1936 covered £60,800,000 out of US exports to the United Kingdom of £93,200,000: 65 per cent.[16] Reductions of duty on US goods ranged across the board from the abolition of the 2s. duty on wheat 'with the consent of Canada, Australia and India' to cuts 'as a rule from the level of 20 per cent to 15 per cent' on manufactures.

The dependent Empire fared little better, 'one of the most notable concessions made by the Colonial Empire' being the abolition of the duty on unmanufactured US tobacco 'throughout the West Indies'.[17] As Locock had told Lothian, it had always been in America's interest to import raw materials from the Empire without duty and *The Economist* noted that 'because the majority of colonial products have always been admitted into the United States duty free . . . domestic exports from the Colonies to the United States covered by duty reduction amounted to about £290,000 in 1936':[18] a trifling sum. Ominously for the UK, and in addition to the impact on British manufacturers mentioned in Locock's letter to Lothian, duty reductions on US manufactures into Britain also applied to the Empire, so that American manufactures could now compete directly with those of Britain in the imperial market. This struck at the heart of the triangular trading mechanism between America, Britain and the Empire beloved of those supporters of the Agreement who claimed that, with the Empire included, trade between the two powers broadly balanced.

This view was attractive to American opinion. The *New York Times* stressed to its readers that 'we buy more from the British Empire, exclusive of our trade with the United Kingdom, than we sell to it' and that: 'This definitely means that we Americans have not been the "time-honoured beneficiaries" of British–American trade by buying little from England while selling her a great deal. The bargain we are to strike with the British people themselves, therefore, does not require any major adjustment in either country's favour.'[19] This seemed equitable, but the language of an earlier passage was not. This bemoaned the fact that: 'We had a larger export trade in 1929 than England's by more than 30%, but our losses were so disproportionate during the depression that by 1933 England's exports practically equaled our own. In 1937, for the first year since the depression, the strong advance of our export trade placed us definitely in a superior position.' This, like the imperial provisions of the Agreement sits uneasily with the language of triangular trade and Anglo-American 'balance'.

The *National Review* interpreted American thinking correctly. It noted that the Agreement 'appears to involve the grant to the U.S.A. of the inestimable advantage of functioning as an economic entity, while preventing, for the duration of the Agreement, any attempt to organise the British Empire on a similar basis'.[20] The consequence was that 'this means that the U.S.A. will become the practical economic centre of the British Empire. It is interesting to note, in this connection, that in political circles in the U.S.A. plans for the widespread economic penetration of the Empire are openly discussed.'[21]

6.2 The Cabinet falls hesitantly into line

In the Cabinet, abandonment of negotiations was seriously considered and the president of the Board of Trade, Oliver Stanley, seemed so inclined, though unwilling to make a stand in Cabinet to match his intemperate language. Supporters of the Agreement, unable to highlight desirable aspects, stressed the political consequences of a breakdown in negotiations at such a late stage. On 19 October 1938, the Cabinet was presented with the Committee on Trade and Agriculture's Report on the negotiations, compiled after receipt of a new and more extensive list of American demands, which Hull claimed would have to be met before he would conclude an agreement. The Committee's Report stated plainly that unless the Cabinet wished to make the Americans a final offer on existing terms, and be prepared to break off negotiations if that offer was not accepted, then it would be necessary to make further concessions and grant the Americans free entry on maize and lard.[22]

As it was, the difficulties of presenting to the country an agreement based on existing British concessions were fully appreciated. The chancellor reflected the political misgivings of those who sought an agreement when he reflected that, though 'it would be a misfortune if we were unable to conclude a treaty, there was a limit to the demands which we could concede. It was impossible to say that the treaty, as it now stood, was one which on balance would be approved by the commercial community.'[23] Lord Halifax 'said that his general feeling was that it was desirable to go a very long way in order to reach an agreement. Nevertheless he was convinced that it was impossible to make concessions in regard to some of the requests put forward by the Americans.'[24]

Stanley was unwilling to press for the halting of negotiations, despite his vexation. He stated that 'we should make up our minds now as to how far we should go and should refuse to make any further concessions' but he nevertheless 'also thought that, before the negotiations were finally concluded a personal appeal would be made to the Prime Minister, and he thought that there was much to be said for reserving some final concession which we could offer when this appeal was made to the Prime Minister'.[25] The Committee on Trade and Agriculture's Report reflected the ambivalence of the political dimension of the Trade Agreement by including two appendices, one from Sir Ronald Lindsay stressing its benefits, and one from Stanley detailing its drawbacks.

The note by Stanley brimmed over with resentment. He commented on the extensive concessions already made by Britain and reported the subsequent receipt of the American list of final demands. These were

far reaching and with the exception of those on maize and possibly lard, are to my mind quite unacceptable. Experience over the last three months has shown that the grant of a concession by us has been followed not by the display of a reasonable spirit and a with-drawal of other demands, but by a flood of further demands.[26]

Stanley did not recommend outright rejection but had 'no doubt there-fore that we should treat this consolidated list of demands as a final list and should answer by the offer of what we can concede and a definite intimation that that is the full extent of our concessions'. Stanley concluded boldly: 'If the United States Government are not willing to conclude an agreement on the basis thus reached, we must, with great regret, recall our Delegation and announce the breakdown of the negotiations.'

Lindsay's comments began in contrast to the position of his Depart-ment's American and economic experts. He complained of the current situation that:

The protracted negotiations which have led to this have brought me personally to that state of bitterness and exasperation which usually results from dealings with the United States Government. Their delays and tergiversations have been intolerable, they can see no point of view but their own and their demands cause His Majesty's Government loss of revenue and administrative difficulties out of all proportion to the benefits likely to accrue from American trade.[27]

As with Stanley, however, this spleen was misleading, Lindsay attributing American behaviour to Britain's being 'put through the mangle of American politics' rather than to any overtly hostile intent. Initially, he made no attempt to defend the Agreement on economic grounds, stating that:

I myself have always advocated the Trade Agreement less on eco-nomic than on political grounds. Political grounds today are as over-whelmingly strong as ever before. Not wishing to overstate my case, I have never said that even complete surrender by us would secure the whole-hearted friendship of the United States Government and people but it is certain, in case of failure, that blame will be laid on us in American eyes and we shall alienate the sympathy we can ill afford to lose. We should commit a first class political crime and our justification, even though it might be a real one, would consist of a multitude of minor economic factors which could hardly be understood by any but experts and which would not be perceived at all by the public.[28]

However, after a plea on behalf of Hull, failure of whose 'effort will bring about a tremendous recession' made 'disastrous if it were possible to say, as would be said both here and in England, that death blow to his policy was our failure to come to terms now with the United States',[29] Lindsay proceeded to provide economic justification for the Agreement. With regard to 'the actual merits of agreement',[30] Lindsay conceded that

I put forward my own opinion with diffidence owing to its technical nature and because factors of other than commercial nature come into consideration some of which are beyond my powers of appreciation. But I am advised by my commercial staff that American concessions to us will be of very great value and even essential to our export trade and I believe from a purely commercial point of view that it would in the last resort be worth our while to agree to it as it stands.

Lindsay's attitude was typical for a British official. None had suffered more than he during negotiations. The penalties of the Agreement were clear in his eyes, and yet, an instinctive and unlearned faith in free trade as an ideal had led him to reject his doubts and rely on the 'expert' opinions of his colleagues, thus leaving himself free to embrace the imagined political benefits of the Agreement.

The views of Foreign Office experts, however, were extreme. When Lindsay had telegraphed the Department fearing a breakdown of negotiations in October, his colleagues in London had minuted bitterly against the economic connections within the Empire. Assuming that capitulation to US demands would in some way benefit British consumers, Mr Thompson commented that 'it is not too much to say that the point has been reached at which the interests of some forty million people in the U.K. are to some extent jeopardised by our endeavours at every point to meet the Dominions, India and the Colonies'.[31] He went on: 'I think myself that the day is rapidly approaching when a more independent attitude will be necessary.' Sensing no irony he continued: 'as I see the situation, the first obligation of H.M.G. in the U.K. is to seek the well-being of the inhabitants of these islands. Any increase in our prosperity and purchasing power can only react favourably on conditions in our Empire overseas.'

These views attracted his colleagues. Balfour, by way of corroboration, cited the denunciation of the Anglo-Colombian Trade Agreement over banana exports, and the possible effects on textiles. He opined that 'the livelihood of many thousands of Lancashire cotton operatives was thus placed in jeopardy for the sake of the welfare of the Jamaican negroes. Such occurrences demonstrate the penalty of Empire to which Mr Thompson draws attention.'[32] The terms of the American Trade Agreement would bring little joy to Lancashire, however, and a prop of the moral case against Ottawa was that it had denied cheap foreign goods to the inhabitants of the colonies, Jamaican negroes presumably included. However, home interests notwithstanding, Balfour stressed that 'it is open to the Cabinet to consent as a last resort to the free entry of lard which has apparently been requested in the consolidated list. I submit that we should vigorously support such a concession when the moment arrives.' Moves towards the US position on lumber 'should have convinced them of our readiness to comply with their wishes to the fullest possible extent compatible with our commitments in other directions'.

This hostility to the Empire and eagerness to comply with US demands was unlikely to appeal to Cabinet and the full force of such thinking did not reach ministerial ears. Lindsay's memorandum concluded with an appeal to the broad view:

> Value of agreement however is not to be measured in terms of good-will nor are its disadvantages to be valued in terms of departmental difficulties or disturbance of trade or even loss of revenue or protection. Infinitely wider issues are at stake and I myself (though I should hope to obtain some minor adjustments) am so impressed with their importance that I should prefer to accept the draft as it stands rather than break.[33]

The sheer extremism of liberal opinion in the Foreign Office, though veiled from public expression, even to the Cabinet, can be seen to have exerted an influence on policy. This was obvious to the advocates of protection, who were very conscious of the fact that they were on the outside of policy formation, looking in. The *Journal of the National Union of Manufacturers* contrasted the openness of the American end of the negotiations, where the US government was required to hear the opinions of affected business interests, and British secrecy. The NUM pointed out that:

> These negotiations may perhaps bring home to us that there is something wrong with a system under which business arrangements of such great magnitude and importance can be launched without any kind of prior consultation with the business community, and can be carried through by the officials without the business community having any real say in the matter.[34]

It was then noted, perceptively, that:

> The incident may show us, in a way that perhaps nothing else could, the essential weakness of the bureaucracy in the matter of the formulation of policy, and the tremendous power it has in forcing a policy through once it has been adopted; also the almost complete want of anything like real cooperation in questions of policy or of execution between the Government and the business world.

Criticism of the Agreement had indeed been written off in advance, and the policy machine was by no means confident in the technical basis of its opinions. Cadogan and Halifax formulated a position consistent with that of Lindsay which, while milder in tone than that of Foreign Office experts, yet bowed to the American position. Cadogan minuted that criticism of concessions made to America was likely but noted that:

> We have already made large concessions (which will come in for criticism anyhow, and which may involve loss to the Exchequer) and the further concessions now demanded seem to me hardly to balance against the great disadvantages of a break. Though I confess it is difficult to judge of these matters without detailed and skilled knowledge.[35]

Halifax, in a marginal note, abandoned any pretence of an economic justification of the Agreement and noted that: 'I am afraid that the political reasons for getting a treaty through must outweigh trade and economic considerations and I suppose the Americans have a shrewd realisation of this too.'

Chamberlain appeared to balance himself artfully between the extremes, but in truth Stanley's refusal openly to advocate the breaking off of negotiations and his willingness to countenance some final concessions left this position open. He had 'taken great interest in these negotiations', but had 'never hoped that we should obtain any great economic or political support from the United States as a result of making this Agreement. The advantages to be derived were of a somewhat negative kind.' Chamberlain 'was in favour of sending a reply to the American Government on the lines of the report of the Cabinet Committee. He thought that they should wait and see whether an appeal would be made to the Prime Minister before considering whether any further concessions could be made.'[36]

Perhaps fortuitously, Ambassador Kennedy was fully exposed to Stanley's ill temper and reported his attitude to be representative of the Cabinet. Hull, sensing that the American government had pushed its luck to the limit, decided to settle on existing terms. Although the USA had been able to conduct the negotiations as if from a position of strength, Hull settled at the first sign of impatience in London. This rather supports the Board of Trade view that the American position was based on bluff. The compliant attitude of the British government had made possible the arrogant style of American negotiation, but the swift endgame showed that America needed the Agreement more than Britain. This was reflected in the signing ceremony at the White House, where the full American ceremonial was deflated by the absence of any British Cabinet minister.[37] Sir Ronald Lindsay, whose enthusiasm for American appeasement had been sorely tested but not extinguished, represented his government.

6.3 Irrational hopes and fears

The British fear of facing a three-front war alone, along with a certain sentimental belief in American assistance, became the overriding factors in Cabinet thinking and the practical consequences were embodied in the Trade Agreement. Prior to its conclusion, work had been done in translating such perceptions into policy. After Munich the fourth arm policy was ostensibly unshaken, and Chamberlain reasserted in Cabinet his opinion that: 'It must be remembered that our financial resources would be one of our greatest assets in any long war.'[38] This view met no dissent in the official machine. The permanent under-secretary at the Foreign Office, Sir Alexander Cadogan, produced at this time a number of policy papers in which he attempted a synthesis of the economic and diplomatic realities then facing Britain.

These documents have been interpreted as fatalistic assertions of the various reasons why Britain 'could not rearm as quickly as Germany', largely revolving around the 'greater integration of the British economy with world trade and finance rather than differences in political systems'.[39] In fact, Cadogan's thinking embodied all the contradictions inherent in fourth arm ideology. Initially, he asserted the physical impossibility of more determined preparations for war. He opined: 'It is not a question of this country being unwilling to make the sacrifices required', but that

> Germany is far more nearly self-sufficient than these islands can ever hope to be and, with her closed economy, can concentrate the greater part of her industry on the production of engines of war. We have to import the greater part of our food, and consequently to maintain the value of the £ on the foreign exchanges. It is vital to us, therefore, to maintain our ordinary export trade.[40]

This was current orthodoxy, but Cadogan sensed alternatives. He perceived that although Nazi Germany could intimidate its neighbours into joining its autarkic system, 'the Argentine and other parts of the world' were less likely to 'be caught in the toils of German "autarky"'.[41] Cadogan believed that 'Germany as an "autarkic" Power looks pretty formidable – almost as formidable as the British Empire might be',[42] but having come tantalisingly close to stating that Germany could not compete with Britain in a struggle of economic blocs, the idea left him for an assumption of the superiority of the liberal system and the hope that Germany might perceive some 'limit to "autarky"' and be induced to change 'from her closed-economy, autarkic system to a system of free exchange and trade'.

Cadogan argued paradoxically that Germany's system was a source of weakness but that it somehow gave her an advantage over Great Britain, enmeshed in the supposedly superior internationalist system. It has since been argued that *in extremis* Nazi Germany 'could deal with a shortage of foreign currency by conquest; this option was not available for the United Kingdom'.[43] The obvious answer to this point, and to

Cadogan's confusion, is that the United Kingdom had done its conquering many years previously and that its Empire and the sterling bloc were obliged to accept sterling in payment for their commodities. Cadogan half grasped this point but fell back instinctively on the liberal view.

In Cadogan's opinion, German autarky was limited not in comparison to the economic weight of the Empire but to the liberal system. The danger for the British in this line of thinking, as demonstrated by the Anglo-American Trade Agreement, was that 'their' system included the United States, and although Cadogan argued that 'we must cut our losses in central and Eastern Europe' and 'do everything possible to foster our trade with other parts of the world and with the Empire', he added in the next breath that Britain 'must do what we can to foster commercial exchange with the United States'. Thinking 'not only in the economic field but also politically in the Far East' he concluded that the 'Trade Agreement with America would be worth considerable material concessions'.[44]

The economic position adopted by Cadogan in these papers has been described as 'identical to the one held by the Treasury (and by Inskip)',[45] and though Cadogan confessed that 'I am not an expert in economics and am ready to admit that I may misunderstand the problem',[46] his views embodied the prevailing economic doctrine of the British government. Cadogan's political master, Halifax, echoed them in a letter to Phipps in Paris,[47] and in addition to his regular and reassuring despatches to Roosevelt reassured Joseph Kennedy, who was summoned to spend 'an hour and a half with Halifax this afternoon, drinking tea in front of his fireplace' that Britain would be 'staying very friendly with the United States'.[48] Thus, whatever the harmful effects of the Anglo-American Trade Agreement on the British-imperial economy, Chamberlain could claim that this was offset by his belief that 'the psychological effect on the world was of great importance'.[49]

The opposite view was put by the *National Review* which, discussing the appeasing attitude of the British government, noted that: 'The Americans are in no way to blame for this. They have told us in season and out of season that they will have nothing to do with us. That they are isolationists, that they regret their participation in the war and that their motto is "never again".' In these circumstances: 'The U.S.A. has now been entreated to come and help us to break up our Empire preferences! It seems like insanity.'[50]

7
A 'Maginot Line for the Pound': Profligacy in Defence of a Bankrupt Policy, November 1938–January 1939

In the torrid months after March 1938, the British authorities had demonstrated their commitment to 'business as usual' in international finance, culminating in the Anglo-American Trade Agreement. Renewed attacks on sterling at the end of the year actually hardened London's orthodoxy, provoking American fears that British financial collapse might take budding US economic recovery with it. However, the massive commitment of Britain's remaining gold stocks in January 1939 was to calm American anxiety, as indeed it should have. The move ensured that British wealth would continue to fuel America's reflationary economic policy, and that the drain of British economic and financial strength, lingering rather than sudden and catastrophic, would not imperil America's growing domination of a functioning international economy.

7.1 Holding the line

The British Treasury before the outbreak of war was sustained by 'the dislike of German methods and the fear of bureaucracy'.[1] 'Is not freedom', wrote one official, 'our greatest asset?' In Britain, therefore: 'A Schachtian army of foreign exchange controllers must be avoided except in the very last resort.' The Bank of England was less fervent, and though 'greatly attracted by the policy of freedom to which Treasury arguments pointed, thought the risks too great'. This dissent was easily stifled. Even in the 1938 crisis, Simon was only prepared to incorporate the Bank's fears to the extent that 'some preparatory steps should be taken in case "a full exchange control" should after all prove necessary upon the outbreak of war'.[2]

In the interim, informal steps were taken. At the end of November, details of British moves against speculators emerged. Bolton told Knoke that the British 'had $150,000,000 of forwards maturing (this was the bulk of their total short position in dollars). They were going to let them all run off and they were going to ship gold here for that amount less any spot dollars which they might be able to buy.' Concurrently, the clearing banks were asked to deny their funds for use in forward exchange contracts. These actions would hopefully 'raise the sterling spot rate or else put a big premium on forward dollars, thereby, and to that extent, reducing the profit of the speculators. The arrangement with the clearing banks was a confidential one; the market knew nothing about it and there would be no publicity of any kind.'[3]

These were the first British measures of any sort to restrict exchange movements since the *Anschluss*. 'Bolton thought that this program was the only one of a technical nature which they could at this time embark upon short of a general embargo. The latter, very obviously, would advertise the weakness of sterling and have most unsatisfactory repercussions.'[4] This rather complex position was translated for Morgenthau by Knoke in a telephone conversation, and the secretary initially remarked: 'Well, they're getting a little sense aren't they?';[5] but on being told that Knoke had discovered 'the figure that the forward contracts outstanding are between thirty-five and forty million pounds', he responded incredulously: 'And you mean to say those damn fools have been financing forward contracts on gold?'

As if to rub home the enormity of this information, Knoke reminded the secretary of the 'gentleman's embargo' which had existed 'preventing operation of forward gold . . . earlier in the year', though 'when things began to look a whole lot more normal they thought it would be the right gesture for them to – to remove whatever restrictions had been on the forwards'.[6] This revelation that the British were only restoring a pre-crisis level of financial control spoke loudly to the US authorities of a possible lack of British competence, an impression reinforced when Butterworth, temporarily back from England, told a meeting that 'my sense is that the British have no real long-range policy; that their policy consists of a series of daily improvisations, and that in many instances they haven't been as skillful as we have always been led to believe that they are; that there is a general jittery political atmosphere'.[7]

7.2 Thinking the unthinkable: exchange control

Butterworth believed that the British were not yet ready to compromise their liberal principles, expecting them 'to move along the lines that they have just undertaken yesterday, with various rather minor devices'.[8] However, if they were 'to change the character of London as a money market, with all that that means in their services – I should think that it would be a long and difficult period that they'd have to go through with before they would move in that direction'. White argued that if the British knew the sterling crisis to be politically motivated and likely to continue, they had

> a definite responsibility to the world, because a decline in sterling has other repercussions than merely British considerations. So if they can envisage only a continuation for some time to come of a downward course in sterling, responding to the political pressure, may they not have to give more serious consideration, much as they dislike it, to taking the steps necessary to remove the spearhead of that downward pressure?[9]

This was the first mention in the US Treasury of British exchange control. Despite the American interest in the British 'business as usual' policy, if sterling seemed likely to collapse and isolate the dollar world again the purity of Britain's liberal economics would become worrying. The need was not to do something more, but to do something different. *In extremis*, as the French knew, the imposition of exchange controls was the response preferred by the American Treasury. London, however, would never compromise on this issue.

In the aftermath of Munich, Debenham's CEI paper of October 1937 contemplating autarkic measures was once again considered by the British Treasury. Sir Frederick Phillips asked the opinion of the former secretary of the Economic Advisory Council, Hubert Henderson, who wrote that: 'I agree with almost everything in it.' Further,

> I also suspect that we should make preparations for evolving some system of exchange restrictions appropriate to our conditions, in case something of this sort should become imperative later, in a more serious situation. I'm sure we shall have exchange control in France

before very long, and I doubt whether we can long maintain essentially laissez-faire methods in a world predominantly ruled by autarkic systems.[10]

Uneasy at such professional revisionism, the Treasury turned to its own economist, Ralph Hawtrey, who bolstered his superiors with a series of memoranda hostile to any alteration of liberal practice. Interpreting Henderson's letter without heed to the danger of war he wrote: 'I am not sure whether he would regard exchange restrictions as an appropriate retort to the German measures. In my opinion the adoption of them would be a deplorable blunder.'[11] Restrictive measures 'need not be interpreted narrowly to mean exchange control', though 'whatever the method adopted the outcome would inevitably be a serious further diminution of the whole of the international trade of the world in general and of our own external trade in particular'. Later, in another paper, Hawtrey displayed an extraordinary detachment from current circumstances, stating that: 'For the moment the danger of the pound being over-valued is obviated by capital movements. No doubt these are in their nature temporary and will be reversed later on, and all we have to do is see that when they are reversed we do not let the pound rise higher than is appropriate to our circumstances, including our armament expenditure.'[12]

7.3 American fears

In the absence of British initiatives, the US Treasury returned to a consideration of the possibilities for American action. A gathering took place at the Treasury on 29 November, including outside experts. They were presented with a hawkish memorandum prepared by White which he called, inaccurately as it transpired, the 'Agenda for Conference on the Sterling Situation, November 29 1938'.[13] This described events to date, criticised British policy and suggested various responses.

This hostile paper was not received well by the experts, who criticised its narrow-mindedness and rejected it as a basis for the meeting. The discussion which did take place ranged widely, but this served only to reveal and exacerbate the utter confusion already existing. Walter Stewart pointed out that Morgenthau was hampered because being 'in an executive position', he had 'to deal with these problems as they come to you, day by day as they come to you'. Considering the problem as an outsider, he recommended what used to be called moral suasion, constantly asking the British for information and thereby subjecting them to a 'series of additional pressures, without any manifestation of an outward move on your part'. This approach was necessary because: 'There aren't many things, as I see it, on the dollar – actions on the dollar–sterling rate that we have in our hands to do.'[14]

The discussion dwelt on the undesirable short-termism of US Treasury operations, and while Morgenthau defended the professionalism of his advisers he confessed that 'I personally am dissatisfied with what I personally am trying to do on the – not day-to-day but the trends over a period of years, see? And that kind of thinking neither my staff nor myself have time to do.' Expert advice was required because 'we have unlimited money but we have very limited brains'. Morgenthau was so harassed that 'if Harry White comes in and talks about the pound I'm going to be very cross, because I've got to do my financing'.[15]

Morgenthau wanted to consider 'forming a group to take the long distance view on this thing and not just come down when we're in trouble; because I don't know what position the United States is slipping into, and I can certainly say – in the world's market – and as far as I know there's nobody in Washington that knows'.[16] It was suggested that a committee formed with the British could determine 'the best way to restrain the movement of the exchanges'. This could be 'a very fruitful field for discussion; it could be entirely sympathetic and we might all learn something by it, we as well as they'.[17] This current of moderation was added to by Warren, who remarked on 'the unwillingness of the group to discuss these [White's] very drastic proposals at this time'.[18] Morgenthau replied: 'You and I both.' He was, though, 'fearful that we're going – that the thing is going to get worse. I'm very discouraged, very discouraged. I mean I think the whole trend is against us.' Warren reassured him with the comment that the trend 'may not be as precipitous as it has been, let's say, for the last two weeks'. Morgenthau, partly reassured said: 'I think that's right, but I – in these times. . . .' Warren concluded, 'I hope it's right.' Washington remained on edge.

7.4 British reassurances

On 30 November, information from London was delivered by Bewley. He 'asked that no verbatim record be made of his remarks', and proceeded to 'read out what was obviously a telegram he had received from the British Treasury'. Bewley struck an upbeat note for the future when 'he expressed the hope that the technical measures undertaken would gradually operate to strengthen the pound, but that that, in turn, presented a problem of policy as to the degree to which the pound would be permitted to rise in relation to the amount of resources to be recouped'.[19]

This bravado echoed Hawtrey's evidently infectious optimism, and the delirium of denial had gripped the British Treasury. Morgenthau caught it too and 'replied by saying that, at first blush, he hoped that in their desire to replenish the Fund that the British authorities would not weigh too heavily against letting the pound rise'.[20]

Bewley expressed his satisfaction the following day in his report to Waley in London. Remarking on the British Treasury's earlier grumbling about American 'weakening', he stressed the unanimity 'between the two Treasuries' in their commitment to maintain the existing international structures. He went on: 'Morgenthau is at heart a firm believer in permanent stabilisation on gold, and moreover regards the stabilisation of 1934 and the Tripartite Declarations as his personal successes.' In putting the British view to Morgenthau, therefore, Bewley was 'pushing at a door already wide open'. He guessed with absolute accuracy that in requesting information Morgenthau wanted 'to keep us up to the mark as much as possible: not that he really thinks the pound has been indifferently supported, but that he thinks the knowledge of his serious concern can do no harm and may possibly stimulate us to even greater exertions'.[21]

Thus the approach that the Americans thought to be based on subtle psychological pressure was utterly transparent to the British, whose chief concern was to support a sympathetic Morgenthau against imagined domestic pressures. Bewley thought the secretary to be 'afraid of what political agitation there may be, especially after Congress meets, and he is looking for anything that will help him combat it successfully'.[22]

Bewley felt that it was 'hard to believe that at present levels there is any real danger', but that in the event of much more serious sterling pressure, Roosevelt 'might well overrule the Treasury'. To guard against such remote contingencies, Bewley thought that: 'As regards any possible help from us, the more Mr Morgenthau can say that we are keeping him fully informed, loyally cooperating, and so on, the better.' Bewley enclosed a leading article from the *New York Times* supportive of the liberal view and noted that: 'Of course New York is far ahead of the rest of the country on this sort of topic but you may like to see that the true doctrine gets some vigorous publicity.' Later, Hopkins in London wrote on a note attached to Bewley's letter, that: 'I assume the Chancellor has seen this from Washington. For the moment all seems to be fairly well.'[23]

7.5 Hard facts and righteous satisfaction in London

In early December the figures requested by Morgenthau were finally furnished to the Americans in a meeting between Bewley, prominent US Treasury officials and Cochran from the State Department. The information had arrived in leisurely fashion on the *Queen Mary* and Bewley noted that it was 'not as complete as the Secretary requested, most importantly because such detailed information as the Secretary desired was not available to the British Treasury, due in part to the British regard for the professional attitude of the banks toward the confidential character of their clients' transactions with them'. However, Bewley 'did give specific figures in regard to the gold holdings of the exchange equalisation account'.[24]

These revealed to the Americans that gold holdings of £297 million 'at the end of March 1938' had, including the loss of £40 million 'required to cover future operations maturing in December', dwindled to 'approximately' £60 million. These figures, said Bewley, 'proved conclusively that the British officials had been taking every appropriate and possible measure to stop the decline of sterling'. The figures certainly crushed into silence White's argument of half-hearted sterling support.

Bewley then contrasted British probity with French practice, noting that Morgenthau had told him 'that the French had not seen fit to follow American advices'. He asked an uncomfortable Taylor for more information, to which Britain was entitled as a party to the 'tripartite arrangement'. Responding formally to this goading, 'Mr Taylor thought it would be necessary for him to speak further with Secretary Morgenthau before he could elaborate upon the point with Mr. Bewley'.[25] Bewley had reason to be pleased with this exchange and the meeting, which further emphasised impeccable British credentials on matters associated with the Tripartite Agreement. This could not disguise, however, that the figures he had given to the Americans revealed a desperate situation, from which there seemed little escape if the rules of the game continued to be applied.

In the 3 December meeting, Bewley revealed a British plan to increase EEA holdings by moving £60 million from the Issue Department of the Bank of England, the sole remaining reserve of gold.[26] This did not shake his complacency, and he responded to a request from Morgenthau for the latest news, that he would try to obtain 'this information by Monday, but that it might be a little difficult as the week-end was probably in the process of occurring'.[27]

Bewley then went on to the offensive, producing an article from the *Journal of Commerce* by one Clarence Linz which 'mentioned that people here felt dissatisfied with the manner in which the British authorities had handled the pound, et cetera, et cetera'. Bewley said that if the Americans 'did have any feeling such as those [*sic*] expressed in the Linz article, that he felt that we should discuss them frankly with his Government'. Taylor assured Bewley that Morgenthau had been completely frank with him about his views on the pound and that 'he need have no fears along those lines'.[28]

Bewley persisted, and 'emphasized the desirability of complete frankness on our part if we should ever feel that matters were not being handled to our mutual satisfaction, because otherwise the close co-operation and consultation contemplated by the Tri-partite Agreement and subsequent cooperative efforts could not be effective'. Taylor 'assured him that we felt exactly the same way and would not hesitate to tell the British anything we had on our minds and that they should feel the same way'. Bewley's indignation was not authentic. He sent the Linz article to Waley and simply noted that: 'As I thought the enclosed was a rather mischievous article I asked Taylor about it.'[29]

7.6   The bear squeeze fails

British hopes for a sterling recovery were quickly crushed. On 21 December Phillips informed his colleagues that: 'The Bank of England are once more in a state of deep depression as to the future of the sterling exchange.'[30] Governor Norman had 'expressed doubts whether it would not be wiser to transfer a larger sum from the Bank of England, say £100 million of gold or even more'. In view of the fact that the situation was likely to be very much worse in the new year, Norman was 'very anxious in these circumstances that we should inform Mr Morgenthau immediately of the view which we hold of the future and in that connection he thinks it would be desirable if we were to discuss the position orally with an American representative'. Phillips concurred, as:

In the light of the view which the banks take as to the future course of exchange I am inclined to agree with them that an immediate message of warning to Mr Morgenthau would be a wise precaution. It does not seem to me that there is really the least hope that the Americans will be able to give us any assistance since they could only do that by buying sterling and holding it without converting it immediately into gold. But if in fact the rate is bound to fall in the near future obviously such an idea would not be attractive to them.

Hopkins wrote 'I agree' in the margin.

Bolton, however, jumped the gun. That day he telephoned Knoke 'and unburdened himself', saying:

We have been sending you warning cables that the undertone of sterling is worrisome. At the moment the sterling rate is simply being maintained by means of the squeeze which we have engineered and money rates are rising. Over the turn of the year, that is from December 30 to about January 3, the exchange market is ready to borrow sterling against dollars at between 7 and 10 per cent per annum. That is just a measure of their conviction that sterling is bound to go down and of their determination to maintain their long dollar position. The best we have been able to do during the last three weeks by the squeeze was to keep some sort of stability in the rate. Now, with the news of some dissension in the Cabinet, the situation will become much more difficult for us and there is very little likelihood that this matter of Cabinet dissension will be cleared up before the middle or the end of January. Over the turn of the year there will be a large scale raid on sterling and unless there is some improvement in the political situation from January 3 on, I think we are going to find ourselves in an untenable position.[31]

This would mean that: 'On January 3 we shall have to give up the sterling squeeze', because:

In the long run it is impossible politically and economically. I am still discussing all these things with Governor Norman and, of course, he is discussing them with the Treasury. What will come of it I don't know but there will be a very heavy pressure against sterling from the end of the year onward; so heavy I am afraid that we will have to let the rate go down a bit more. Personally I don't want to see the rate drop below the present level which I think is low enough already. We shall resist to the extent of our resources but we shall probably be up against an impossible movement which may well carry us below 4.61. I shouldn't doubt if in the first week in January we shall lose £50,000,000 of gold.[32]

Bolton thought that, although: 'We have a fortnight before anything is likely to happen', nevertheless: 'Unless there is some political improvement our position is going to be very very difficult.' Bolton then detailed the measures likely to be taken (and which were taken) before concluding that:

> I may be exaggerating the dangerousness of the situation and if I am I shall be only too glad to be wrong. Everybody is convinced that Hitler is going to make a move early in 1939. Hope is low that Chamberlain's meeting with Mussolini will bear fruit. Domestically there is very strong objection against Chamberlain's foreign policy. There is also the belief that certain of our defense ministers have not done their job very thoroughly. In addition there is a growing movement in the Conservative Party to make major changes in the Government. I repeat I am giving you my personal opinion but what I am telling you is necessarily for free discussion. I am putting you under no obligation to keep it to yourself.[33]

Bewley called on Morgenthau on 23 December with the message decided upon on the 21st. It covered much the same ground as Bolton's outpouring to Knoke, though more calmly expressed. Far from being shocked, Morgenthau admitted, according to Taylor's record of the meeting addressed to the secretary,

> that as a result of Bolton's message, the news of the situation . . . did not come to you as a complete surprise, and that whereas you had no specific suggestion to make, you wished to emphasize the fact that you would cooperate in any way possible with his Government in order to help meet the situation; that naturally his Government was in better position to determine what the specific measures might be.[34]

In other words, no special cooperative arrangements would be made to deal with the sterling crisis, though Butterworth was made available for liaison.

On 28 December he attended a meeting with Sir Frederick Phillips, Waley, and Catterns, the deputy governor of the Bank of England. Phillips described 'recent measures taken by the British monetary authorities . . . as being on the whole a success'. However, 'he added that only the normal tightness of money towards the end of the year had made them practical expedients and consequently with the beginning of the New Year their efficacy would be largely impaired'. Butterworth was being consulted because

> the British authorities had been canvassing the situation and had made it a point not only to consult each other but to feel out the temper of foreign centers as regards the general attitude of those who might hold sterling balances in London. Practically without exception they had found that the view held was that sterling would depreciate further and that there was every expectation that after the year-end the movement out of the pound would be renewed.[35]

Butterworth continued:

> Phillips said that he realized that this would coincide with the convening of Congress and consequently he had been desirous of communicating to you the position as they saw it. He said he was sorry to have to convey such doleful tidings for the New Year but it was a painful fact which they themselves were in the process of facing and he wished to play straight and fair with you. He said that the expectation was that sterling would touch the 'Munich' level of 4.61 and even go lower. He went on to say that 80% of the trouble lay in the international political field and those who held foreign balances in London would find little or no comfort in the course of international events.[36]

Butterworth 'did not conceal the fact that I considered this very disturbing news and I pointed out that the average American, including the average members of Congress, looked upon the dollar rate as a sort of monetary barometer and I also emphasized the relation of the commodity price level to our recovery'. This well-tried gambit of threatening the British with the xenophobia of Congress drew a terse response: 'Catterns then said that they realised that this might produce "fireworks" in the United States; that in fact it would produce them everywhere and that no one regretted it more than they did or wished to avoid such a contingency more than they did. But unfortunately political fireworks were going on all over the world which they were not able to control.' When Butterworth asked uneasily

> whether they had in their mind even a tentative figure below 4.61 at which they were prepared to resist, both Catterns and Phillips said that while they hoped that the rate would not in the near future go much below that level, they did not see how they could do more than what they had been doing, which was to use their best efforts and their gold in resisting the trend.[37]

Catterns went on to say that he saw

> only three possible courses of action: (one) to adopt a Schacht system, which as far as he knew was not even up for consideration; (two) to peg the rate at [a] definite point, which he was convinced was 'sure death' (incidentally this was the phrase used by Montagu Norman when I talked to him the day before I sailed); or (three) to do what they had been doing, namely to use their skill and their gold with a view to maintaining the rate as best they could. When pressed on the matter of how liberally they were prepared to use their gold, Catterns stated that they were prepared to resist 'until the last shot is left in the locker'.[38]

This would prove no idle boast but Butterworth was not to know that, and received further discouraging news when he

> pointed out how desirable it was for the American Treasury in such difficult circumstances as the present to have a well rounded picture of the situation, upon which Phillips commented that he had never found the Bank of England's figures worth anything to him and Catterns went on to express very much the same view about this matter as I gave you in Washington, namely that the figures were admittedly so inadequate as to be practically useless.[39]

This conversation was not cheering to American ears, but Butterworth perceived a silver lining and reported to his chief that:

> I think I should point out that 'it is not done' for any official of the Bank of England to participate together with Treasury officials in such a conversation as today's, and the fact that the Deputy Governor was present can only be interpreted as indicative of the concern of the

British monetary authorities and of their desire to obtain your sympathetic consideration.[40]

In December, public opinion had a chance to catch up with recent events when the six-monthly publication of the holdings of the EEA revealed the losses that had taken place between the *Anschluss* and the Munich Crisis. Butterworth reported a stoical reaction, noting that 'the London financial press in general plays down the gold losses as much as the facts permit; no doubt at the suggestion of the British authorities'.[41] The authorities, though, knew what was coming. If they were hoping that a diplomatic breakthrough would transform the situation and enable them to keep the 'last shot' stored in the locker they were sadly mistaken.

On 3 January 1939, Bolton told Knoke that: 'Since they had started dealing for January, that is since December 27, their daily losses had been from £3,000,000 to £4,000,000. He knew', Bolton continued, 'that there was a big speculative account open against sterling and he also knew that that account was growing.' Bolton was clear enough about the causes of this constant pressure: 'The predominant factor was the belief that there was going to be another war scare in the near future.' At this stage, the mere prospect of a war scare was enough to begin a stampede out of sterling. Bolton had little confidence in countervailing forces, noting that: 'One weak step taken to counteract that in the near future was Chamberlain's visit to Mussolini and nobody believed that this visit would bear any fruit.'[42]

7.7   Desperate remedies: 'absolutely shooting the works'

In the face of the alarming trend in the currency market, the Bank took further, though minor, restrictive action. Knoke reported Bolton's description of this 'program' which was to consist of 'a letter' to the 'Bankers Association, asking their members to prohibit completely all advances against gold and all forward gold transactions. Similarly, they would be asked to scrutinize and reject any transactions in exchange which they believe to be speculative in origin.' In addition it was hoped that: 'To some extent the banks might also be able to limit speculative transactions in foreign exchange but as to the success of that he was not very hopeful.' In addition to these limited measures 'towards the end of the week a substantial transfer of gold would be made from the issue department to the exchange account. As to the exact amount to be transferred, no decision had as yet been made.'[43]

Bolton said that: 'Everybody had agreed to this program and Mr Morgenthau would be duly advised by cable.' It was clear that American pressure played no part in this decision, which was ideologically based. Bolton told Knoke that: 'The only alternative to this program was complete restriction (I suppose he meant of the German kind) and that, they thought, was politically impossible under the present conditions and would be complete frustration of all they had done.'[44]

The term 'politically impossible' did not refer to the voters. The political difficulty of full exchange control would be the certainty of its exploding completely the political and economic basis of the fourth arm policy, the fantasy of 'business as usual', which prevented Britain from becoming that different kind of nation the National Government so feared. However, the rejection of sterner measures of exchange control implied a policy simply of hoping for the best. Bolton said of the British authorities that:

> For the time being they were inclined to encourage the growth of the bear account now open and to wait for some new factors with which to fight it back. This would at least technically weaken the bear position and give them a better chance to combat it with success later on if and when the political outlook had improved, for one thing was clear to everybody, namely that the basis of the present problem was primarily political.[45]

This attitude was reckless. The authorities knew that the prevailing political climate was bleeding Britain's gold. An actual war scare would clearly obliterate the EEA. The British had painted themselves into a corner, and only one move of any magnitude could sustain existing policy. Accordingly, on 6 January 1939, the US Treasury received a strictly confidential triple priority telegram from Butterworth. He stated that:

> The British monetary authorities informed me last evening of the following steps which they are taking:
>
> (a) It will be announced at 4 o'clock this afternoon London time the transfer from the issue department of the Bank of England to the Exchange Equalization account of some pounds 200,000,000 of gold valued at the old statutory price of 85 shillings per ounce. There will remain in the Bank of England some pounds 126,000,000 valued at 85 shillings an amount which is roughly equivalent to

the amount of gold in the possession of the Bank of England when it abandoned the gold standard in 1931.

> The object of the transfer of so large an amount instead of the contemplated pounds 60,000,000 is to attempt to impress the market that henceforth the account possesses ample resources to meet the call upon it and that all the gold resources acquired since 1931 are available for that purpose.[46]

This action risked utter ruin to uphold liberal financial principles. The ground had been prepared in terms of public opinion and Butterworth noted that: 'The nature of the announcements and editorial comment indicates that the press is complying with the British authorities' desire that the measures be launched in a favorable atmosphere, the steps being generally characterized as desirable and not unexpected, the only editorial criticism being that the action might well have been taken earlier.'[47]

Wayne Taylor remarked in the daily US Treasury meeting on 6 January that the British announcement was 'the big news of the day. It means they are absolutely shooting the works.' Duffield asked: 'Have they got anything left after they do that?' After Lochhead replied that the British were down to the 1931 position, of 'about a hundred twenty-one million pounds', Taylor again emphasised that 'it is certainly laying it all on the line'.[48]

An intriguing feature of the British move was an initial tendency on both sides of the Atlantic to regard it as an aggressive act. Lochhead, reflecting on a slight initial jump in the sterling rate, stated: 'I think a lot of people like the idea that England is taking a little more aggression than they have done. A lot of people figure England has been drifting the last two or three months with a hopeless spirit. This shows more of a fighting spirit, which they like.'[49] Butterworth noted that 'the strengthening of the EEA's gold reserves is universally approved' as 'a bold and judicious means of making clear to the world the full amount available to defend sterling. Such phrases as the MANCHESTER GUARDIAN'S "reserves are being moved up to the front for a firm defence of sterling" and the FINANCIAL TIMES' characterization of the "Maginot Line for the pound" are typical.'[50]

The latter comparison was unwittingly apt. After the replenishment of the EEA in January, the pound would remain in the vicinity of $4.67 until August, and as was its way, the US Treasury ceased to worry about the matter. This did not mean that the problem was any less acute for Britain: quite the reverse. Multiplying war scares would now simply be reflected in a pronounced increase in the gold drain to America. By 1939, however, the US administration had convinced itself that all measures likely to result in reflation of their economy were welcome, and in pursuit of a national income of $80 billion from the 1938 figure of $65 billion, very large sums indeed would be required.

7.8 A parting of the ways

The measures adopted by Morgenthau in 1938 to absorb the gold flow and his support for the British defence of sterling through a passive 'business as usual' policy had answered American needs quite brilliantly. This was by no means appreciated in Britain, where there existed an ingrained lack of understanding of, and a certain condescension towards, American economic thinking.

In January 1939, *The Economist* wrote on what it referred to as 'The Dogma of Purchasing Power'.[51] This referred to the importance Americans attached to the maintenance and increase of what Keynesians would later call aggregate demand. It was lamented that 'these views are now held in a dogmatic or doctrinaire fashion. That is to say, they are accepted as, say, the gold standard was formerly accepted – as something so generally accredited that to doubt it would be economic heresy if not social perverseness.' The 'purchasing power doctrine' held that 'purchasing power is regarded as antecedent to production; that is, purchasing power is not so much the reward of production as the initiating force of the demand that calls production into being'.

Such thinking led directly in the opposite direction from the British fourth arm policy to 'the view that the cash deficit of the Treasury represents a contribution by the State to the national income – regardless of whether the deficit is financed by increasing the supply of money or by savings'. This led to the logical conclusion that 'since the largest possible national income is admittedly desirable, any argument in favour of a balanced Budget is economically subversive, so long as the national income is below some acknowledged "normal" level'.[52]

It was noted that 'emphasis on the expression of the purchasing power theory in terms of the national income is of relatively recent growth', replacing earlier, and unsuccessful, American attempts to end the Depression by raising commodity prices. 'Confidence that the price level can be controlled, or the rate of industrial activity determined, by solely monetary devices has been considerably weakened in recent years; but to a considerable and growing extent the public demand is shifting to the belief that the national income can be raised to, and maintained at, a desired level.'[53] This belief was greatly supported by the influx of foreign gold.

The Economist's summary of American opinion was largely reiterated in the President's annual State of the Nation message to Congress which stated: 'The first duty of our statesmanship to-day is to bring capital and man-power together. We want to get enough capital and labour at work to give us a total turnover of business, a total national income, of at least eighty billion dollars a year.'[54] The developing gulf between the practice of the British and American governments can perhaps best be stated by the difficulty of imagining Sir John Simon rising to express similar sentiments to the House of Commons. By 1939 British and American economic thinking had bifurcated completely, and Britain had taken the wrong turn.

The British were left with their financial probity intact and their war-fighting economic potential disintegrating about their ears. There was no one else to blame. The United States Treasury had been puzzled, had not subjected the British to any material pressure and indeed had not been sure what British action it would have liked. American enjoyment of the fruits of British folly, whilst not especially laudable, was nevertheless far removed from forcing the British to sterling's support. Morgenthau was later inclined to claim credit falsely for the British action in January, but his achievement had been one of encouragement rather than coercion.

7.9   Defence pays the price

Cabinet rearmament debates were not helped by the quality of expert economic advice. In December 1938 the CEI presented a report to Cabinet entitled 'Problems of Rearmament'.[55] This acknowledged the problem caused by loss of gold and foreign currency reserves. The Committee 'felt that we could be most useful in setting forth a list of the various available remedies without advocating any one in particular to the exclusion of others'.[56] If this seemed indecisive, the Committee added that 'we desire to emphasize in conclusion our strongly held opinion that action along one or other of these lines is urgently required and that the present position has potentialities of real danger'.

The report was a curious mixture of complacency and fear, as if struggling to reconcile events in different worlds. The Cabinet was reassured that: 'Our gold reserves are large; fully sufficient, if we had to take account only of the adverse balance of payments in the next three or four years on current account.' However, the reserves 'have been entirely accumulated through short-term capital movements which may be reversed. It is the combination of a continuing drain on current account with a sudden drain on capital account which would be dangerous.' The report pointed out that: 'The greater part of our gold reserve has been acquired since the beginning of 1932. Between that date and the end of 1937 we had an aggregate adverse balance of payments estimated by the Board of Trade at about £80 millions.' Net repayments on foreign loans of £50 million did not offset this figure and the situation 'would, in the absence of short term capital movement, have resulted in a loss of gold in the period'. The position was, therefore, that 'the inflow of short term money in the six years was at least large enough to finance our actual gold acquisitions'.[57]

This understated an encouraging tale of success, but the report chose to stress an earlier crisis arguing that: 'The position has potential dangers, not less than those discovered by the Macmillan Committee shortly before our departure from the gold standard.' The report strangely ignored the gold losses since March and stated that: 'In spite, therefore, of the apparent strength of our reserves, we cannot regard the position of sterling as unassailable.' This curious unreality continued with the statement that, despite the previous assertion that the balance of payments was immaterial to the state of the reserves: 'A series of adverse balances of payments which led to a substantial loss of gold might set in motion a withdrawal of short-term funds from London which would quickly exhaust the resources available to meet it.'[58]

The detachment of the Committee from the full urgency of the situation might be explained by the fact that some members had not been absolutely frank with their colleagues. Sir Frederick Phillips, writing to Catterns at the Bank of England during the preparation of the report, informed him of 'some suggestions which Keynes has put in to the Economic Advisory Committee: you will appreciate on reading them how careful I am not to impart indiscreet information to that body'.[59] However, impending war could not easily be ignored. In a Treasury summary of the report, Phillips noted that 'the Committee of course have not got access to the position of the Exchange Equalisation Account but they conclude that the situation is unsatisfactory and that anything possible to improve our adverse balance of payments should be effected as rapidly as possible'.[60]

Indiscreet information could only have strengthened the Committee's recommendation that Britain might 'have to consider protecting the sterling exchange by the most stringent and unsatisfactory form of exchange control, that is to say, exchange control which applied to foreign, as well as to British capital'.[61] This was the rub. The report concluded that with regard to the outflow of 'the liquid resources of nervous foreign holders . . . it is doubtful whether there are appropriate financial measures for checking it, short of exchange control'.[62] The stark position was that, because such movements 'depend primarily on political confidence and secondarily on the expectations held abroad as to the future of the sterling exchange' the British authorities faced a very clear choice: 'Unless and until we are prepared to impose a general exchange control, we have to let these resources go to the extent they want to.'

The Committee then expressed the incredible opinion that the loss of all short-term balances was preferable to the unpleasantness of exchange control. It stated that 'the amount of such withdrawals is not unlimited' and that: 'They are a perpetual source of danger which we are perhaps better without.'[63] In effect, the British government's expert economic advisers had concluded that the loss of the bulk of Britain's reserves was preferable to exchange control, and that the problem of falling reserves would cease when all these reserves had gone.

The CEI's report was supplemented in January 1939 by a statement to the Cabinet from the chancellor of the exchequer on currency legislation.[64] In this, Simon sought to explain the transfer of the Bank of England's monetary gold stocks into the EEA for the support of sterling, and at the same time obtain the Cabinet's permission to legislate for a compensating increase in the issue of paper money. This statement, taken with the CEI's effort, demonstrated the manner in which defence, finance and the international political situation had become utterly interwoven. However, it also indicated the government's continuing orthodoxy. The statement was merely for the information of the Cabinet, which was invited to give retroactive approval to official action. Simon did not raise the possibility of any remedial action save that which he had already taken, nor were opinions sought.

The statement was prepared by Treasury civil servants and a draft was sent to the Cabinet secretary, Sir Edward Bridges, by Hopkins. This draft was 'a copy of the stuff which we have suggested to the Chancellor that he should say at the Cabinet tomorrow. The Chancellor has not said whether he likes it or not. I assume that he will talk more or less on these lines.' In fact the draft statement formed the Cabinet record, which was regarded before the event as a matter of some sensitivity. Hopkins explained to Bridges that 'we have suggested that the Cabinet Minute about the statement should go on the Secret Cabinet file, but should not be circulated'. In an explanatory marginal note, he added: 'comparisons with 1931 not good for too wide circulation'.[65]

The chancellor's statement was a weak attempt to rationalise appalling facts incompatible with the fourth arm mentality. Simon revealed the full extent of sterling losses since April 1938, avoiding comment on the proximity of this date to the *Anschluss*. He did concede that the prospect of war was affecting the exchanges, and in brazen self-justification argued that 'The £800 millions worth of gold which we held last April represented in considerable measure the accumulation here of refugee money',[66] which, quoting a note added to the draft by Hopkins, 'gave to our financial position an appearance of strength which was in part misleading'.[67] Simon went on: 'Since last April anxieties on the part of foreigners as to the fate of this country in the war which they regarded as impending had led to a great efflux of these funds, chiefly to America, which was regarded as a safe repository.'[68] However, the 'appearance of strength' which this fugitive money was giving to the United States was anything but 'misleading'.

Simon confessed to a bitter blow for government policy lamenting that: 'One would have hoped that with the Munich settlement the drain on the pound would have subsided, but that was not what had occurred. It appeared only too evident that the view continued to be persistently held abroad that war was coming and that this country might not be ready for it.'[69] Simon then turned his reasoning to add that 'lying behind that anxiety there was, of course, the further anxiety created by the obvious worsening of our financial position, by the heavy increase in the adverse balance of our trade, and by the growth of armament expenditure'.[70] This muddied the waters and concealed the significance of the next statement that: 'In the three months from the 1st October the drain had continued, the value of the pound falling from a top figure earlier in the year of 5 dollars to a figure little above 4.60.' Simon was suggesting that the fall in the pound was equally attributable to conventional economic causes beyond the control of the government, whilst linking the reserve drain firmly with fear of war. He thus separated cause and effect, and more than implied that government was an entirely passive spectator, with no hand in events. The chancellor then made a spurious comparison, stating that he 'was afraid that it must be said that the recent conditions had been painfully reminiscent of those which obtained in this country immediately prior to the financial crisis of September, 1931'.

In equating a purely financial crisis with one based on impending war, Simon served his case well. The government could claim the crisis to be technical, and the Cabinet could be conditioned to accept the squandering of the gold reserve as a financial response to financial crisis. Though he knew the crisis atmosphere behind the gold drain to be intensifying, Simon stated that he 'hoped that this measure would have a good effect, though another shock would await when the figures of our finances for the next Budget came to be portrayed'. He felt able to state that: 'The big transfer from the Bank of England to the Exchange Equalisation Account appeared to have had a considerable effect on "bear" speculators, as showing that we had every intention of maintaining the pound.'[71] The impact on bear speculators was no doubt considerable, because the government's action promised them spectacular riches.

The Treasury made determined efforts to uphold the fourth arm policy even as it became impossible for the government to resist demands for increased armaments expenditure. In January 1939, the war scare over a supposed Nazi threat to Holland saw measures for the acceleration of defensive preparations put on the agenda of the Foreign Policy Committee, for immediate authorisation without further reference to Cabinet. It was felt, however, after 'general discussion' in Cabinet 'in regard to the state of our defensive preparations as compared with the position last September, and to the steps which could be taken to accelerate production' that:

> The view generally expressed was that virtually all the action which could be taken to accelerate production over the next two or three months had already been taken, and that any extension of the range of our defensive preparations which it might now be necessary to consider could not affect the position in the immediate future.[72]

The Cabinet thus concluded that:

> while there was little scope for acceleration of the Defence Programme over the next two or three months, it was important to take all practicable steps to put the Defence Services into a state of

readiness to meet the contingency of a possible emergency in the near future.[73]

In the FPC, chaired by Chamberlain, these practicable steps amounted in their entirety to certain measures to improve the AA position and a request to the king not to travel to Canada on the battlecruiser *Repulse*, as preparations for the Royal quarters involved the removal of anti-aircraft equipment. The king would be asked to charter a liner instead.[74]

This level of complacency was not sustainable and in Cabinet on 2 February, Hore-Belisha presented unstoppable proposals for the equipment of the Army on a continental scale. However, both Chamberlain and Simon resisted them and reiterated the fourth arm policy. Chamberlain 'said he thought that this was a rather new conception so far as our plans were concerned'. He pointed out that although Hore-Belisha 'had described his proposals as modest', nevertheless 'the total cost of the items in the Secretary of State's paper amounted to £81 millions'.[75]

Noting that Simon 'would deal with the financial side of the proposals', Chamberlain carefully prepared the ground for him by stating that:

> Speaking generally, he thought it was clear that an unanswerable case could be made out for increased armaments in every arm, if the financial aspect of the proposals was ignored. But finance could not be ignored since our financial strength was one of our strongest weapons in any war which was not over in a short time. The Chancellor of the Exchequer would, no doubt, say whether he thought that we could continue adding to defence expenditure at the rate of the last few months. As a former Chancellor of the Exchequer, the financial position looked to him extremely dangerous.[76]

Considering the scale of Britain's financial commitment, he thought that the French should be told not to expect the creation of a large British Army.

Simon took his cue and reminded the Cabinet 'that it was necessary to include financial resources among our total available resources'. He noted that Hore-Belisha's proposals at £81 million 'were . . . broadly equivalent to the whole cost of the Army in 1937–38', at £82 million. He did not add that they amounted to less than a quarter of the sum transferred from the Bank of England's gold reserve for the defence of sterling. Simon added that in the next financial year, the estimates in 'total for the three Defence Services would be over £500 millions' and that he, therefore, 'entirely accepted the view that, in the present circumstances, there was no alternative but to use borrowing powers'.[77]

Incremental borrowing, however, left the fourth arm philosophy intact. Simon's greater concern was 'that there were limitations to what we could borrow. It was already clear that the existing borrowing powers were inadequate and shortly he would be putting before his colleagues proposals for doubling the existing borrowing powers. Further, it was clear that even this increase would not meet the aggregate defence needs over the 5 years to March, 1942.' Simon then sought to alarm his colleagues with the budgetary implications of rearmament. He said that 'for the financial year 1938–39 . . . he had provided for the largest sum ever provided out of taxation by this country for defence'.[78] Interestingly, 'out of taxation' was added by hand to the record in place of the original 'for', indicating that the authors of Simon's statement had overlooked the First World War.

Simon anticipated 'a substantial Budget deficit' in the current financial year. He further stated that:

> In the ensuing year there would be a vast gap to bridge between the sum available for defence from the Budget and a defence expenditure of over £500 millions. Further, he was extremely anxious as to the position in later years. The peak year of defence expenditure was always receding, and under present plans the rate of defence expenditure in 1940–41 would exceed defence expenditure in 1939–40. Further, it was now becoming clear that the maintenance of the defence forces now being equipped would cost an annual figure far in excess of any figure which we had ever raised out of revenue to meet defence services. It would be substantially in excess of £300 millions a year. It was out of the question to conemplate [*sic*] borrowing for a continuing annual charge. It was impossible to escape the conclusion that we were advancing to a position in which the financial situation would get altogether out of hand.[79]

Ignoring the possibility that measures appropriate to wartime might be considered, Simon made an impassioned plea for the restriction of defence expenditure. He reminded his colleagues that: 'A year ago, the Cabinet had very deliberately decided to work on the ration principle and had reached a conclusion that a total of £1650 millions should be made available for defence purposes.' Since Inskip 'had been given the task of allocating this sum', Simon noted that matters had developed rapidly and it was clear that the total defence expenditure which we were now faced with over five years, April 1937 to March 1942, enormously exceeded the total of a year ago. Every addition, such as was involved in the proposals now made by the Secretary of State for War added to our already gigantic financial burden for defence.[80]

Simon 'did not dispute' the case that Hore-Belisha's proposals 'could properly be represented as both urgent and necessary. But had they any better claims to be so described than, for example, proposals in regard to further financial assistance to agriculture and shipping.' Simon

was satisfied that, not only he himself but all his colleagues would find themselves greatly embarrassed by the problem of how all these proposals could possibly be financed. He agreed with the Prime Minister's view that our financial strength was an element of the greatest importance, but he was gravely disturbed lest that strength might be slipping away.[81]

Simon then mentioned exchange difficulty in support of his argument:

During the previous autumn he had been faced with serious difficulties in maintaining the level of the pound. Once a loss of confidence showed itself on a wide scale, there would be no means of arresting it. We might be faced with a financial crisis as grave as that of 1931, but with the added difficulty that the foreign situation was now far more serious.[82]

He 'felt bound to ask whether it was really necessary to adopt all the proposals made by the Secretary of State for War, at any rate, in their present form, and whether a substantial reduction could not be effected'.[83]

7.10   Policy consumes itself

Simon's argument revealed that his front in Cabinet with Chamberlain was intact, and both were as convinced of the fourth arm argument as in 1937. Simon's inability to comprehend the seriousness of the international situation aided his assumption that defence expenditure was the root of all financial difficulty. Stanley and Halifax dissented, both feeling that war was imminent. Their interventions, however, demonstrated that their opposition to fourth arm thinking was not homogeneous, and that distinct schools of thought were emerging within Cabinet. Dangerously for Chamberlain, they were both predicated on fourth arm logic.

Halifax appropriated the ultimate refuge of economic liberals, namely total economic dependence on the United States. He 'was satisfied that the present state of tension could not last indefinitely and must result either in war or in the destruction of the Nazi regime. We could argue, therefore, that we were borrowing in respect of a period which could not last indefinitely.'[84] He was to develop this argument to answer criticism of the dangers it might present in the event of a long war, stating during the climactic July Cabinet, at which the Treasury expounded its position, that he thought the Treasury gave 'too gloomy a view'. If a war 'should last longer than we anticipated, it would be reasonably safe to assume that when the war had continued for some time the attitude of the United States would be sufficiently favourable to us to enable us to win the war'.[85] This was a precarious hope on which to base policy, but the concessions already made to Washington left Chamberlain with no effective answer.

Halifax had effectively questioned the point of American appeasement if it was not intended to rely on America in war. This harmonised with the comforting illusion that Britain could not lose in its dealings with the United States. The currency and trade agreements had seemed to point to the ultimate restoration of a global trading system, itself a liberal dream. If war were avoided and a settlement with Germany were reached, this momentum could only be increased, while the pressure on sterling caused by fear of war would of course be removed. If war came, on the other hand, US involvement would save the current system. Britain's fate in an American world was not considered, but Halifax 'was the first to admit his relative ignorance of financial matters' and noted in his diary, when the consequences of such ignorance had been revealed, that the area formed 'one of the subjects that I made up my mind long ago I should never understand, and so I do not make any attempt'.[86] The fourth arm policy though, was designed to beguile the ignorant, not be usurped by them.

Halifax's argument that the crisis was at hand had broad support. Stanley made this clear: 'The Foreign Secretary had expressed what many of them were feeling. From one point of view we were already at war and had been for some time.'[87] The illiberal implications of this realisation had been stressed in Cabinet by Hore-Belisha in March 1938, but their accuracy was now inescapable.

Stanley's reasoning developed differently from that of Halifax, though the final version of his argument was also expressed in the July Cabinet. Stanley thought: 'The point would ultimately come when we should be unable to carry on a long war. There would, therefore, come a moment which, on a balance of our financial strength and our arms strength, was the best time for war to break out.'[88] Stanley's logic contained a grim imperative. According to this view, British finances did matter, as the government said, and Britain must fight soon. War would bring with it exchange controls and an end to the pointless and debilitating drain of foreign exchange and gold. The same was not true of undeclared war, if 'business as usual' were maintained. The loss of gold and currency would continue, with each day bringing collapse measurably closer.

Neither Stanley nor Halifax doubted Simon's financial premise. Stanley did not consider that policy might change in peacetime, and Halifax hoped for American charity in the worst case. Because of this, however, they both struck at the heart of fourth arm policy. The danger arose that fourth arm logic might actually drive Britain precipitately into war rather than preserve 'business as usual' for the peace saved by Chamberlain. Ultimately, the 'now or never' point of view represented by Stanley did help to bring war about, and damage already done made the Halifax position prophetic.

Chamberlain, witnessing his own and Simon's arguments turning in upon themselves, urged that the new minister for coordination of defence, Chatfield, 'should have an opportunity of considering these proposals before any final decision was reached'. This breathing space was provided by the prime minister's forcing of Inskip's resignation days previously.

The confusion evident in official circles as to the potentialities and dangers of Britain's financial position is reflected by historians, and much of the Treasury's alarmism, especially concerning the external position, continues to be taken at face value or misinterpreted. Chamberlain's critics have tended to adopt either the Halifax or the Stanley position, sometimes both, thus remaining within the confines of fourth arm logic. It has been written, from the Stanley perspective, that, despite the defeats it suffered over increased defence expenditure in 1939, the Treasury, 'like the Government . . . chose to carry on as though nothing had changed, ignoring the first signs of economic disintegration that were embodied in the country's increasing loss of gold'.[89] The gold drain, though, was politically driven, as was the economic damage caused by Chamberlain's determination to continue 'as though nothing had changed'.

The gold drain was in no way the result of the rearmament process,[90] and the Treasury knew it. Like accelerated rearmament itself, the gold loss was the result of a worsening diplomatic situation, but unlike increased expenditure which created its own impetus against the fourth arm policy, the gold loss could only have been halted by a conscious decision to abandon this policy which never came.

A directly causal chain has been assumed along the lines that 'appeasement failed and war became imminent, rationing was abandoned and gold fled Britain's shores',[91] by both critics and defenders of the Treasury. Accordingly, the fourth arm policy has been praised as enabling Britain to survive until American aid became available. This argument depends on the loss of reserves being unpreventable. The 1956 official history of financial policy argued that on the outbreak of war no power on earth could be expected to prevent these funds leaving Britain 'at some fairly early stage in the proceedings, and to do so with such certainty that no step taken by the British authorities could influence their withdrawal'.[92] This is untrue.

Nor is it true that in Britain's position of gold haemorrhage, the only possibilities were to ration expenditure or fight quickly. As we have seen, the British government was unwilling, not unable, to enforce effective exchange control and thus give imperial war potential a chance. As growing Cabinet dissension showed, Chamberlain could no longer rely on argument to sustain his policy which was now being clubbed to death with its own logic. As 1939 progressed, therefore, it would be necessary to rely on naked political force to maintain the fourth arm policy at home, and perhaps more importantly on secrecy. To abandon the fourth arm policy would have been to reveal shocking information, as was realised when some attempt at economic preparedness had to be seen to be made.

8
'Not a Damned Bit Good': the Concealed Catastrophe, 1939

In the spring of 1939, fourth arm policy faced ever more adverse circumstances. In March, Hitler's move into Prague imposed a more bellicose public stance on Chamberlain, and even natural supporters of 'business as usual' were becoming resigned to war. This was uncomfortable for the government, which had neglected warlike economic and financial preparations in good faith that Chamberlain would secure peace. Nevertheless, an early war would have the advantage of forcing a change in policy while disguising the full picture of existing unpreparedness and waste, which remained unknown outside a small circle of officials and the inner Cabinet. Similarly, if normality were by some miracle restored, these facts need never come to light. However, in this period of impending war the government encountered growing pressure from influential groups outside the solely political world for far-reaching economic measures, and the situation demanded at least the appearance of action. The expert stonewalling that followed ensured that when policy did collapse in August, the near-immediate outbreak of hostilities concealed the traces of what had gone before with such thoroughness that even 60 years later the story has not been fully uncovered.[1]

8.1 The 'large blank spaces on the map'

In April 1939, Sir John Anderson, the lord privy seal, wrote to inform the chancellor that he had received a memorandum from a prominent group of industrialists headed by Sir Arthur Salter, a fellow of All Souls and MP for Oxford University, entitled 'Economic Defence'. Anderson noted that it was a document 'which I am assured has influential backing'.[2] It called for an 'Economic General Organisation Staff to which industry, trade and finance could have access on questions of economic defence in time of war' and asked if 'the Government would welcome the formation of an Association for economic defence, representative of industry, trade and finance, to work in conjunction with and assist the official organisation suggested'.[3]

It was difficult to ignore this appeal. Anderson noted that it 'practically synchronises with a very important memorandum put forward by the Prime Minister's Panel of Industrialists on "Industry in War" '.[4] The Salter paper had also been forwarded by Colonel Greenly, the chairman of the Prime Minister's Panel, and Anderson saw that action would be necessary. He suggested 'that the two should be considered together, preferably by an ad-hoc Committee of the Committee of Imperial Defence'. Anderson noted that the Salter memorandum

> suggests certain measures for the fuller development of economic planning for war and for bringing outside opinion into closer touch with Government policy. While I do not feel particularly drawn to the specific course of action suggested, I certainly feel, and have felt for some time, that it would be of great advantage to clew up more firmly the various measures that have been under examination as separate problems, to fill in certain obvious blanks and to place commerce and industry in a position to relate their own plans more closely and more intelligently to the policy of the Government.

Control of the matter soon passed to Sir Horace Wilson, the government's chief industrial adviser, who canvassed the views of leading Treasury civil servants. Between them they sought to absorb these new demands within the existing machinery of government. Hopkins agreed that 'there is everything to be said for some type of organisation wh. Wd. [sic] coordinate the action of the different Depts in this very important field and survey the results as a whole'.[5] This would however be kept within government and would 'not of course be the kind of thing Mr. Falk and his colleagues would like – a lot of economists operating in vacuo – but perhaps an organisation similar to that wh. [sic] has been run by Sir A. Robinson in connection with supply'. In a marginal note Warren Fisher agreed: 'What is wanted is a civil CID. . . . What is *not* wanted is a panel of economists and doctrinaires.'

After such analysis, Anderson's idea for a full committee was abandoned and he was persuaded to accept instead an interdepartmental survey of financial and economic matters. A draft for Simon was discussed and 'it was arranged that the next step should be a talk on the draft between Sir Horace, Sir William [Brown], Sir Richard Hopkins and Sir Frederick Phillips'.[6] Wilson then wrote to Simon that

> Sir John does not wish to press his suggestion for a C.I.D. Committee. He would be content – and indeed would, I think, prefer – that there should be selected someone with the necessary knowledge and experience to undertake a review of the plans and proposals that have hitherto been prepared by the various Departments (including the Treasury) for the purpose of keeping the country going during war, in order to advise whether the various plans and proposals are consistent in themselves with one another and at the same time adequately cover the ground.[7]

After this was done: 'The report made as a result of the review, in addition to indicating defects or gaps that might have been perceived should include recommendations as to how these defects and gaps may be dealt with.'

It had been hoped, naturally, that 'it would be possible to select a senior civil servant, but there does not seem to be anybody available who has both the necessary knowledge and experience and is at the same time sufficiently free'.[8] Instead, Wilson and his colleagues had decided upon Lord Stamp, who as a director of the LMS railway could only do the job part-time.[9] He requested the assistance of the economists Professor Clay, then working at the Bank of England, and Hubert Henderson, which Wilson arranged. There were indeed compelling reasons, as far as the Civil Service was concerned, why urgency might prove unpalatable. The Salter memorandum had noted that:

> One major field in which industry is entirely uninformed concerns finance. How is the next war to be paid for? Is it to follow the previous method of 1914–18 viz. of business as usual, with resort to borrowing on a grand scale, accompanied by additional taxation to cover the annual service of the new loan? Or is there, in the alternative, to be a war economy in which all productive and other services are to be placed at the disposal of the country for war purposes?[10]

In truth, the government had no idea. Wilson had written to Hopkins that 'Stamp's main functions would be I think to deal with the large blank spaces on the map which represent at present our policy for controlling imports, for encouraging exports and for controlling the general course of production in the event of war'.[11]

On 22 June, A. Nevil Rucker, Chamberlain's parliamentary private secretary, wrote to the Cabinet secretary, Bridges, that:

> I have discussed the whole matter with H.J. [Wilson] and he thinks that it would be best not to take action at your end, at all events at present. He has had discussions with the departments concerned on the wider questions of industrial planning and he thinks that this matter should continue to be examined inter-departmentally rather than that an *ad-hoc* Committee should be set up. He does not think we need take up at the moment the question of a special Department under the Board of Trade or the Lord Privy Seal.[12]

In July Wilson stated the position to Bridges more bluntly, when the latter sent him papers that had been collected for 'circulation to the sub-committee on the Central Control of Business'. Bridges told Wilson that: 'These papers do not cover the whole ground. For example, they do not cover the measures for the control of exchanges, or for the control of new capital issues. These are Treasury matters, and while they are listed in the War-Book, we have no details of them. You will, no doubt, obtain information of this from the Treasury.'[13] Wilson replied that 'in my view they only exhibit the bareness of the ground in our particular sphere of war planning'.[14]

When the Stamp Survey convened, it immediately sought the views of the Treasury's leading civil servants. Hopkins, Phillips and Waley attended its second meeting, where it 'emerged' that: 'No central planning body had been established by the Government for the consideration of war plans in the economic and financial spheres, each Government Department being charged with the responsibility for preparing its own plans.'[15] This dissipation of effort meant that there were 'in many cases plans affecting two or more departments, and in these cases the work was done mainly through the medium either of inter-departmental committees and subordinate organisations or the Committee of Imperial Defence'. Such was the labyrinthine system of war planning bequeathed by Hankey.

However:

> As regards the Treasury itself, their plans were in the main self-contained. The Treasury proposed to use the Board of Inland Revenue

as agents in regard to questions arising from the destruction of property, and the Bank of England as agents for exchange control. The Treasury were, therefore, not faced with the necessity of building up a special staff and organisation of their own.

The Treasury remained aloof and unaccountable, the government's only point of contact with wartime financial machinery, and its sole conduit to the Bank of England. The Bank's misgivings about the Treasury's exchange policy were thus unlikely to emerge.

The Treasury was able to give the Survey the impression that all was under control, stating that:

> General exchange control would be essential from the outset; and this would be operated in conjunction with the Board of Trade measures for the control of imports. In the operation of exchange control bankers and bullion brokers would be appointed as authorised agents; the necessary forms, etc., had already been printed; and the Dominion Governments informed privately.

These confident assertions disguised the Treasury's abiding reluctance to enforce comprehensive exchange control.

In the meantime the Stamp Survey was provided with draft copies of various forms and a Bill to be put before Parliament on the outbreak of war. Interestingly, a summary entitled 'Treasury Financial Arrangements for War' to be employed 'to deal with the first shock' was also provided,[16] which revealed both the inadequacy of existing arrangements and the great potential for positive action given a different attitude. It began by asserting that: 'According to present intentions, foreign exchange control will be imposed in the United Kingdom immediately on the outbreak of war, for the purpose of economising and using to the best advantage the gold and foreign exchange resources of the country.'

If 'present intentions' did not change and controls were introduced, they would not be comprehensive. The capital of non-residents could be removed from the country, subject to applications 'to be considered individually by the Bank of England with a view to permitting such withdrawal of capital to be made in an orderly and controlled way'. To ease this process: 'If dollars are not available, non-residents may be allowed to ship gold if it is possible for them to secure transport.' There were other yawning gaps. It was explained that on ideological grounds 'accounts of non-residents will not be blocked, as they are under

German and other exchange control systems: this may lead to a "Black Bourse" rate for sterling, but the Treasury have felt extreme reluctance to block "non-resident" accounts'.[17]

Having revealed its inclination to shrink from firm action, the Treasury then gave tantalising hints of possibilities it was unwilling to exploit, noting that the 'Dominion; Colonial; etc., Governments have been informed on the above lines and asked to consider to what extend [sic] and with what modifications a similar scheme should be introduced in other parts of the British Empire'.[18] This request was peremptory:

> It has been suggested to the Authorities concerned that within rhe [sic] British Empire, an area dominated by British sterling, local exchange controls must be imposed in order to protect the local currency from the risk of a capital flight which if not checked by a control would involve either q [sic] depreciation of the exchange or a drain on sterling funds to support it.[19]

Here the Treasury was baldly stating the totality of sterling area dependence on Britain, and it included an extract from the communication in question. The recipients were told that

> arrangements will be required to ensure that the entire credit facilities of each area will become available for the financing of exports necessary for the conduct of the war and other essential purposes. It is obvious that the more complete the local control in any area is, the greater will be the latitude permissible for United Kingdom transactions with that area and the less hampering will be the financial formalities between that area and this country. Pending the conclusion of satisfactory arrangements by the area concerned its currency, even if linked to sterling, will, from the point of view of the British regulations, be treated as a foreign currency.[20]

Unfortunately, this lack of charity did not begin at home.

8.2   The 'time which we dare not regard as peace'

In July 1939, the CEI once again advised the Cabinet on the economics of defence. In contrast to its position of December 1938, the Committee's Twenty-Seventh Report made no pretence that peacetime conditions prevailed, although it still could not bring itself to advocate complete defensive preparations. It acknowledged that 'our defence programme has nothing to lose and everything to gain by the adoption of remedies less drastic than those required in war, but appropriate to a time which we dare not regard as peace'.[21] The Committee now confessed that:

> It would be surprising indeed if adequate defence preparations could be achieved on top of the undisturbed normal economic activity of the country without special measures. We believe that the attempt to do so would produce dangerous repercussions on the price level and the balance of trade.

This was a complete reversal of fourth arm logic, which had claimed since 1936 that any 'dangerous repercussions' would come from attempts to interfere with 'normal economic activity'. The Committee had also acknowledged that the international recession of 1937–38 was offset in Britain by rearmament. It noted that in civilian investment 'a decline of no less than £120 millions attributable in part to a reduction of stocks of raw materials and semi-finished goods' had taken place:[22]

> Normally this decline might have produced a serious slump, but its effects were mitigated in 1938 by the expansion of defence demand. This decline in ordinary domestic demand, however, made possible a simultaneous expansion of defence expenditure and an improvement of the export surplus of the investment industries, after paying for their raw material imports, of £42 millions compared with 1937.[23]

It has been argued that Keynes had converted leading Treasury figures to his views on the management of the domestic economy and rearmament made his case.[24] The economic requirements of defence, however, remained in the background. The Committee thought that import controls seemed a logical answer to balance of payments difficulties:

> But it must be remembered that we are debarred from increasing duties on a wide range of engineering products, e.g., by our recent trade agreement with the United States, and from imposing quantitative limitations on imports that do not apply to home production by that and other trade treaties. Even so it is possible that the present

pressure on our balance of payments may be so accentuated by the increase in our defence expenditure that more fundamental remedies, in the direction of import and exchange control, may have to be considered.[25]

In this respect the Committee's thinking was unchanged. Action might be needed only to correct poor balance of payment figures, not the continuing drain of reserves caused by the proximity of war. Exchange control remained a regrettable possibility, not an urgent necessity.

As at the turn of the year, the Cabinet received Treasury advice in close proximity to the CEI's contribution. On this occasion, however, the presence of Hopkins was required to shield Simon from terse and searching questions. The Cabinet was invited to consider the Treasury's 'Note on the Financial Situation',[26] which sought to convince it of the Treasury's interpretation of recent events. This document was thought so sensitive that ministers were asked to hand it in at the end of the meeting. A striking feature was the title of its first section: 'The War Chest'. For the first time Britain's reserves of gold and foreign currency were explicitly referred to as assets for use in war. This, however, was the full extent of the Treasury's mental adjustment.

The report downplayed the effect on the exchanges of Hitler's actions and said that

> the recent development of events – particularly the growth of the defence programme and the persistent demand for loans and credits from foreign countries – has added to the problem of finding money for defence a new anxiety as to our ability to defend the £ and to continue to purchase vital necessities from abroad, both in present conditions if they continue, and above all, in war.[27]

This dishonest attempt to link the gold drain to defence spending prefaced a variety act of desperate dissembling. The Treasury's report repeated the assertion that although the £800 million gold stock of the previous year 'looked imposing' it, 'in fact, gave a rather misleading appearance of strength'.

The report stated that 'In less than 15 months of international tension nearly 40 per cent of our gold stock has disappeared.' However, in giving 'reasons for our gold loss of over £300 million in 15 months', international tension was not mentioned. A curious collection of reasons was put forward: the 'economic setback of 1937' was cited which 'profoundly disturbed world conditions, the effect being especially marked among the best customers of our export trade'. British gold reserves, though, grew throughout 1937. The return of a 'great deal of fugitive French money'[28] was also mentioned.

Another reason given was revealing: 'The balance of our trade is adverse, but the essential point for sterling is the aggregate balance of trade of the sterling bloc which banks in London. It is estimated that for a period of 18 months to December last, the sterling balances held in London by the countries of the sterling bloc were falling at the rate of some £80 million a year.'[29] The reasons for this phenomenon were many and complex, and were, incidentally, aggravated by the Anglo-American Trade Agreement, but the point is disingenuous. By deliberately excluding Britain herself as a member of the sterling bloc it excluded the effect of debt repayment to her by the bloc, that is the sizeable portion of the £80 million quoted which simply moved to British accounts and thus remained in London. The demands of war were to lead to a dramatic reversal of this position as Britain incurred massive obligations to the newly named Sterling Area, while abrogating the American Agreement. This money also remained in London.

After this list of red herrings the report came to the international situation as an aggravating rather than fundamental cause of gold loss, though it was known and repeatedly stated that the political situation was the real culprit:

These economic factors leading to a depletion of our gold stocks have been reinforced by the effect of political conditions. A great deal of fugitive money in London has been transferred by foreigners to the United States or other supposedly safe countries, and probably there is a small trickle of British investments to the United States, though the amount is not significant.

The report then detailed the adverse effects of war preparation on the visible balance of payments and the cost of foreign loans, before stating with breathtaking disingenuousness that:

The following measures have been taken to protect the exchange. The value of sterling has been let down from 5 dollars to 4.68. The embargo on foreign issues has been greatly tightened up. A very large *bloc* of gold has been transferred from the Bank of England to the Exchange Equalisation Account for use in active defence. Sweeping measures to discourage and impede speculators have been taken.

A subtle shift in reasoning had been used here to disguise the true situation. The report had previously discussed the defence of the reserves. Now it was describing the defence of the exchange, for which the reserves were being used.

Anticipating calls for devaluation the report extended its flimsy web of contradictions contending that 'very little more could be done even with the most far-reaching powers. A further small depreciation of the £ would be ineffective: a large depreciation even if it were on balance desirable, is not at present practical politics.' This statement was made a month before sterling's defence was abandoned and the currency 'let' down to $4.03. Even as they spoke in Cabinet, Simon and Hopkins were aware of enormous and increasing pressure on sterling. The report stated, however, that: 'Up to the present the disadvantage of our gold loss has been largely political. It must discourage our friends and encourage the Axis powers.'

In addition to its desire to downplay the scale of the disaster, the report betrayed a growing confusion as to the boundaries of political and economic reality in peace and war. If the gold loss 'continues swiftly it will soon become also a serious economic anxiety even in peace. But the greatest anxiety is that it may gravely affect our staying power in war. Our gold stock, together with such assets as we may be able to sell or mortgage in wartime to countries overseas, constitutes our sole war chest.' A comparison with 1914 revealed the difficulties for Treasury officials grappling with these concepts.

The report acknowledged that First World War financial conditions had been sustained by borrowing in America, and made the obvious point that 'under the Johnson Act we cannot borrow in the United States, either privately or from the Government' and that 'unless, when the time comes the United States are prepared either to lend or to give us money as required, the prospects for a long war are becoming exceedingly grim'.[30] In these circumstances it made little sense to continue donating gold to the United States. However, this paradox was dictated by fourth arm logic, which had to conform to Great War practice to remain consistent. Consequently: 'At the rate of £20 million a month, at which we have been using gold, our reserves would barely last three years and considering the increased demands likely in war, this estimate of the period is very likely too optimistic.' Despite the Treasury's pessimism it was necessary to present the Cabinet with a plan of action. The report concluded that: 'Apart from increased taxation, the following means of arresting the general deterioration suggest themselves.'[31] The first of these was to state the obvious: 'The primary need is to conserve our resources in gold and foreign exchange, which represent our staying power in war.' Inflation and tax increases were mentioned and the opinion expressed that 'in the course of time general controls are likely to become necessary and the standard of living must be directly or indirectly affected'. The avoidance of foreign arms purchases was recommended on the grounds that: 'Further expenditure on Armaments in this country cannot be undertaken without counting the cost in gold.' In terms of defence expenditure generally, 'as there is a prospect of the continuance of the present armed peace, if not of the outbreak of war, finality of expenditure (unless for overmastering reasons) should now be declared'.

This statement was an unrealistic attempt to reimpose rationing and dissent was anticipated: 'If, nevertheless, substantial new expenditures are contemplated, the Cabinet should be provided not only with estimates of cost but so far as possible with estimates of the extra strain involved upon the exchanges.' Next came a confession that little had been done to lay in stores 'of food and of vital raw materials, the acquisition of which from overseas is essential to our continued existence'. This should be 'carried further in spite of the immediate gold losses which this course involves'.[32] Such a confused and dishonest document, containing veiled confession of monumental failure, might have been expected to produce an explosion in Cabinet, and Hopkins was there to face it.

8.3 A minor revolt

The Cabinet response to the Treasury's paper ranged from bewilderment to anger. The sharpest questioning came from Hore-Belisha, who appeared to sense the document's fundamental dishonesty. He was the only minister to put a specifically technical question when he 'asked Sir Richard Hopkins what were his views on the general level of sterling, and whether it was fair to say that we were weakening our position by not allowing the natural level to operate'.[33] Hopkins replied vaguely that 'in the opinion of some the level of sterling was rather too high. Any difference of opinion on this matter, however, related to a relatively small margin, say $4.55 to $4.68, and this would have but little effect on gold losses.' He then diverted attention from this questionable statement with a rambling discourse on the effects of devaluation on competitiveness, which were in Hopkins' opinion, 'likely to be transient'.[34] This was no answer to Hore-Belisha's question.

Ministers were now unsettled, and the secretary of state for air, Kingsley Wood, 'asked Sir Richard Hopkins whether his view was that we were not in a position to fight a long war'. Hopkins stated the obvious at length. He

> said that the situation undoubtedly grew more difficult with every month that passed. If war should break out in the near future, we should have in our war chest the existing gold stock less those foreign balances which would be removed. If, however, war occurred say a year hence, those stocks would have been diminished by the drain in the intervening year. So long as we continued on the present course our financial position was being weakened.[35]

Wood persevered and 'said that he had understood that it was a fundamental feature of our policy that we should conserve our strength for a long war, and he asked Sir Richard Hopkins whether that strength had gone'.[36] Hopkins 'said that this was not his view, but the memorandum drew attention to very serious matters which must be borne in mind'. Wood for the third time 'asked whether we were in a worse position to fight a long war than in 1914'. Hopkins replied 'that this must be the case subject to the question whether the United States was prepared to help us with finance'.

This led Stanley to ask whether the Americans 'were in a better position' to do this than in 1916. Hopkins' reply followed the question in ignoring neutrality legislation, and said of the Americans that 'he did not think that their vast gold stocks would be of much help to them in financing us in war'. All the more reason, it might be thought, for not adding Britain's to them. It was a surprising assumption that the Americans might even have contemplated such a use for their gold.

Hopkins foreshadowed lend-lease by stating that: 'The primary need would be that they should give us a share of their production without our paying for it.' The Neutrality Acts were not mentioned. Hopkins then agreed 'that the production of gold from South Africa could be increased, but South African gold belonged to South Africa, and we should have in effect to pay for it, either by exports to South Africa or by a loan from that country'.[37] This statement was also untrue. South

Africa was inside the sterling bloc and would have to accept sterling payment for its gold. In Civil Service tradition, Hopkins' spirit of economy extended to the truth.

The paper on Britain's financial position was accompanied by another entitled 'The German Financial Effort for Rearmament.' This 'Note by the Chancellor of the Exchequer' formed 'an analysis of the present financial effort of Germany as compared with that of this country'.[38] Also, because 'the question is often asked why this country cannot at all times do what Germany does it may be well to make one or two general observations on that subject'. After listing supposed German advantages, such as a 'docile population' willing to tolerate high levels of tax, paragraph 6 of the report turned to Germany's external position, stating that:

> As Germany cannot expect in war to import from overseas, the policy has been to acquire great stocks of imported necessities, to produce at home substitutes for particular types of essential imports, though involving great economic waste, and to acquire power over adjacent territories which can supply German needs. The question of the means of payment for overseas imports in war – an ever present anxiety in our case – scarcely arises in Germany. We cannot be self-supporting even if we wish to.

In the subsequent discussion, nobody sought to contrast this dubious statement with the official policy of blockading Germany into surrender. The report expressed astonishment at the yield of taxation likely to be achieved by the Germans, as this method of finance replaced earlier borrowing, stating that 'the implications are staggering'.[39] This was because 'from roughly the same kind of total national income',[40] the Germans 'will have over £880 millions a year for defence *without* borrowing against our £247 millions and unless their Budget breaks down they can keep it up indefinitely'.[41]

Contradictions in policy were by this stage painfully apparent and Hore-Belisha, obviously well briefed, pointed to inconsistencies in Treasury thinking. He

> drew attention to a statement in paragraph 6 of the Introductory Section of C.P. 148(39) which referred to the self-sufficiency of

Germany. He contrasted this with a paper prepared by the Industrial Intelligence Centre which reached the conclusion that Germany would not last out for more than a year of war. He also referred to a paper which the Director of the Industrial Intelligence Centre had read to the Imperial Defence College which indicated that Germany would have to produce at seven times her existing rate if she was to maintain 100 divisions in the field.[42]

Hopkins replied that 'he was not qualified to speak on the capacity of Germany to wage a world war' (any more than on that of Great Britain it seemed):

> no doubt the views in the paper expressed by the Director of the Industrial Intelligence Centre did not purport to be more than estimates. He did not think that our war plans were prepared on the assumption that war could not in any case last for more than a year. The important point was, he thought, that for whatever period the war lasted, whether a year or longer, we should have to continue to import food and raw materials. Germany, on the other hand, had not got command of the seas and could not expect to import goods except from adjacent countries. Her plan, therefore, had been drawn on the basis of self-sufficiency.[43]

This was a weak answer and the minister of labour 'asked whether the logic of this argument was not that we should make every acre of this country as productive as possible?'[44]

Hopkins, with his assurance rapidly deteriorating under unaccustomed questioning, made an obvious reply, trapped within peacetime thinking. He

> said that no doubt this process could be carried out to a certain further stage with reasonable economy. He thought, however, that to apply our resources to the uneconomic development of the agricultural capacity of this country would probably involve an even greater strain on our resources than dependence on imports. It seemed to him that the right course was that we should seek to reserve a reasonable part of our foreign exchange resources in case we were in a tight corner. He also thought that we should consider every possible method of forcing the export trade in time of war.[45]

In response to a helpful prompt from the prime minister 'that the point of paragraph 6 . . . was that Germany relied on the policy of stocks or self-sufficiency', Hopkins 'agreed. If at any time Germany was short of a particular commodity and had to buy from countries overseas, her lack of gold would be the determining factor.' This was nonsense, as was soon to be pointed out.

Next, Hore-Belisha summed up his tidy inquisition, stating that

these papers held out a dismal prospect for this country but not for Germany. Thus paragraph 19 of C.P. 148(39) appeared to indicate that Germany could keep up her expenditure on armaments indefi-nitely. In this connection the Secretary of State for War drew atten-tion to paragraph 5, on page 2 of C.P.148(39). He asked whether it was in fact the case that Germany was in no way relaxing her efforts and that she would keep up expenditure on armaments indefinitely.[46]

Hopkins' reply drew a distinction between internal and external finance, stating

that so far as concerned internal finance, he thought that this seemed to be the case. So far as concerned obtaining necessities from abroad, there was a great difference between the position of this country and that of Germany. Germany was largely self-supporting in food. A commodity such as rubber was now produced in Germany by syn-thetic processes, though at great cost, thereby limiting the need for imports from abroad. So far as concerned overseas finance, Germany was bankrupt and the position was kept going only by severe controls which limited the imports of what we should regard as necessary commodities.[47]

Kingsley Wood returned to the attack and 'asked whether a financial breakdown in Germany could be regarded as either inevitable or indeed likely'.[48] Despite his distaste for German methods, Hopkins admitted that he 'saw no reason to anticipate a breakdown, at any rate within an early period of time'. Wood then, like Hore-Belisha, provided a damning summary:

Sir Richard had said that Germany was spending more than we were spending on armaments, that there was a prospect that Germany could fight a war as long as we could, and that none of the remedies proposed seemed likely to see us through a life-and-death struggele [*sic*]. Was it not necessary that we should consider whether we should do more to model ourselves on German methods?[49]

Hopkins referred him to paragraphs 36 and 40 of CP 149(39) which considered the possibility of action when full employment was reached. Hore-Belisha then moved in again and

> said that C.P. 149(39) seemed to indicate two alternative courses; that we should copy Germany's taxation or that we should adopt the measures of control therein indicated. Possibly both these courses should be adopted. He noted that the various measures of control were being studied, and he assumed that before the Cabinet was invited to reach any conclusions they would be informed of the results of that study.[50]

Hopkins once again referred to paragraphs 36 to 40 of CP 149(39). Silent to this moment, Chatfield then delivered a withering comment on the Treasury's competence when he referred to 'paragraph 6 of the Introductory Section of C.P. 148(39), where it was stated that Germany could not expect to import goods from overseas in war. He said that in the last war Germany had imported large quantities of goods from Scandinavia, and would be able to do so again.'[51] Hopkins could only reply 'that it had not been within his knowledge that Germany had been able to secure a large volume of imports in the last war. Any large volume of German imports in War would *pro tanto* modify the arguments in the paragraph referred to.'[52]

8.4 The crunch: 'a real bad day'

By August, the gold committed in January was almost gone. Change became inevitable, and as the British authorities still recoiled from Schachtian devilry, a floating pound was preferred. On 10 August, Bolton's deputy, Hawker, called Knoke and told him that:

> War fears on the Continent and in the Far East were developing as the recently much talked of August 15 (the day on which German mobilization supposedly reaches its climax) was approaching and the Japanese situation was steadily growing worse. As a result of all this, the demand for spot and forward (for end August and for three months delivery) dollars today, both from the Far East and from the

Continent, had been heavy and the British fund had sold about $30,000,000 in support of sterling. In other words today had been a real bad day; the first one, as a matter of fact, in many weeks. Talk in the street and in the press about a possible further devaluation of sterling in the next three months was increasing and Morgenthau's visit to Europe was causing further rumors.[53]

Knoke thought that: 'All one could say as to the future of sterling was that it really should be weak in view of all these fears and talk of war the world over and of the strain on Britain's finances which the rearmament programme was bound to cause. One must expect to see sterling under attack so long as this war fear and tension in Europe continues.'[54]

The plight of sterling once more appeared in meetings of the US Treasury, initially in renewed concern at the amount of gold that the US had to absorb. On 24 August, however, Butterworth was sent for by Phillips and told that 'that the mounting European crisis was producing an increasing drain on their gold resources and the rate of increase was very alarming'.[55] In the first three days of that week £35 million of gold had gone and the British

> had been hanging on 'from day to day' and after raising the bank rate this morning they had reluctantly come to the conclusion that they must adopt one of two courses to conserve their gold resources; either put on exchange control or let sterling depreciate. They had decided not to adopt the former course principally because if the crisis should pass many months would ensue or perhaps as long as a year before they could remove the controls but if they let sterling depreciate, if the political crisis should pass they were convinced sterling would rapidly rebound to near the current level.[56]

Consequently, 'when London opened tomorrow the British fund would stay out of the market and let sterling find its own level'.[57] Butterworth

> asked him to what level he expected sterling to depreciate and how long the British fund proposed to stay out of the market. He said that they would stay out until sterling found a new level which would certainly take a day or two and that it was difficult to prejudge what rate it would be since political events were moving so fast, but he implied that he did not expect the depreciation to be drastic.

In conclusion, 'Phillips emphasized the confidential character of this message and the fact that he was sorry that such short notice was being given but they had been hanging on from day to day and the decision had only just been made'.[58] In a supplementary telegram, Butterworth noted that he had 'pressed strongly for information regarding the actual state of the British equalization fund', and was told that total British gold reserves now totalled £400$^1/_4$ million, down from £590 million in March.[59] He further reported that: 'In supplying these figures Phillips took pains to emphasize that at the moment it was the pace that was killing.' Knoke was given the same news by Hawker, although he already knew through the Treasury Department of Phillips' conversation with Butterworth. Asked for his personal opinion Knoke said that the news 'would naturally be a terrific shock although people had more and more generally figured in recent weeks that something was bound to happen'.[60] Knoke

> felt that restrictions as a first step would have been less of a shock to the public here. That was what I would really have expected though fully aware of the fact that restrictions would not be very effective in the long run. Nevertheless, I would have thought that, considering the great tension in the international atmosphere, they would have considered it preferable to carry on with restrictions at least until the crash had come (if there was to be a crash) rather than risk giving Hitler a chance to use this development as a further inducement to stand pat.[61]

The Americans were not told the whole truth. The unwillingness of the British authorities to impose exchange controls was hardly the result of likely difficulty in removing them. A briefing document was prepared for the chancellor,[62] weighing up available options. This acknowledged that 'from the summer of 1938 onwards it became apparent that international politics were the dominant influence on the exchanges and on sterling in particular'. It surveyed, wistfully, the damage already done to the gold reserves by existing policy: 'If we were in a period of assured peace, such a reserve, though somewhat narrow, could be regarded with equanimity', but: 'Actually our position is one in which we are threatened with war and gold is exceedingly necessary to us as a reserve for purchasing food and munitions under actual war conditions. For this purpose our present reserve of 469$^3/_4$ millions must be regarded as altogether too low already.'

This belated clarity of vision makes the document's recommendations seem bizarre, especially in their continuing insistence on a razor-sharp dividing line between peace and war. It was conceded that 'we could proceed to apply measures of exchange control similar to those enforced in Germany and to the extent to which we were successful we could no doubt maintain the £ at almost any rate we chose'. Further comment on this seemingly attractive option, however, was not persuasive in intent:

adopting exchange control may be inevitable in actual war. If a country is prepared largely to sacrifice its export trade (relying on subsidies from the taxpayer to enable its goods to be sold abroad), to enforce rigorously a lower standard of living on the population, and to abandon its position as a great financial and banking centre, there is no reason why it should not adopt exchange control in war, and we should no doubt do so in a great war in which we had not from the start the help of the United States. But the adoption of exchange control in time of peace is another matter. It might well mean the final loss of much of our financial power, which is a lesser sacrifice than losing a war but still not to be contemplated with equanimity. Exchange control was no doubt for this kind of reason rejected even by the French in their worst period last year.

The option actually taken sounds rather less attractive. If support for the pound were withdrawn:

The heavy fall in sterling might be widely regarded as a sign of fundamental weakness in the British economic system, with adverse repercussions on the diplomatic situation. This danger would be particularly great if the freeing of sterling were unaccompanied by any other measure suggesting that an active policy was being pursued, since it might in these circumstances convey an impression of helpless feebleness.

This was sound prediction. The same day, US Treasury officials came to terms with the situation. Hanes encapsulated the position, stating 'it's an accomplished fact and they're simply saying to us this is what we're going to do'. He wondered 'should we make any answer or should we tell Butterworth we have no comment to make. We regret this move of course but we have no further comment to make.'[63] Lochhead added: 'I think that's the safest thing because of course it's water over the dam.

I'm terribly sorry they didn't try to use exchange control but that – it's too late, I mean they're not going to – they've made up their minds.' The option of announcing a breach of the Tripartite Agreement was hardly discussed. Lochhead commented that 'we could take the attitude that this is an exceptional time just now and we're reviewing the situation. In the meantime the tripartite will continue.' The British had after all 'actually made their decision on it, and nothing we're going to say is going to change it', and so 'we should just simply tell Butterworth that we regret very much the decision and not make any more comment on it'.[64] Hanes remarked that 'I think that jibes with everybody's opinion here too, Archie'.

Lochhead had also discussed the matter with Harrison at the Federal Reserve Board who 'said the same thing. He said that's the safest.'[65] In terms of action Lochhead thought 'there's nothing certain that I can see that we can do. We can't tell them you can't do it', and consequently 'it looks to me as if we're going to have to swallow something, for a short time at least'.[66] Lochhead explained matters by telephone to Morgenthau, currently in Europe, saying that after the British announcement 'the boys came in right away and wanted to know whether the tripartite had busted up', and whether Hanes 'was considering devaluing the dollar under the power you have and Johnny said – spiked that right away – said we hadn't thought or talked about it'.[67]

The French were old hands at this game, and the views of the Finance Minister Paul Reynaud, as expressed to the American Embassy, remain instructive. Reynaud 'thought the British idea somewhat sketchy, of what constituted consultation under the tripartite agreement'. Nevertheless, 'he hoped that the United States Government would also pretend that it had been informed in advance'.[68] Reynaud went on to say that:

> According to his private opinion, the matter had been foolishly handled by the British. They would have had a cheap money and a strong one which would have drawn gold, had they abolished all restrictions on gold exports and simultaneously stopped operations of the stabilization fund, and let the pound drop with a resounding thud to a very low point indeed and then pegged it there.[69]

This was once true, but folly to attempt with war imminent.

8.5 Preparations for war: 'well into the 1917 stage'

Butterworth remarked perceptively of the British authorities that 'these people are awfully determined, – not because they want to do anything but because they don't see any way out'.[70] He encapsulated the situation neatly: 'They're on the horns of the dilemma; either they fight – and it's going to be awful – for if they don't fight and do another Munich, they'll never be able to hold their Empire and the Allies together again.'

Butterworth reported that, 'the atmosphere is not a damned bit good over here'.[71] He had observed in a telegram the day before that:

> The City is naturally bewildered and despairing at the speed and turn of events. Its mood at the moment is to see no alternative to fighting regardless of the character or condition of the so-called peace front. An incident may serve to paint the emotional picture: a lieutenant in the Guards' scarlet uniform happened to pass through the City in an automobile. Crowds gathered from nowhere and he was cheered to the echo by top-hatted senior partners and messengers alike. How long this mood will last remains to be seen. But at any rate it is well to doubt that it is shared by those who hold the political power of decision.[72]

On 28 August, Butterworth reported a lunch appointment 'with Clay at the Bank of England'.[73] The latter

> confirmed . . . that in the event of war Great Britain would become economically and financially a totalitarian state as rapidly as possible and problems would be regarded in the light of manpower, tons and tonnage rather than pounds, shillings and pence. Clay felt that their plans were sufficiently developed so that they would start off at well into the 1917 stage.[74]

The City was ready, if only to decamp. Butterworth noted that: 'Preparations for war are far advanced in the city. [sic] The clearing banks have already transferred their head offices to the country where the section of the Bank of England with which they deal is also now located.' In fact: 'All financial institutions have during the past year duplicated their records and have made arrangements to continue as much of their operations as possible in places of comparative safety.'[75]

This seems unheroic, but Simon's view of the Treasury as one of the fighting services was vindicated and financial honour preserved because: 'The hard nucleus of the Bank of England and the Treasury are remaining in London' along with the bulk of the populace. This was only fair, for as Butterworth noted in his next telegram on 30 August, the Treasury was expecting much from the ordinary citizen. The Treasury told Butterworth

> that sales of securities by British residents to non-residents will be permitted, provided the foreign exchange is turned over to the British monetary authorities in return for sterling at the going rate. The British Treasury is, of course, aware that there is nothing to prevent the recipient of such sterling from converting it back into say dollars and having those dollars placed in another name, but it is at the present time content to rely on the 'general trustworthiness and patriotism of the man-in-the-street' not to make use of such loopholes. Furthermore, the Treasury points out that to close such loopholes would necessitate a complete exchange control system. The Bank of England has been besieged with requests for rulings covering unanticipated contingencies.[76]

When war came, the British government was moving away from the other great powers of the day in economics. Liberal ideology had climbed back to the summit of British thinking on the back of the economic recovery its eclipse had made possible. The result was to export British growth across the Atlantic, as a gift to the United States.

The appalling consequences of the fourth arm policy became apparent with the outbreak of war, when exchange controls were introduced automatically at the newly depreciated exchange rate of $4.03 to the pound. This was a desirable peacetime level, but in war the existing trade gap with the United States was bound to widen massively. The utility of devaluation lay in the American desire that it should be avoided. If the Tripartite Agreement had been a genuine cooperative pact, the Americans could have been prevailed upon to use their enormous gold reserves to support sterling. Britain could have concentrated American minds by reserving the sanction of letting sterling go, as Reynaud suggested, much earlier than actually happened. The Americans had no power to resist this outcome when it did come.

The British gained nothing from their late devaluation, and were left only with its adverse effects in wartime. Nor did they reap the available benefits from exchange control. Had controls been introduced in March

1938, the massive sums of gold expended in sterling's defence against political pressure would have been saved, money which could have bought time to develop home and imperial war potential. Even in war, however, the British authorities were half-hearted about exchange control. They permitted the existence of an unofficial 'black bourse' in sterling for the surprisingly large number of transactions not immediately covered, so that the situation was worsened by the existence of a second value of sterling at a considerable discount to the official rate.

There was precious little to show in the political sphere for the financial sacrifices of 1938–39. The curious belief that the United States would somehow underpin the British war effort without exacting a political price would soon prove false. The tragedy for the British was that their financial weakness in war was the freak consequence of bad policy, which had undermined the strong economic foundations of rearmament.

Britain had, as a result of the economic status regained since 1931, managed to accumulate considerable reserves of gold and foreign currency by the beginning of 1938, and these, being composed largely of foreign balances accumulated against an adverse balance of payments, were a tribute to the strength of the new economic system. As gold began to drain, was permitted to drain, across the exchanges, nothing was done by the British government to preserve this financial credibility. And here was the irony of the situation. The fourth arm policy relied on the maintenance of Britain's external credit, but this credit had been built by determined intervention in the workings of markets. The 'business as usual' attitude of fourth arm economics, clearly demonstrating an unwillingness to intervene in British interests, destroyed it.

The Stamp Survey stumbled upon the true ghastliness of the situation too late. Indeed much of the initial effort expended on it by Wilson and other senior civil servants was aimed at keeping the lid on the appalling picture of unpreparedness that the Survey should have uncovered. In August 1939, the Survey reported optimistically that 'we have made a preliminary survey of practically the whole ground and have arranged for the choice of documents to be supplied to us. A consideration of these and of our notes, after the holidays will provide the basis for a more detailed enquiry on particular points.'[77] It was too late.

Conclusion

The history of the fourth arm policy is one of paradox. Weak and incompetent, it was executed with ingenuity and determination. Many respected figures outside government, even Keynes, would have been hard pressed to distance themselves from at least some of its aspects,[1] whilst important figures within it, notably Hore-Belisha, rebelled against its operation. It was formulated around a common acceptance of liberal economics, yet united disparate constituencies. Their objectives overlapped but were not identical, and the concept of an unholy alliance between the City of London, the Treasury and the Bank of England is overstated. There is no indication that the City welcomed the uncontrolled panic conditions of 1938–39, which favoured its great rival New York, and the Treasury ignored the Bank over exchange control. Conversely liberals of all hues, even progressive economists whose radicalism was confined to the domestic economy, rallied to the fourth arm argument at one time or another.

The political interaction of these interest groups, forming around Neville Chamberlain and the government machine, ensured that Britain in the late 1930s witnessed what was effectively a liberal coup d'état. The common ground for those who participated was the need to defend liberal values or lose what they held dear. This was true of both pan-Anglo-Saxon dreamers like Lothian and the Civil Service heirs of the 'nightwatchman' state. In the inter-war world of shattered polities and ideological flux, everything was at issue and the stakes were high.

In a time of danger liberals knew that the defence ground they had recaptured in the 1920s must be held tenaciously, for if it fell to protectionists the size and importance of the imperial economy and the wider sterling bloc were such as to place the liberal system in jeopardy on a global scale. To the architects of fourth arm policy Hitler was a possible opponent but protection and imperial preference were mortal enemies.

The fourth arm policy was not merely a shield against innovation. It enforced the application of liberal finance and economics, weakening Britain's strategic position. This increased the attractiveness of appeasement, German and American, which weakened the economic and military situation still further. Spiralling failure drew the various adherents to the fourth arm policy closer together. In 1939 the position was reached that they would hang together unless Chamberlain won an unlikely reprieve through diplomacy to add to the stay he had gained at Munich.

Under the most severe pressure, therefore, Simon continued to resist additions to the defence budget, the Treasury and the Bank watched as speculative assault on sterling spilled Britain's war chest across the exchanges and a Trade Agreement was concluded with the United States that prevented any strengthening of the sterling bloc in the year before open war was declared.

A.J.P. Taylor stated that: 'Historians often dislike what happened or wish that it had happened differently. There is nothing they can do about it.'[2] Historians, though, should surely be aware of what did not happen and why not, if they are to complete Taylor's thought and 'state the truth as they see it without worrying whether this shocks or confirms existing prejudices'. Thus, to understand the full significance of the fourth arm policy we should be aware of the opportunity cost of the actual course of events, of the dog that did not bark. For all who sought to shape the future of Britain, the cost of defeat in the struggle to control economic policy could not have been higher. In this conflict, the resurgence of the liberal view was an event of the highest importance, whilst the achievements of its advocates were very great and measurable in the economic distress of 1945.

The move towards a more liberal economic outlook on the part of the British government between 1936 and 1939 went against the grain of economic progress since 1931 and the initial inclination of the government itself, explicitly stated to US representatives, to depend on Empire and sterling bloc resources to meet the growing crisis. This political choice went to the heart of the matter. Everything about the bloc was big: its actual size; its growth potential; its schismatic political power in Britain, and the horror it provoked amongst Atlanticists on both sides of the ocean. The successful interventions of the US Treasury and State Departments under Morgenthau and Hull in the British debate reflected an overriding American interest in Britain's failure to develop.[3]

Britain's economy was, nevertheless, thrown back on to the newly formalised Sterling Area as soon as war broke out, despite the liberal sentiments of her policy makers and the anger of the Americans.[4] However, it was far too late for the potential of the Area to be fully

184 Britain, America and Rearmament in the 1930s

developed, and it has been portrayed as a failure ever since.[5] Much of
the case for fourth arm policy is sustainable only in ignorance or denial
of the potential of the sterling bloc before 1939.

The opportunities forgone in the 1930s can be judged from the partial
achievements that followed in the far worse circumstance of war in
progress. The formal creation of the Sterling Area after the outbreak of
war eased Britain's financial position, as witnessed in the switch from
US to sterling sources of supply. After the collapse of France, the dependence on American supply and the scale of lend-lease are much quoted
as justification for pre-war economic appeasement. However, it should
be remembered that half Britain's reserves had been squandered before
1939, and much of the American weaponry recorded at sale price, item
by item, in lend-lease was produced in factories built with the capital
provided by British (and French) orders, yielding little of value before
1942. It must be asked if the crisis would have occurred had these
resources of capital been used to create capacity in the Dominions or at
home.

A general failure to consider such possibilities stems from omissions
in the inter-war documentary record, often deliberately contrived,
and their consequences for historians. It is no coincidence that the Sterling Area is written about with greater confidence by historians of the
immediate post-war period, when it was keeping the nation afloat and
was prominent in the documentary record. However, even in these
studies the consequences of failure to adequately consider the lessons
of the 1930s are apparent in strange contradictions. Correlli Barnett pro-
vides a classic example. Hostile to free trade and liberal internationalism, yet strangely partial to liberal financial mechanisms, he initially
traduces the Sterling Area along the now familiar lines that it was too
small (for what is not made clear), and somehow archaic. Strangely,
for something brand new and born of Britain's departure from gold
'for the first time during a peace' it was nevertheless 'the detritus of
successive episodes of history'. Ignoring its role in feeding and fuelling
Britain in war to the tune of £3 billion, Barnett describes it simply as
a means for Britain to 'strut her Victorian role of central banker' on a
'diminished stage'.[6]

The sterling paid to the members of the wartime Area naturally
ensured that their holdings of pounds grew phenomenally during the

war, as of course sterling was not convertible and Britain's exports were necessarily reduced. Barnett describes this as the obtaining supplies 'on tick', and that by '1945 the United Kingdom's sterling debts (or "balances") had risen to £2969 million'.[7] However, the Sterling Area was hungry for British exports after the war, having access to dollars only through London, and to the unmitigated benefit of the British economy it had sterling to pay for them.

However, this money is habitually described as the 'sterling debt' – a post-war liability. Much is made of the fact that London undertook to meet the dollar deficits of the RSA (Rest of the Sterling Area), largely from the proceeds of the 1945 US loan of $3 billion. However, for exclusive access to a proven market of £3 billion, this seems a small price to pay. The fundamental economic concept involved was expressed succinctly by Ralph Hawtrey. Writing of the newly restored gold standard in 1926, his comments can be repeated without risking accusations of hindsight. The true status of the sterling balances can be explained in terms of Hawtrey's statement that: 'The idea of money is derived from the idea of a debt'[8] and his subsequent explanation:

A debt is one of the fundamental concepts of economics. It must not be thought of as arising only from the borrowing of money or from the postponement of payment. Every sale of goods or service rendered gives rise to a debt. The debt may be immediately discharged, but that does not affect its nature from the point of view of the means of payment.[9]

The sterling balances were no more 'debt' than any money is debt, and were far more effectively employed than gold sent across the Atlantic after March 1938. The money involved retained its utility for the British economy, rather than that of the United States. The soundness of Hawtrey's comments was unwittingly endorsed by the American government after the war, which in return for the 1945 loan insisted, fruitlessly as it transpired, on the convertibility of sterling by 1947, so that it might gain a slice of the sterling 'debt' cake.

To think in terms of sterling as a source of weakness in the post-war world it is necessary to hold conflicting views. Barnett considers the Sterling Area 'a legacy of history now too burdensome for the United Kingdom to carry except at the expense of damage to her own progress as an industrial society'.[10] However, 'British industry . . . continued to seek refuge, as it had done since the late Victorian era, in the easy markets of the sterling area (above all the Commonwealth)'.[11] How it could be that the Sterling Area was at once an intolerable burden and yet a soft option awaits explanation.

It is also unclear how the markets of the Sterling Area were any 'easier' for the British than were the protected markets of Britain's competitors for their own producers, in which British exporters faced discrimination or exclusion. In this connection it has been observed that, 'if German and American businessmen and entrepreneurs were so superlatively great at being entrepreneurs, why did they need high tariff walls to keep out their creampuff, backward, epicene British rivals?'[12] The strange contradiction of viewing the Area as both burden and crutch is the logical conclusion of an argument that can be traced backwards to the acceptance the fourth arm argument hook, line and sinker.

Barnett is by no means unique in the completeness with which he does this, arguing in relation to material needs of rearmament that: 'By 1938 the volume of all these imports was running Britain straight towards a balance of payments crisis', and quoting Sir John Simon's lamentations to Cabinet without qualification or analysis. Barnett states, solely on the basis of such official pessimism, that: 'With a fall of a quarter in Britain's total gold and convertible currency reserves since the previous year, national bankruptcy, a distant iceberg on the horizon in 1937, now began to loom huge and jagged in the offing.'[13] Acceptance of the fiction that the gold drain was economically motivated suggests the spurious conclusion that: 'By the spring of 1939 the contrast between Britain's self-perpetuated role of first class world and imperial power and her backward industrial economy had brought her within the zone of icy chill that spelt inevitable shipwreck.'[14]

However, it was admitted within government before 1939 that the deficit on the balance of payments current account posed no immediate threat to British solvency, and that the gold drain was a political phenomenon. British industrial 'backwardness' had no connection with the loss of reserves: indeed, even the government line was rather that the voracious appetite of the buoyant industrial machine was sucking in imports.

It is a truism that the final and spectacular US recovery from the Depression was the result of rearmament, which mobilised the 'spare capacity' in America's economy. However, the inadvertent British role in US recovery before the war cannot be ignored. The volume of gold fed into the American economy from London was in itself vast but there were two other factors of importance. The gold was distributed through the Federal Reserve system as a *basis* for the creation of much larger amounts of money in the form of bank credit. Then, once this money was in circulation there was of course the multiplier effect, discovered in Britain by Kahn and in the late 1930s becoming understood through the mechanism of Keynes' general theory. A remarkable combination of Morgenthau's intuitive, though unlearned, grasp of America's economic interest and the corresponding ignorance of his supercilious British counterparts, paved the way for American success. The foundation of US recovery was thus well in place before significant orders for weaponry were placed.

The concept of 'spare' American capacity is, however, too glibly stated. British shipbuilding fell to 7 per cent of its pre-war total before rearmament[15] yet nowhere is it argued that there was spare capacity for the industry to increase its production more than fourteenfold, and with good reason because this was not so. Nor was it in the United States. Lost productive capacity is lost forever. New capacity can be created only when new capital mobilises resources, and realising this America triumphed. The United States flourished because the Federal government accepted by 1938 that capital scarcity was its single greatest problem and took action accordingly.

The British in contrast, blinded by a fourth arm perspective, believed their capital stock ample to finance their modest military programme, until war showed the need for the gold surrendered to America. The British government was oblivious, both of the scale of production required and that which was possible from a sound foundation. This gulf of comprehension was the single largest factor working for the United States. It is small wonder that the US economy recovered, or that British economic independence was lost.

Against this loss, in the years of American non-belligerency Britain's return on the money poured into US contracts was small indeed: 'Munitions production in the U.S. was quite small even at the time of the entry of the U.S. into the war. What expansion had been realised was in part the legacy of cash orders placed by the U.K. and other Empire governments with individual firms and with the encouragement of the U.S. Administration.' Indeed: 'Deliveries on these orders in the eighteen months up to the end of 1941 were 40 per cent of all aircraft production in the U.S., and even then the contracts were by no means fully delivered.'[16] The legacy of the fourth arm policy can be seen in the later explosion of American war production. If '[i]t was British ordering which established U.S. production of such important types as the Mustang fighter (developed from the Spitfire design)'[17] and the progress of U.S. contracts was so painfully slow, it can be argued that it would have been better to build up Canadian and other dominion armaments industries sooner than was done and to use resources for the development of equipment in the more advanced British rearmament machine.[18] This would have avoided the wasteful situation where America 'remained a large producer of weapons and ammunition of British design until quite late in the war, but her contribution might have been larger had there been a greater standardization of types and calibres'.[19]

The economic events of the war, though, were but echoes of past mistakes. Far from constructing the impressive military capacity of which they were capable before 1939, the British actually worked hard to weaken their war potential. The drain of gold, the Tripartite Agreement, the Anglo-American Trade Agreement and the rationing of defence expenditure were all aspects of the same philosophy: that the fight against Nazism was a struggle of ideals, not of nations, and if the price of maintaining these ideals in victory was to pass the torch to the United States then so be it. However, this issue was hardly faced by liberals, who took an absurdly unrealistic view of American altruism and selflessness.

British failure was compounded by the importance of the time factor in the economics of war potential, a consideration which nevertheless undermines concepts of British structural weakness and long-term decline. Economic power is a protean force, which can be made or wasted with phenomenal speed. Success lies in getting the equation right and continuing to get it right with each new day. The war and its aftermath demonstrate this point, whether in the explosion of U.S. wartime production, or the recovery of defeated Japan and Germany to having the second and third largest economies of the capitalist world within a few decades of being reduced to bare subsistence on the victors' rations.

War, as Hitler knew well, could transform the relative wealth of nations at speed. A successful economy had to be protected by force to prevent its wealth becoming plunder. This truth was expressed succinctly in Chamberlain's observation that: 'We are a very rich and a very vulnerable Empire, and there are plenty of poor adventurers not very far away who look on us with hungry eyes.'[20] The British practice of sharply delineating wartime and peacetime in finance was, therefore, desperately dangerous. Lord Swinton, pressing for increased estimates after the *Anschluss*, argued that 'it was the only insurance. Without it we could not live to use our resources.'[21] More cruelly, Simon was criticised as husbanding funds, even into wartime, to 'ensure that the country had enough money left to pay indemnities to the victors'.[22]

The decline of Britain from a position of prosperity to the wartime consumption of its remaining capital stock and dependence on America was not an inevitable, or indeed logical, outcome. The post-1931 recovery was based on a new system that proved conducive to rearmament, and strong growth was continued into the rearmament period, at which time the *financial* problem was to contain sterling's upward surge. After the *Anschluss*, the financial indicators went naturally in the other direction. In these circumstances it was necessary to consolidate the sterling bloc and to bring the financial system into line with economic progress by introducing exchange controls, to conserve the capital necessary to maintain economic impetus into wartime and fuel further expansion. Then the economy could have continued to grow, the capital stocks to increase and the reserves to accumulate.

The fourth arm policy froze these levers and prevented their use. Financial disaster ensued, resulting in the ironic paradox that the weakness produced by the policy of fending off war preparation kept bringing forward the optimum date for the commencement of hostilities. This was the practical consequence of the belief that only the actual outbreak of war would impel the adoption of a financial and economic policy more suitable to Britain's actual situation of undeclared war. By early 1939 it was obvious to members of the Cabinet that under existing policy, and with war seemingly inevitable, the crisis should not long be delayed. Had policy remained on the course pursued until 1936, the question might not have seemed so urgent. On 3 September 1939, Britain, being rich, had no excuse for being vulnerable.

Notes and References

Preface

1. PRO CAB 24/273, p. 268. CP 316(37) Defence Expenditure in Future Years. Interim Report by the Minister for Coordination of Defence, 15 December 1937, p. 2.
2. G. Schmidt, *The Politics and Economics of Appeasement: British Foreign Policy in the 1930s* (Leamington Spa, 1986), p. 3.
3. S. Newton, *Profits of Peace: the Political Economy of Anglo-German Appeasement* (Oxford, 1996), p. 69.
4. R.A.C. Parker, 'British Rearmament 1936–9, Treasury, Trade Unions and Skilled Labour', *English Historical Review* 96 (1981), p. 314. This position is also taken in the following influential articles: R.A.C. Parker, 'Economics, Rearmament and Foreign Policy: the United Kingdom before 1939: a Preliminary Study', *Journal of Contemporary History* 10 (1975), pp. 637–47; and G.C. Peden, 'A Matter of Timing: the Economic Background to British Foreign Policy, 1937–1939', *History* 69 (1984), pp. 15–28.
5. Newton, *Profits of Peace*, pp. 68–9.
6. Schmidt, *Politics and Economics*, p. 3.
7. C. Barnett, *The Collapse of British Power* (London, 1972), epitomises this approach. Barnett combines contempt for political liberalism with a commitment to liberal financial orthodoxy worthy of Montagu Norman.
8. For example, B.J. Eichengreen, *Golden Fetters: the Gold Standard and the Great Depression, 1919–1939* (Oxford, 1992); S. Howson and D. Winch, *The Economic Advisory Council, 1930–1939: a Study in Economic Advice during Depression and Recovery* (Cambridge, 1977); and I.M. Drummond, *The Floating Pound and the Sterling Area, 1931–1939* (Cambridge, 1981), are among works indispensable to a serious study of British war potential.
9. K. Middlemas, *Diplomacy of Illusion: Britain and Germany 1937–39* (London, 1972), p. 8. The point has recently been repeated by McDonough, though he is apparently unaware of the problem in the field of defence finance, and thus of its scale and wider importance. F. McDonough, *Neville Chamberlain, Appeasement and the British Road to War* (Manchester, 1998), p. 7.
10. For example, see D.C. Watt, *How War Came: the Immediate Origins of the Second World War, 1938–1939* (London, 1989), p. 307; Parker, 'Economics, Rearmament and Foreign Policy', pp. 643–4; Newton, *Profits of Peace*, pp. 114–17; G.C. Peden, *British Rearmament and the Treasury, 1932–1939* (Edinburgh, 1979), pp. 102–3.
11. Chamberlain to Mrs Morton Prince, 16 January 1938. Quoted in K.G. Feiling, *The Life of Neville Chamberlain* (London, 1946), p. 324.
12. B.J.C. McKercher, *Transition of Power: Britain's Loss of Global Pre-eminence to the United States, 1930–1945* (Cambridge, 1999), p. 259.

1 New Rules for an Old Game

1. Cd 8462 of 1917. Dominions Royal Commission, *Final Report of the Royal Commission on the Natural Resources, Trade and Legislation of Certain Portions of His Majesty's Dominions*.
2. B.J. Eichengreen, *Sterling and the Tariff, 1929–32* (Princeton, 1981), p. 38.
3. W.C. Hancock, *Problems of Economic Policy 1918–1939* Part 1 (Oxford, 1940), p. 109.
4. Cmd 3897 of 1931. Committee on Finance and Industry [Macmillan Committee], *Report*, para. 46.
5. PRO CAB 47/1. CID Advisory Committee on Trade Questions in Time of War. Reports and Proceedings 1924–1938. Reports – Advisory Committee on Trading and Blockade. Fifth Annual Report Covering Note by Chairman, 29 April 1929.
6. Hancock, *Problems of Economic Policy*, p. 111.
7. Cd 8462. Dominions Royal Commission, *Final Report*, para. 327.
8. Hancock, *Problems of Economic Policy*, p. 100.
9. Cd 8462. Dominions Royal Commission, *Final Report*, para. 333.
10. Hancock, *Problems of Economic Policy*, p. 101.
11. Cd 8462. Dominions Royal Commission, *Final Report*, para. 369.
12. Cd 9032 of 1918. Committee on Commercial and Industrial Policy, *Interim Report on Certain Essential Industries*, para. 7.
13. Ibid., para. 12.
14. Cd 9035 of 1918. Committee on Commercial and Industrial Policy, *Final Report of the Committee on Commercial and Industrial Policy after the War*, para. 123.
15. Hancock, *Problems of Economic Policy*, p. 99.
16. Cd 9182 of 1918. Currency and Foreign Exchanges, *First Interim Report of the Committee on Currency and Foreign Exchanges after the War* [Cunliffe Committee], Introduction.
17. Ibid., para. 15.
18. Ibid., Introduction.
19. PRO CAB 27/71. War Cabinet Finance Committee. Minutes of Meetings, 24 July 1919–31 July 1922. Minutes of Third Meeting, 20 August 1919.
20. Ibid.
21. Ibid., Minutes of Eleventh Meeting, 22 October 1919.
22. Ibid.
23. D.E. Moggridge, *British Monetary Policy 1924–1931: the Norman Conquest of $4.86* (Cambridge, 1972), p. 24.
24. CAB 27/71. War Cabinet Finance Committee, Minutes of Ninth Meeting, 17 October 1919.
25. PRO CAB 4/12. CID Paper 599B. Note by the Chancellor of the Exchequer. War and Financial Power, 26 March 1925.
26. J.R. Ferris, *Men, Money and Diplomacy: the Evolution of British Strategic Policy, 1919–26* (Ithaca, 1989), p. 34.
27. Ibid., pp. 34–5.
28. Ibid., p. 34.

29. A contemporary, P.J. Grigg, observed that 'Hawtrey was "Director of Financial Inquiries" at the Treasury, which meant that he was a sort of economic consultant'. Grigg, principal private secretary to successive chancellors in the 1920s, noted that Churchill 'used to accuse us of giving Hawtrey too little scope. I remember his demanding from time to time that the learned man should be released from the dungeon in which we were said to have immured him, have his chains struck off and the straw brushed from his hair and clothes and be admitted to the light and warmth of an argument in the Treasury board room with the greatest living master of argument.' P.J. Grigg, *Prejudice and Judgement* (London, 1948), pp. 81–2.
30. CAB 47/1, p. 76. Advisory Committee on Trading and Blockade, Fifth Annual Report, April 1929, p. 27.
31. Ibid., p. 62. Fifth Annual Report, Covering Note by Chairman.
32. Ibid., p. 29. Advisory Committee on Trading and Blockade. Third Annual Report, December 1926, p. 9.
33. H. van B. Cleveland, 'The International Monetary System in the Interwar Period' in B.M. Rowland (ed.), *Balance of Power or Hegemony: the Interwar Monetary System* (New York, 1976), p. 18.
34. D.H. Aldcroft, *The Interwar Economy: Britain, 1919–39* (London, 1970), p. 244.
35. Ibid., pp. 243–44.
36. B.J. Eichengreen, *Golden Fetters: the Gold Standard and the Great Depression, 1919–1939* (Oxford, 1992), p. 32.
37. Ibid., p. 37.
38. I.M. Drummond, *The Gold Standard and the International Monetary System 1900–1939* (Basingstoke, 1987), p. 9.
39. Moggridge, *British Monetary Policy*, p. 7.
40. Cleveland, 'The International Monetary System', p. 17.
41. Drummond, *Gold Standard*, p. 21.
42. Eichengreen, *Golden Fetters*, p. 31.
43. R.G. Hawtrey, *The Gold Standard in Theory and Practice* 2nd edn (London, 1931), p. 1.
44. K. Burk, *Britain, America and the Sinews of War, 1914–1918* (London, 1985), p. 177.
45. In other words: 'The symbolic character of the monetary unit has emerged into the foreground, while its relation to some actual physical material has receded.' Cmd 3897. Committee on Finance and Industry [Macmillan Committee] *Report*, para. 20.
46. Cd 9182. Committee on Currency and Foreign Exchanges [Cunliffe Committee], *First Interim Report*, para. 31.
47. Eichengreen, *Golden Fetters*, pp. 198–201, dissents from the view that world gold stocks in the 1920s were too low in total, but acknowledges that progressive maldistribution of reserves, especially in favour of the USA and France, meant that gold in circulation was inadequate to satisfy demand worldwide, enforcing reliance on the risky gold exchange standard.
48. PRO T 185/1, p. 26. Committee on Currency and Foreign Exchanges after the War [Cunliffe Committee], *Proceedings*.
49. Eichengreen, *Golden Fetters*, p. 194.

50. C.H. Feinstein, P. Temin and G. Toniolo, 'International Economic Organisation: Banking, Finance and Trade in Europe between the Wars', in C.H. Feinstein (ed.), *Banking Currency and Finance in Europe between the Wars* (Oxford, 1995), p. 12.
51. F.C. Costigliola, *Awkward Dominion: American Political, Economic, and Cultural Relations with Europe, 1919–1933* (Ithaca and London, 1984), p. 112. Costigliola's work is amongst a number by American authors which earn a blistering rebuke from R.W.D. Boyce for adopting a position which 'seriously misrepresents British policy' in the 1920s, by neglecting the fact that British policy makers 'remained committed to multilateralism and strenuously resisted a retreat into Imperial protectionism'. Boyce contends that American work fosters the view that 'anything Britain did in the international arena is regarded as self-evidently designed to regain Britain's "financial leadership", while any American initiative is seen as a contribution to an "open world economy"'. Costigliola is actually more even-handed than this attack implies. R.W.D. Boyce, *British Capitalism at the Crossroads, 1919–1932: a Study in Politics, Economics and International Relations* (Cambridge, 1987), p. 375, fn 1.
52. Costigliola, *Awkward Dominion*, p. 56.
53. For example, see B.D. Rhodes, 'Reassessing "Uncle Shylock": the United States and the French War Debt, 1917–1929', *Journal of American History* 55 (1969), pp. 787–803.
54. Cleveland, 'The International Monetary System', p. 43.
55. S.V.O. Clarke, *Central Bank Cooperation: 1924–31* (New York, 1967), p. 92.
56. Hawtrey, *The Gold Standard in Theory and Practice*, p. 125.
57. D. Williams, 'London and the 1931 Financial Crisis', *Economic History Review* Second Series 15 (1962–63), p. 518.
58. Aldcroft, *The Interwar Economy*, p. 269.
59. Williams, 'London and the 1931 Financial Crisis', p. 519.
60. Ibid., p. 524.
61. Aldcroft, *The Interwar Economy*, p. 270.
62. Williams, 'London and the 1931 Financial Crisis', p. 527.
63. S. Howson, *Sterling's Managed Float: the Operations of the Exchange Equalisation Account, 1932–39* (Princeton, 1980), pp. 4–5.
64. Ibid., p. 4.
65. PRO PREM 1/97, p. 70. Note to Prime Minister's Office from Treasury, 15 October 1931.
66. Ibid., p. 8. Note of a Conference Held in the Prime Minister's Room at 10 Downing Street, 6 October 1931.
67. Ibid., p. 3. Memorandum from Hopkins to PM, 4 November 1931.
68. Feinstein, Temin and Toniolo, 'International Economic Organisation', p. 55.
69. I.M. Drummond, *The Floating Pound and the Sterling Area, 1931–1939* (Cambridge, 1981), pp. 7–8.
70. PRO T 172/1768, p. 6. Memorandum from Hopkins to Chamberlain, 18 January 1932.
71. M.M. Postan, *British War Production* (London, 1952), p. 13. This quotation is used approvingly by Parker in defence of the government's rearmament policy. R.A.C. Parker, 'British Rearmament 1936–1939, Treasury, Trade Unions and Skilled Labour', *English Historical Review* 96 (1981), p. 306.

72. A. Barkai, *Nazi Economics: Ideology, Theory, and Policy* (Oxford, 1990), pp. 55–6.
73. Ibid., pp. 104–5.
74. W. Michalka, 'Conflicts within the German Leadership on the Objectives and Tactics of German Foreign Policy, 1933–9' in W.J. Mommsen and L. Kettenacker (eds), *The Fascist Challenge and the Policy of Appeasement* (London, 1983), p. 51.
75. W. Carr, *Arms, Autarky and Aggression: a Study in German Foreign Policy, 1933–1939* (London, 1972), p. 41.
76. T 172/1768. Hopkins to Chamberlain, 18 January 1932.
77. Hawtrey, *The Gold Standard in Theory and Practice*, p. 151.
78. *Parliamentary Papers* Vol. 10 (1931–32): Cmd 4175, p. 167. Quoted in Drummond, *The Floating Pound and the Sterling Area*, pp. 26–7.
79. Hawtrey, *The Gold Standard in Theory and Practice*, p. 106.
80. Ibid., p. 144.
81. Ibid., p. 151.
82. Drummond, *The Floating Pound and the Sterling Area*, p. 132.

2 'On the Upgrade'

1. P.J. Cain and A.G. Hopkins, *British Imperialism: Crisis and Deconstruction 1914–1990* (New York, 1993), p. 75.
2. B.J.C. McKercher, '"Our Most Dangerous Enemy": Great Britain Pre-eminent in the 1930s', *International History Review* 13 (1991), p. 757.
3. Ibid., p. 766.
4. Neville Chamberlain Papers 18/1/819, Chamberlain to Hilda Chamberlain, 4 March 1933. Quoted in I.M. Drummond, *The Floating Pound and the Sterling Area 1931–1939* (Cambridge, 1981), p. 140.
5. An excellent account of the origins and management of the EEA is provided in S. Howson, *Sterling's Managed Float: The Operations of the Exchange Equalisation Account, 1932–39* (Princeton, 1980).
6. A recent summary of this viewpoint, factually incorrect but accurately representing the fourth arm argument as it was constructed by the government in 1937–38, argues that 'from 1931 the country ran persistent peacetime balance of payments deficits [presumably this refers to current account], reflecting both its weakening competitive position industrially and the reduction of its invisible earnings. Frequently it was pressure on the balance of payments and especially on sterling which hobbled defence policy – retarding rearmament in the 1930s.' D. Reynolds, *Britannia Overruled: British Policy and World Power in the Twentieth Century* (London, 1991), p. 17.
7. D.H. Aldcroft, *The Interwar Economy: Britain, 1919–39* (London, 1970), p. 245.
8. It has been noted that: 'In the thirties, as the British economy somewhat disengaged itself from its long involvement with external markets of all kinds, all export markets became sharply less important – in spite of devaluation and of the Ottawa agreements.' I.M. Drummond, *British Economic Policy and the Empire, 1919–1939* (London, 1972), p. 19.

9. The economist Colin Clark produced a paper for a 1931 Cabinet Committee on international trade containing both prime minister and chancellor, of which he was secretary, which argued that 'it was possible to think of shifting resources towards industries producing for the home market, if only because a smaller volume of exports now sufficed to purchase Britain's food and raw material imports'. S. Howson and D. Winch, *The Economic Advisory Council, 1930–1939: a Study in Economic Advice during Depression and Recovery* (Cambridge, 1977), p. 84.
10. A detailed account of this pre-Ottawa willingness to interfere with markets is provided in J.M. Atkin, 'Official Regulation of British Overseas Investment, 1914–1931', *Economic History Review* 2nd Series 23 (1970), pp. 324–35.
11. C.H. Feinstein, *National Income, Expenditure and Output of the United Kingdom, 1855–1965* (Cambridge, 1972), T.14. Table 5, Gross Domestic and Gross National Product by Category of Expenditure at Constant Prices 1870–1965, ii) 1913–48 at 1938 prices.
12. Ibid., calculation from Table 5.
13. F.C. Costigliola, 'Anglo-American Financial Rivalry in the 1920s', *Journal of Economic History* 37 (1977), p. 934.
14. D.H. Aldcroft, 'Economic Growth in Britain in the Inter-War Years: a Reassessment', *Economic History Review* Second Series 20 (1967), pp. 313–14.
15. The figures quoted are conservative. It has been noted with regard to Aldcroft's article that: 'Even those who have sought to question the more exaggerated claims for the thirties as a period of rapid economic growth have conceded that the annual growth rate for the decade averaged between 2.3 and 3.3 percent, depending upon the indices of production taken.' J. Stevenson and C. Cook, *The Slump: Society and Politics during the Depression* (London, 1977), p. 9.
16. Aldcroft, 'Economic Growth in Britain', p. 313.
17. Cain and Hopkins, *British Imperialism*, p. 86.
18. *The Economist*, 26 November 1938: Supplement 'The British–American Trade Agreement', pp. 2–3.
19. In 1913, 80 per cent of Britain's imports had come from foreign sources. In 1938 this had fallen to 61 per cent, a 'foreign' total which of course included non-Empire members of the sterling bloc, significant exporters to Britain who were bound to accept payment in sterling. Drummond, *British Economic Policy and the Empire*, p. 21.
20. CAB 24/265, p. 230. CP339(36), Memorandum on the Balance of Payments by the Chief Economic Advisor to His Majesty's Government, 18 December 1936, p. 9. Leith-Ross, in addition to his independent role, was a senior Treasury official, and his paper does not chime with more recent orthodoxy which claims that: 'Throughout the 1930s the Treasury and the Bank were haunted by 1931', and that: 'For the Treasury the payments position was its prime economic concern for most of the 1930s.' Reynolds, *Britannia Overruled*, p. 125.
21. For a detailed development of this argument see Cain and Hopkins, *British Imperialism*, Chapters 8 and 10.
22. The point has been made that if the British were intent on the imperialist exploitation of their colonies, their methods left much to be desired. I.M.

Drummond, *Imperial Economic Policy 1917–1939: Studies in Expansion and Protection* (London, 1974), pp. 427–46.

23. *FRUS 1936*, Vol. 1 (Washington, 1953). Memorandum by the Secretary of State, 20 July 1936, p. 677.

24. Amery to Lord Linlithgow, 25 January 1941. Quoted in W.R. Louis, *In the Name of God, Go! Leo Amery and the British Empire in the Age of Churchill* (New York and London, 1992), p. 25.

25. Ibid., p. 81.

26. Ibid.

27. Cain and Hopkins, *British Imperialism*, p. 94.

28. F.C. Costigliola, *Awkward Dominion: American Political, Economic, and Cultural Relations with Europe, 1919–1933* (Ithaca and London, 1984), p. 67.

29. *The Economist*, 'The British American Trade Agreement', p. 1.

30. Ibid.

31. Quoted in J.M. Blum, *From the Morgenthau Diaries* Vol. 1, *Years of Crisis, 1928–1938* (Boston, 1959), p. 45.

32. Ibid., p. 52.

33. SD 611.4131.115$^1/_2$. Memorandum. Functions of a British Empire Committee, 12 September 1934.

34. Sir F. Leith-Ross, *Money Talks: Fifty Years of International Finance* (London, 1968), p. 160.

35. House of Assembly, *Debates* Vol. 18, 28 January 1932, cols 429–30. Quoted in Drummond, *The Floating Pound and the Sterling Area*, p. 91.

36. Hull's treatment during the conference and his subsequent return to favour are described in T. McCulloch, 'Anglo-American Economic Diplomacy and the European Crisis, 1933–1939' (unpublished D.Phil. thesis, University of Oxford, 1978), pp. 67–8, 87.

37. He was well suited to the task. On the successful passage of the Trade Agreements Act through Congress it has been noted that: 'Hull, whose abiding interest was trade policy, as had been evident at the London Economic Conference, was delighted. It made up for all the disappointments he had suffered since March 1933 and before.' Ibid., p. 123.

38. SD 611.4131/115$^1/_2$. Memorandum on Work of British Empire Committee, 12 September 1934.

39. Ibid., memorandum, Functions of a British Empire Committee.

40. Ibid., memorandum on Work of the British Empire Committee, 13 September 1934.

41. Ibid.

42. SD 711.41/280. Note of Meeting between Lord Lothian and Under-Secretary of State Phillips, 11 October 1934.

43. PRO PREM 1/105, p. 13. MacDonald to Vansittart, 15 May 1931.

44. Ibid., p. 8. Minute, J.H. Thomas to MacDonald, 16 May 1931.

45. Ibid., p. 12.

46. Ibid., p. 29. Letter, Treasury to Foreign Office, 8 May 1931.

47. D.N. Chester and F.M.G. Willson, *The Organisation of British Central Government, 1914–1964* (London, 1968), p. 19.

48. Stephen Roskill, *Hankey, Man of Secrets* Vol. 2, *1919–1931* (London, 1972), p. 125.

49. Ibid., p. 129.

50. For this correspondence see the Leith-Ross papers, PRO T 188/175.
51. Lord Bridges, 'Whitehall and Beyond', *The Listener*, 25 June 1964, p. 1016. Quoted in G.K. Fry, *Statesmen in Disguise: the Changing Rôle of the Administrative Class of the British Home Civil Service, 1853–1966* (London, 1969), p. 60.
52. The hierarchical British governmental structure of this time has been contrasted favourably with the apparently chaotic American and German systems, and in many ways the two resembled each other more than either did the British system. It has been said of Roosevelt that: 'By pitting Welles against Hull, political envoys against career diplomats, Treasury against State, Stimson against Morgenthau, and a host of other official and personal representatives against each other for influence over foreign policy, he became a court of last resort on major issues and kept control in his own hands.' This is more than suggestive of similar descriptions of Hitler's methods, for example Speer's comment that Hitler 'did not like establishing clear lines of jurisdiction. Sometimes he deliberately assigned bureaus or individuals the same or similar tasks. "That way", he used to say, "the stronger one does the job".' Perhaps the contrast with British practice is illusory. The political infighting in the American system particularly, to which British condescension is encapsulated by Keynes' bafflement at 'how decisions are ever reached at all', was at least conducted in public by elected representatives. In Britain, the same horse trading took place behind closed doors amongst civil servants, and the public was presented with a facade of good order and streamlined efficiency. R.F. Dallek, *Franklin D. Roosevelt and American Foreign Policy, 1932–1945* (New York, 1979), p. 532; A. Speer, *Inside the Third Reich* (London, 1970), p. 210; J. Charmley, *Churchill's Grand Alliance: the Anglo-American Special Relationship, 1940–57* (London, 1995), p. 45.
53. P.J. Grigg, *Prejudice and Judgement* (London, 1948), p. 94.
54. R. Skidelsky, *Politicians and the Slump: the Labour Government of 1929–1931* (London, 1967), p. 6.
55. Ibid., p. 79.
56. Neville Chamberlain Papers: Chamberlain to Amery, 10 March 1933. Quoted in Drummond, *The Floating Pound and the Sterling Area*, p. 19.
57. D.C. Watt, *Personalities and Policies: Studies in the Formulation of British Foreign Policy in the Twentieth Century* (London, 1965), p. 29.
58. Ibid.
59. Ibid.
60. Boyce notes shrewdly that one of the Round Table movement's 'contributions was the subtle one of diverting imperial sentiment away from aggressive economic policies'. R.W.D. Boyce, *British Capitalism at the Crossroads, 1919–1932: a Study in Politics, Economics and International Relations* (Cambridge, 1987), p. 26.
61. Quoted in J.R.M. Butler, *Lord Lothian (Philip Kerr) 1882–1940* (London, 1960), p. 170.
62. Howson and Winch, *Economic Advisory Council*, p. 1.
63. Ibid., p. 157.
64. For an excellent summary of Keynes' involvement in Liberal policy formation see J. Campbell, 'The Renewal of Liberalism: Liberalism without

Liberals' in G. Peele and C. Cook (eds), *The Politics of Reappraisal, 1918–1939* (London and Basingstoke, 1975), pp. 88–113.
65. Watt, *Personalities and Policies*, p. 30.
66. I.M. Drummond and N. Hillmer, *Negotiating Freer Trade: the United Kingdom, the United States, Canada, and the Trade Agreements of 1938* (Waterloo, 1989), pp. 4–5.

3 'The Destiny of Tomorrow'

1. I.M. Drummond and N. Hillmer, *Negotiating Freer Trade: the United Kingdom, the United States, Canada, and the Trade Agreements of 1938* (Waterloo, 1989), p. 37.
2. *FRUS*, 1936, Vol. 1 (Washington, 1953). Memorandum by the Secretary of State, 22 January 1936, p. 629.
3. Ibid., pp. 629–30.
4. Ibid., p. 630.
5. Ibid., p. 631.
6. Ibid., p. 630.
7. Ibid., p. 631.
8. PRO BT 11/589, pp. 278–9. Enclosure, 26 February 1936: FO A1505/890/45. Lindsay to Eden, 8 February 1936.
9. *FRUS* 1936, Vol. 1. The Secretary of State to the Chargé in the United Kingdom (Atherton), 13 February 1936, p. 636.
10. Ibid., p. 635.
11. Ibid. The Chargé in the United Kingdom (Atherton) to the Secretary of State, 26 February 1936, p. 644.
12. PRO BT 11/589, pp. 282–8. Enclosure, 14 February 1936: FO A 6260/890/45. Lindsay to Eden, 23 January 1936.
13. Ibid., pp. 286–7.
14. Ibid., p. 288.
15. Quoted in *FRUS* 1936, Vol. 1. The Chargé in the United Kingdom (Atherton) to the Secretary of State, 28 February 1936, p. 645.
16. Ibid. The Secretary of State to the Chargé in the United Kingdom (Atherton), 28 February 1936, p. 645.
17. Ibid. The Chargé in the United Kingdom (Atherton) to the Secretary of State, 29 February 1936, p. 646.
18. Ibid. Memorandum, in The Secretary of State to the Chargé in the United Kingdom (Atherton), 28 March 1936, p. 648.
19. Ibid. Memorandum by the special Assistant to the Secretary of State and Chief of the Division of Western European Affairs (Dunn), 30 March 1936, p. 649.
20. Ibid., p. 650.
21. Ibid. Memorandum by the Secretary of State, 1 April 1936, p. 650.
22. Ibid. The Ambassador in the United Kingdom (Bingham) to the Secretary of State, 7 April 1936, p. 655.
23. Ibid. Memorandum by the Secretary of State, 1 April 1936, pp. 650–1.
24. Ibid. The Ambassador in the United Kingdom (Bingham) to the Secretary of State, 7 April 1936, pp. 655–6.

25. Ibid. The Secretary of State to the Ambassador in the United Kingdom (Bingham), 11 April 1936, p. 656.
26. Ibid. The Ambassador in the United Kingdom (Bingham) to the Secretary of State, 28 April 1936, p. 660.
27. Ibid. The Ambassador in the United Kingdom (Bingham) to the Secretary of State, 29 April 1936, pp. 660–1.
28. Ibid. The Ambassador in the United Kingdom (Bingham) to the Secretary of State, 1 May 1936, p. 662.
29. SD 611.4131/139. American Consulate, Birmingham, to Secretary of State, 30 April 1936.
30. Quoted in *FRUS* 1936, Vol. 1. Bingham to Hull, 1 May 1936, p. 662.
31. Ibid. The Ambassador in the United Kingdom (Bingham) to the Secretary of State, 26 May 1936, pp. 663–6.
32. SD 611.4131/177. The Chargé in the United Kingdom (Atherton) to the Secretary of State, 12 June 1936.
33. Drummond and Hillmer, *Negotiating Freer Trade*, p. 38.
34. *FRUS* 1936, Vol. 1. Memorandum by Mr William A. Fowler of the Division of Trade Agreements, 17 June 1936, pp. 666–7.
35. Ibid. Memorandum by Mr Richard Eldridge of the Division of Trade Agreements, 24 June 1936, pp. 670–1.
36. Ibid. The Chargé in the United Kingdom (Atherton) to the Secretary of State, 26 June 1936, p. 672.
37. Ibid. The Chargé in the United Kingdom (Atherton) to the Secretary of State, 19 June 1936, p. 669.
38. Ibid. Memorandum by the Secretary of State, 20 July 1936, pp. 679–80.
39. Ibid., pp. 675–6.
40. Ibid., pp. 677–8.
41. Ibid. The Secretary of State to the Ambassador in the United Kingdom (Bingham), 25 July 1936, p. 680.
42. Ibid. The Ambassador in the United Kingdom (Bingham) to the Secretary of State, 28 July 1936, p. 680.
43. Ibid. The Secretary of State to the Ambassador in the United Kingdom (Bingham), 3 September 1936, pp. 680–4.
44. Ibid. The Ambassador in the United Kingdom (Bingham) to the Secretary of State, 19 September 1936, p. 685.
45. Ibid. Memorandum by Mr John R. Minter of the Division of Western European Affairs, 21 September 1936, pp. 685–6.
46. S.V.O. Clarke, *Exchange-Rate Stabilization in the Mid-1930s: Negotiating the Tripartite Agreement* (Princeton, 1977), p. 18.
47. Ibid., p. 50.
48. Morgenthau clarified this point in conversation with his advisers on 18 September 1936: 'This is a notice to Japan, Germany and Italy that we won't stand any monkey business. . . . This is a notice to the boys – *Achtung!*' Quoted in J.M. Blum, *From the Morgenthau Diaries* Vol. 1, *Years of Crisis, 1928–1938* (Boston, 1959), p. 166.
49. Clarke, *Exchange Rate Stabilization*, p. 52.
50. Ibid., p. 53.
51. For an interesting account of this attempt to establish an economic voice for the FO, see D.G. Boadle, 'The Formation of the Foreign Office

Economic Relations Section, 1930–1937', *Historical Journal* 20 (1977), pp. 919–36.
52. FO 371 19933 C4758/99/18, p. 171. Minute by Jebb. Origin of the Hall memorandum, 25 June 1936.
53. Ibid., C4759/99/18, p. 191. Hall Memorandum, p. 8.
54. Ibid., C4758/99/18, pp. 171–2. Origin of Hall Memorandum.
55. Ibid., p. 180. Record of a Conversation between Sir R. Vansittart and Mr Gwatkin.
56. G. Schmidt, *The Politics and Economics of Appeasement: British Foreign Policy in the 1930s* (Leamington Spa, 1986), pp. 221–2.
57. PRO BT 11/589 p. 29. Minute by W.B. Brown, 14 July 1936.
58. CAB 24/264, p. 311. CP 277(36) International Action Towards Relaxation of Obstacles to Trade. Board of Trade, 23 October 1936.
59. Ibid., pp. 1–2.
60. Ibid., pp. 3–5.
61. Ibid., p. 1.
62. The Belgian Premier was prevailed upon to contact governments with a view to arranging an international conference. The central role of Leith-Ross in this initiative can be traced from the extensive correspondence contained in PRO CAB T 188/175.
63. PRO CAB 24/265, p. 275. CP 339(36) The Balance of Payments of the United Kingdom, 18 December 1936.
64. Ibid., p. 277. CP 339(36), p. 2.
65. Ibid., p. 3.
66. Ibid., p. 4.
67. Ibid., p. 5.
68. Ibid., p. 6.
69. Ibid., p. 9.
70. Ibid., p. 12.
71. PRO FO 371 19933 C4760/99/18, p. 204. Note by Jebb, 2 July 1936.
72. PRO CAB 24/265, p. 310A. CP 341(36) Economic Advisory Council. Committee on Economic Information, Twenty-First Report. Survey of the Economic Situation, December 1936, p. 32.

4 The Devil in the Detail

1. PRO PREM 1/291, pp. 43–7. Letter from Runciman to Baldwin, 'Secret' 6 January 1937.
2. Ibid., p. 55. Memorandum by Runciman. Conversations with President Roosevelt and Mr Hull. Runciman met Hull on 23 January 1937.
3. Ibid., p. 53. Runciman to Baldwin, Secret, 8 February 1937.
4. Ibid., pp. 53–4. Runciman to Baldwin, 8 February.
5. Cordell Hull, Secretary of State to Roosevelt, 22 January 1937. In D.B. Schewe (ed.), *Franklin D. Roosevelt and Foreign Affairs*, Second Series, January 1937–August 1939, Vol. 4, January–March 1937, pp. 85–8.
6. PREM 1/291, p. 60. Conversations with President Roosevelt and Mr Hull. Meeting with Hull and Roosevelt, 24 January 1937.
7. Ibid., p. 56. Meeting with Hull, 23 January.

8. Ibid., p. 62. Meeting with Hull and Roosevelt, 24 January.
9. Ibid., p. 63. Final talk with the Premier, 26 January 1937.
10. *FRUS*, 1937, Vol. 2 (Washington, 1954). The Department of State to the British Embassy, 17 January 1937, p. 1.
11. *DBFP*, Second Series, Vol. 18 (London, 1980). Record by Mr T.K. Bewley (Washington) of a Conversation with Mr H. Morgenthau, 23 February 1937, p. 278.
12. Ibid., p. 279.
13. The shuttle of draft replies and amendments between Eden and Chamberlain can be followed in ibid., pp. 348, 381, 415 and 428. The British were puzzled by Morgenthau's motives, and felt the Treasury level inappropriate for such dialogue. However, in absorbing the attention of the two most influential Cabinet ministers, Morgenthau's initiative kept the pressure on London.
14. See Chapter 2.
15. S. Howson and D.Winch, *The Economic Advisory Council 1930–1939: a Study in Economic Advice during Depression and Recovery* (Cambridge, 1977), p. 143.
16. PRO T 188/175, pp. 26 et seq. Letter and Memorandum, Eden to Chamberlain, 24 March 1937.
17. PRO FO 371/17318, pp. 133–4. Memorandum, January 1933. Quoted in Drummond, *The Floating Pound and the Sterling Area, 1931–1939* (Cambridge, 1981), p. 21.
18. David Dilks (ed.), *The Diaries of Sir Alexander Cadogan O.M., 1938–1945* (London, 1971), p. 19.
19. PRO FO 954/29. Anthony Eden, Private Office Papers, US 37/1, pp. 1–2. 17 March 1937.
20. PRO CAB 27/622, p. 162. Cabinet Committee on Foreign Policy, Twelfth Meeting, 11 June 1937.
21. Ibid., p. 165.
22. Ibid., p. 175.
23. Ibid., p. 180. Thirteenth Meeting, 16 June 1937.
24. Ibid., p. 187.
25. Hankey to Phipps, 11 November 1938. Quoted in R. Douglas, *In the Year of Munich* (London, 1977), p. 80.
26. CAB 27/622, p. 187. Committee on Foreign Policy, Twelfth Meeting.
27. PRO T 160/840/F13427/8. Leith-Ross Memorandum, 31 May 1937. Quoted in Drummond, *The Floating Pound and the Sterling Area*, pp. 227–8.
28. PRO DO 35/266/9223F/1. Leith-Ross to E.H. Marsh (Dominions Office), 28 February 1933. Quoted in ibid., p. 159.
29. For example, on 25 November 1937, the High Commissioner in Australia passed on a telegram from London stating 'that negotiations should proceed as rapidly as possible' and that it was 'therefore necessary for the United Kingdom Government at once to invite the Commonwealth Government to give a definite assurance that they will, in connection with a United Kingdom–United States Agreement, be prepared to waive their rights under the United Kingdom–Australia Trade Agreement of the 20th August 1932'. Chamberlain followed this up on 30 November with a personal message to Lyons, the Australian prime minister, in which he said that: 'I am particularly sorry to have to ask you for an early decision on a matter of

considerable difficulty at a time when you have so many pressing domestic preoccupations, but as I explained in my earlier message on this matter it is essential that our negotiations with the United States should now proceed rapidly.' A trade agreement 'would have an importance in world affairs far beyond its intrinsic provisions', and Chamberlain concluded that 'I confidently hope you will be able to let us have the formal consent of the Commonwealth Government at a very early date'. PREM 1/291, pp. 154 and 146–7.

30. CAB 27/622, p. 161. Committee on Foreign Policy, Twelfth Meeting.
31. Baldwin's caution concerning the electoral aspects of rearmament appears to have been personal to him. Even Chamberlain, who was making every effort to limit expenditure on weapons, wished to play up rearmament at the 1935 general election but was restrained by the prime minister, who wished to stress the continuing relevance of the League of Nations. Chamberlain's aim to divert the lion's share of such additional expenditure as would take place on a showy deterrent bomber force can be understood in this context. M. Cowling, *The Impact of Hitler: British Politics and British Policy, 1933–1940* (Cambridge, 1975), pp. 91–4; U. Bialer, *The Shadow of the Bomber: Fear of Air Attack and British Politics, 1932–1939* (London, 1980).
32. PRO CAB 16/123, p. 5. DPR (DR.9) CID Sub-Committee on Defence Policy and Requirements. Programmes of the Defence Services. Report, February 1936.
33. Ibid., p. 87. First Meeting of the DPRC,13 January 1936, p. 7.
34. Ibid.
35. Ibid., pp. 89–90. First Meeting, pp. 9–10.
36. Ibid., pp. 93–4. First Meeting, pp. 13–14.
37. Ibid., p. 10. DPRC Report, February 1936, p. 11.
38. Ibid., p. 15. DPRC Report, p. 20. Annexe C. Industrial Production. Memorandum by Lord Weir.
39. Ibid., p. 11. DPRC Report, p. 11.
40. Ibid., p. 11. DPRC Report, p. 12.
41. G. Post Jr, *Dilemmas of Appeasement: British Deterrence and Defense, 1934–1937* (Ithaca and London, 1993), pp. 312–13.
42. PRO T 161/783/48431/02/1. Hopkins on Defence Finance, 14 May 1937.
43. PRO CAB 23/87, p. 38. Cab. 1(37) Cabinet Minutes, 13 January 1937, p. 7.
44. Ibid., p. 155A. Cab. 5(37) Cabinet Minutes, 3 February, p. 15.
45. Ibid., p. 220. Cab. 7(37) Cabinet Minutes, 10 February, p. 20.
46. T 161/783/48431/02/1. Hopkins to Chamberlain, May 1937. Marginal note by Chamberlain.
47. PRO CAB 24/270, p. 272. CP 165(37) Defence Expenditure. Memorandum by the Chancellor of the Exchequer, 25 June 1937, p. 2.
48. Ibid., p. 1.
49. Ibid., p. 3.
50. *The Economist*, 21 January 1939, p. 115.
51. T 161/783/48431/02/1. Handwritten alteration to Fisher's proof copy of CP 165(37).
52. CAB 24/270, p. 273. CP165(37) Defence Expenditure. Memorandum by the Chancellor of the Exchequer, p. 4.

53. PRO CAB 23/88 p. 333. Cab 27(37) Cabinet Minutes, 30 June 1937, p. 9.
54. PRO CAB 64/30. Minister for the Coordination of Defence. Defence Preparations, Estimates and Expenditure. Letter, Simon to Chamberlain, 22 October 1937.
55. Ibid., Inskip Committee, Minutes of Seventh Meeting, 2 December 1937.
56. Ibid. Minutes of Sixth Meeting, 25 November 1937.
57. PRO T 161/855/48431/01/1. Cost of Defence Requirements. Memorandum by the Minister for the Coordination of Defence, circulated 23 November 1937.
58. N.H. Gibbs, *Grand Strategy* Vol. 1, *Rearmament Policy* (London, 1976), p. 282.
59. PRO CAB 24/273, p. 268. CP 316(37) Defence Expenditure in Future Years. Interim Report by the Minister for Coordination of Defence, 15 December 1937, p. 2.
60. R.P. Shay Jr, *British Rearmament in the Thirties: Politics and Profits* (Princeton, 1977), p. 166.
61. T 161/855/48431/01/1. Memorandum by Bridges, 8 December 1937.
62. CAB 24/273, p. 268. CP 316(37) Defence Expenditure in Future Years, pp. 2–3.
63. PRO CAB 24/274, p. 322. CP 24(38) Defence Expenditure in Future Years. Further Report by the Minister for Coordination of Defence, 8 February 1938.
64. Shay, *British Rearmament*, p. 161.
65. Ibid., p. 168.
66. PRO CAB 58/23. Economic Advisory Council, Committee on Economic Information. Notes on Armament Expenditure, the Foreign Exchanges and Government Finance. Memorandum by Mr P.K. Debenham, 31 October 1937.
67. Quite the reverse. In 1914, The central role of London in world finance and US borrowing in Britain created an effect whereby the exchange rate 'had risen as high as $7 to the pound compared to the normal $4.86'. It took some months for the new realities of wartime to become apparent, but by 'December 1914, for the first time since the war had begun, the rate of exchange in New York went against Britain'. K. Burk, *Britain, America and the Sinews of War, 1914–1918* (London, 1985), pp. 56 and 59.
68. B.H. Liddell Hart, *The Memoirs of Captain Liddell Hart* Vol. 2 (London, 1965), p. 106.
69. Shay, *British Rearmament*, p. 198.
70. PRO CAB 23/92, p. 370. Cab. 13(38) Cabinet Minutes, 14 March 1938, p. 11.
71. Ibid., p. 12.
72. Ibid.
73. Ibid., p. 13.
74. Ibid., p. 15.
75. Ibid., p. 16.
76. Ibid., p. 18.
77. Ibid.
78. Liddell Hart, *Memoirs* Vol. 2, p. 144.
79. It is also suggested that he was happy to work within the limits set by the Treasury. As a former financial secretary to the Treasury, Hore-Belisha may

well have found this a useful budgetary negotiating position to counter charges of profligacy, but his open attacks on the fourth arm policy in Cabinet in 1938 and 1939 clearly place him in opposition to the government's financial restraints. B. Bond, *British Military Policy between the Two World Wars* (Oxford, 1980), pp. 255–7.

5   Between Hitler and Wall Street

1. *The Economist*, 28 January 1939, p. 171.
2. See particularly Schmidt, who compares 'the mobilisation of financial, economic and social resources, and the existing constitution of domestic political forces which allotted to armaments policy its "hinge function" – its function as mediator between foreign policy and the domestic political and social system'. G. Schmidt, *The Politics and Economics of Appeasement: British Foreign Policy in the 1930s* (Leamington Spa, 1986), p. 390.
3. *New York Times*, 13 March 1938, p. 1.
4. Ibid., p. 35.
5. FDR PSF Box 97, Treasury Dept. 26 March 1938. Quoted in R.A.C. Parker, 'The Pound Sterling, the American Treasury, and British Preparations for War, 1938–9', *English Historical Review* 98 (1983), p. 264.
6. FDR MD Book 114, p. 277. Treasury Meeting, 14 March 1938, 9.45 a.m.
7. Ibid., p. 363. Treasury Meeting, 14 March 1938, 2.30 p.m.
8. Ibid., p. 379. Paraphrase of Telegram received from the Secretary of the Treasury from Cochran. American Embassy, Paris. 14 March 1938, 10 p.m.
9. In 1938, White held the US Treasury posts of assistant director, Division of Research and Statistics, and, subsequently, director of monetary research.
10. MD Book 114, p. 279. Treasury Meeting, 14 March, 9.45 a.m.
11. Ibid., Book 123, p. 209. Butterworth to Morgenthau. British Summary of Events, 4 May 1938.
12. Ibid., Book 122, p. 135. Telephone Conversation between Kennedy and Morgenthau, 3 May 1938.
13. Ibid., Book 114, p. 277. Treasury Meeting, 14 March, 9.45 a.m.
14. Ibid., p. 363. Treasury Meeting, 14 March, 2.30 p.m.
15. Ibid., p. 315. Treasury Meeting, 14 March 1938, 11.40 a.m.
16. Ibid., Book 120, p. 316. Treasury Meeting. Re French Monetary Situation, 25 April 1938.
17. Ibid., Book 123, pp. 144–5. Treasury Meeting, 5 May 1938, 9.06 a.m.
18. Ibid.
19. Ibid., p. 262. Telephone Conversation between Morgenthau and Cochran, 5 May 1938, 10.59 a.m.
20. Ibid., p. 321. Telephone Conversation between Morgenthau and Butterworth. Treasury Meeting, 5 May 1938.
21. Ibid., pp. 396–7. Summary of Meeting with the French Ambassador, 6 May 1938.
22. P. Kennedy, *The Rise and Fall of the Great Powers: Economic Change and Military Conflict from 1500 to 2000* (London, 1988), p. 426.
23. *New York Times*, 16 March 1938, p. 22.
24. MD Book 115, pp. 40–1. Treasury Meeting, 16 March 1938.

25. Ibid., p. 46.
26. Ibid., Book 118, p. 215. Memorandum on the Estimated Financial Requirements for the Next Six Months, 7 April 1938.
27. Ibid., p. 218. Treasury Department Inter-Office Communication, To Mr Taylor from Mr White: Shall Excess Reserves be Increased and if so, How? 7 April 1938.
28. Ibid., Book 120, pp. 336–8. Treasury Meeting. Re French Monetary Situation, 25 April 1938.
29. *The Economist*, 15 October 1938, p. 113.
30. MD Book 120, p. 338. Treasury Meeting. Re French Monetary Situation, 25 April 1938.
31. PRO PREM 1/267, p. 8. Letter, Chamberlain to Daladier, 17 August 1938.
32. MD Book 115, p. 27. A Record of Conversation between the President and HM, Jr, 16 March 1938.
33. Ibid., Book 116, p. 261. Treasury Memorandum, 23 March 1938.
34. Ibid., Book 137, pp. 33–4. Letter from Harrison to Morgenthau, 29 August 1938.
35. *The Economist*, 15 October 1938, p. 113.
36. *New York Times*, 1 September 1938, p. 33.
37. Ibid., 3 September 1938, p. 17.
38. Ibid.
39. MD Book 142, p. 16. Treasury Meeting. Re Gold Policy, 21 September 1938, 10.15 a.m.
40. *New York Times*, 4 September 1938, Financial Section, F1.
41. Ibid., 5 September 1938, p. 22.
42. Leffingwell was a former assistant secretary of the Treasury, and was at this time a member of J.P. Morgan & Co. which may account for the sharpness of his exchange with New Dealer Morgenthau.
43. MD Book 138, p. 60. Notes on Meeting at Secretary's Home, Thursday 1 September 1938.
44. Parker, 'The Pound Sterling', p. 270.
45. MD Book 138, p. 142. Inter Office Communication, To Secretary Morgenthau from Mr White, 6 September 1938.
46. Ibid., p. 155. Treasury Meeting, 6 September 1938.
47. Ibid., p. 145. Inter Office Communication. To Secretary Morgenthau from Mr White, 6 September 1938.
48. Ibid., Book 142, p. 54. Treasury Meeting. Re Gold Policy, 21 September 1938.
49. Vice President of the Federal Reserve Bank of New York, and Professor of Economics at Harvard University.
50. MD Book 142, p. 59. Treasury Meeting, 21 September.
51. MD Book 146, p. 152. Telegram, for Treasury from Butterworth, 17 October 1938.
52. PRO CAB 24/273, p. 88. CP 287(37) Economic Advisory Council. Committee on Economic Information, Twenty-Third Report, Survey of the Economic Situation, October 1937, p. 31.
53. MD Book 144, p. 250. Treasury Group Meeting, 7 October 1938.
54. Ibid., p. 86. Telegram, for Treasury from Butterworth, 4 October 1938.
55. Ibid., p. 125. Telephone Conversation with Bank of England, 6 October 1938.

56. *The Economist*, 8 October 1938, p. 74.
57. MD Book 145, p. 195. Telephone Conversation with Bank of England, 11 October 1938.
58. Ibid., p. 195.
59. *The Economist*, 15 October 1938, p. 123.
60. Ibid., p. 124.
61. Ibid., p. 125.
62. MD Book 147, p. 74. Treasury Group Meeting. Re: Sterling Exchange Rate, 21 October 1938, 10.00 a.m.
63. Ibid., p. 87.
64. Professor of Economics, University of Chicago, and US Treasury consultant.
65. MD Book 147, p. 87. Treasury Meeting, 21 October, 10.00 a.m.
66. MD Book 139, p. 130. Business Report by Mr Haas. Quoted in Parker, 'The Pound Sterling', p. 265.
67. MD Book 153, p. 184. Quoted in Parker, 'The Pound Sterling', p. 266.
68. Ibid., Book 142, p. 61. Treasury Meeting. Re Gold Policy, 21 September 1938, 10.15 a.m.
69. Ibid., pp. 338–40. Treasury Meeting, 26 September 1938.
70. *DBFP*, Second Series, Vol. 18 (London, 1980). Record by Mr T.K. Bewley (Washington) of a Conversation with Mr H. Morgenthau, 23 February 1937, p. 279.
71. MD Book 146, pp. 239–40. Copy of Telegram from Wilson in Paris to the Secretary of State, 20 October 1938.
72. Ibid., Book 147, p. 130. Summary of Memorandum to Secretary Morgenthau from Mr White. Subject: The Dollar–Sterling Situation, 21 October 1938.
73. MD Book 147, p. 146. Treasury Meeting. Re Sterling Exchange Rate and Government Loans to South America, 21 October 1938, 3.00 p.m.
74. Ibid., p. 92. Treasury Meeting. Re Sterling Exchange Rate, 21 October 1938, 10.00 a.m.
75. Ibid., p. 96.
76. Warren was Vice President of Case, Pomeroy & Co., and had formerly worked as an economist at the Federal Reserve Board.
77. Ibid., Book 147, pp. 114–16. Treasury Meeting. Re Sterling Exchange Rate, 21 October 1938, 10.00 a.m.
78. Ibid., p. 124.
79. Ibid., p. 146. Treasury Meeting. Re Sterling Exchange Rate and Government Loans to South America, 21 October 1938, 3.00 p.m.
80. Burgess had been a Vice President of the New York Federal Reserve Bank in the early 1930s and attended Treasury meetings as an expert in the management of public debt.
81. Ibid., Book 147, p. 147. Treasury Meeting. Re Sterling Exchange Rate, 21 October 1938, 3.00 p.m.
82. Oliphant was a lawyer and had moved with Morgenthau from the Farm Credit Administration to the Treasury Department in 1934. He held the position of general counsel from that time until his death from a heart attack in January 1939.
83. Ibid., Book 147, pp. 152–8. Treasury Meeting. Re Sterling Exchange Rate, 21 October 1938, 3.00 p.m.

84. Stewart was a former director of the Division of Research and Statistics at the Federal Reserve Board and had been economic adviser to the Bank of England between 1928 and 1930. In 1938 he was President of Case, Pomeroy & Co.
85. PRO T160/871/15777. Letter, Bewley to Waley, 22 October 1938.
86. Ibid., Letter, Bewley to Waley, 2 November 1938.

6 'It Seems like Insanity'

1. *The Economist*, 26 November 1938. Trade Supplement, 'The British–American Trade Agreement', p. 4.
2. I.M. Drummond and N. Hillmer, *Negotiating Freer Trade: the United Kingdom, the United States, Canada, and the Trade Agreements of 1938* (Waterloo, 1989), p. 148.
3. E. Gilman, 'Economic Aspects of Anglo-American Relations in the Era of Roosevelt and Chamberlain' (unpublished Ph.D. Thesis, University of London, 1976), p. 120.
4. *The National Review*, March 1938, p. 288.
5. Drummond and Hillmer, *Negotiating Freer Trade*, p. 152.
6. *National Review*, March 1938, p. 290.
7. Gilman, 'Economic Aspects', p. 123.
8. BT 11/1085. Draft Memorandum, Stanley for Cabinet, no date. Quoted in ibid., p. 123.
9. When the treaty was concluded Stanley was less upbeat. He wrote to Chamberlain that 'I am of course arranging to see the press about it, and I propose some time next week to see Amery, Page-Croft, Herbert Williams and Dorman-Smith who, I think, represent the people in the House most likely to criticise. It is, however, especially vital that industry as a whole should regard the agreement in the best light possible.' To this end Stanley asked Chamberlain if he would think of seeing representatives of 'the Federation of British Industries, the Association of British Chambers of Commerce and the National Union of Manufacturers, and asking them for obvious reasons to do what they can to see that industrial criticism is expressed reasonably. I do not think it would be necessary for you to see them for more than a very few minutes.' This few minutes makes an interesting contrast with the exhaustive consultation required under the American system. PRO PREM 1/291 pp. 9–10. Letter, Stanley to Chamberlain, 11 November 1938.
10. PRO FO 371/A7789/1/45. Note 20 to Chapter 8 in C.A. Macdonald, *The United States, Britain and Appeasement, 1936–1939* (London, 1981), gives the unfortunate impression that the views expressed in this memorandum were Balfour's own.
11. PRO BT 11/1142. Overton to Waley, 25 September 1939, quoted in Gilman, 'Economic Aspects', p. 123.
12. H.V. Hodson, 'The Empire and the Anglo-American Trade Agreement', *Lloyds Bank Limited Monthly Review* New Series Vol. 10, March 1939, p. 84.
13. *National Review*, December 1938, pp. 713–14.
14. Ibid., p. 714.

15. Lothian Papers, GD 40/17/390. Locock to Lothian, 12 August 1939, quoted in Gilman, 'Economic Aspects', p. 122.
16. *The Economist*, 'The British–American Trade Agreement', p. 8.
17. Ibid., pp. 8–9.
18. Ibid., p. 9.
19. *New York Times*, 13 March 1938, Section 4, p. 6.
20. *National Review*, January 1938, p. 40.
21. Ibid.
22. PRO CAB 24/279, pp. 177–8. CP 225(38) Cabinet Committee on Trade and Agriculture. The United Kingdom–United States Trade Agreement. Report, pp. 1–2.
23. PRO CAB 23/96, p. 18. Cab. 49(38) Cabinet Minutes, 19 October 1938, p. 15.
24. Ibid., p. 17.
25. Ibid., p. 15.
26. CAB 24/279, p. 181. CP 225(38) Appendix One. Committee on Trade and Agriculture. United Kingdom–United States Trade Negotiations. Note by the President of the Board of Trade, p. 2.
27. CAB 24/279, p. 196. CP 225(38) Appendix Two. Committee on Trade and Agriculture. United Kingdom–United States Trade Negotiations. FO Telegram No. 217. Immediate. Important. Trade Agreement, p. 1.
28. Ibid., pp. 1–2.
29. Ibid., p. 2.
30. Ibid., p. 3.
31. PRO FO 371/21506/A7561/1/45. Note by Mr Thompson.
32. Ibid., note by Balfour.
33. CP 225(38) Appendix Two, p. 3.
34. *Journal of the National Union of Manufacturers*, February 1938. Quoted in the *National Review*, March 1938, p. 289.
35. FO 371/A7789/1/45 Memorandum by Cadogan, 11 October 1938.
36. CAB 23/96, p. 21. Cab. 49(38) Cabinet Minutes, 19 October, p. 18.
37. T. Rooth, *British Protectionism and the International Economy; Overseas Commercial Policy in the 1930s* (Cambridge, 1992), p. 284.
38. PRO CAB 23/96, p. 58. Cab. 23/96 Cabinet Minutes, 26 October 1938, p. 15.
39. G.C. Peden, 'A Matter of Timing: the Economic Background to British Foreign Policy 1937–1939', *History* 69 (1984), p. 23.
40. David Dilks (ed.), *The Diaries of Sir Alexander Cadogan O.M., 1938–1945* (London, 1971), p. 116.
41. Ibid., p. 118.
42. Ibid., p. 119.
43. R.A.C. Parker, 'Economics, Rearmament and Foreign Policy: the United Kingdom before 1939 – a Preliminary Study', *Journal of Contemporary History* 10 (1975), p. 646.
44. Dilks (ed.), *Cadogan*, p. 119.
45. Peden, 'A Matter of Timing', p. 23.
46. Dilks (ed.), *Cadogan*, p. 118.
47. *DBFP*, Third Series, Vol. 3 (London, 1950). Letter from Viscount Halifax to Sir E. Phipps, 1 November 1938, pp. 251–3.

48. *FRUS*, 1938, Vol. 1 (Washington, 1955). The Ambassador in the United Kingdom (Kennedy) to the Secretary of State, 12 October 1938, p. 85.
49. CAB 23/94. CP 36(38)3. Quoted in Parker, 'The Pound Sterling', p. 270, fn 7.
50. *National Review*, March 1938, p. 291.

7 A 'Maginot Line for the Pound'

1. R.S. Sayers, *Financial Policy 1939–45* (London, 1956), p. 229.
2. Ibid., p. 232.
3. FDR MD Book 153, pp. 81–2. Telephone Conversation with Bank of England, 28 November 1938.
4. Ibid., p. 82.
5. Ibid., p. 143. Telephone Conversation between Knoke and Morgenthau, 28 November 1938.
6. Ibid.
7. Ibid., p. 189. Treasury Meeting. Re Sterling Exchange Rate, 29 November 1938.
8. Ibid., p. 198.
9. Ibid., p. 199.
10. PRO T 160/878/F16506. Mr Debenham's Memorandum on Armament Expenditure and its Effect on UK Finance, Trade and Exchange Position. Treasury Views On. Letter, Henderson to Phillips, 12 October 1938.
11. Ibid. Memorandum by Hawtrey, 25 October 1938.
12. Ibid. Memorandum by Hawtrey, 16 November 1938.
13. MD Book 153, p. 221. Memorandum, White to Morgenthau, 28 November 1938.
14. Ibid., pp. 232–4. Treasury Meeting. Re Sterling Exchange Rate, 29 November 1938.
15. Ibid., pp. 234–7.
16. Ibid., p. 238.
17. Ibid., pp. 241–2.
18. Ibid., p. 251.
19. Ibid., pp. 385–6. Record of Bewley's visit to the Treasury, 30 November 1938.
20. Ibid., p. 386.
21. PRO T 160/871/15777. Letter from Bewley to Waley, 1 December 1938.
22. Ibid.
23. Ibid. Note by Hopkins, 5 December 1938.
24. MD Book 154, p. 232. Memorandum by H. Merle Cochran, 3 December 1938.
25. Ibid., pp. 232–3.
26. Ibid., p. 232.
27. Ibid., Book 155, p. 218. Inter Office Communication. To Secretary Morgenthau from Mr Taylor, 9 December 1938.
28. Ibid., pp. 218–19.
29. T 160/871/15777. Bewley to Waley, 9 December 1938.
30. Ibid., memorandum by Sir Frederick Phillips, 21 December 1938.

31. MD Book 157, p. 217. Telephone Conversation with the Bank of England, 21 December 1938.
32. Ibid., p. 218.
33. Ibid., pp. 219–20.
34. Ibid., p. 282. Inter Office Communication. To Secretary Morgenthau from Mr Taylor, 23 December 1938.
35. Ibid. Book 158, pp. 66–7. Telegram. Strictly Confidential for the Secretary of the Treasury from Butterworth, 28 December 1938.
36. Ibid., p. 67.
37. Ibid., pp. 68–9.
38. Ibid., p. 69.
39. Ibid., p. 71.
40. Ibid., p. 72.
41. Ibid., p. 237. Telegram. For Treasury from Butterworth, 31 December 1938.
42. Ibid. Book 159, p. 71. Telephone Conversation with the Bank of England, 3 January 1939.
43. Ibid., pp. 71–2.
44. Ibid., p. 72.
45. Ibid., pp. 72–3.
46. Ibid. Book 159, pp. 152–3. Telegram. For Treasury from Butterworth. Triple Priority, Strictly Confidential, 6 January 1939.
47. Ibid., pp. 163–5. Telegram. For Treasury from Butterworth, 6 January 1939.
48. Ibid., pp. 179–80. Treasury Group Meeting, 6 January 1939.
49. Ibid., p. 220. Treasury Group Meeting, 7 January 1939.
50. Ibid., p. 233. Telegram. For Treasury from Butterworth, 7 January 1939.
51. *The Economist*, 21 January 1939, p. 120.
52. Ibid.
53. Ibid.
54. Quoted in *The Economist*, 28 January 1939, p. 175.
55. PRO CAB 24/281, p. 296. CP 296(38) Economic Advisory Council. Committee on Economic Information, Twenty Sixth Report. Problems of Rearmament, December 1938.
56. Ibid., p. 11.
57. Ibid., pp. 6–7.
58. Ibid.
59. PRO T 160/771/F19429. Economic Advisory Council. Committee on Economic Information. 26th Report. Problems of Rearmament. Letter from Sir Frederick Phillips to B.G. Catterns, 29 November 1938.
60. Ibid. Treasury Summary of the Committee on Economic Information's 26th Report, 21 December 1938.
61. CAB 24/281, p. 300. CP 296(38) Problems of Rearmament, p. 7.
62. Ibid., p. 10.
63. Ibid.
64. PRO CAB 23/97, p. 39. Cab 1(39) Conclusion 9. Most Secret. Not Circulated. Currency Legislation. Statement by the Chancellor of the Exchequer, 18 January 1939.
65. CAB 23/97, p. 35. Cab.1(39) Appendix. Letter from Hopkins to Bridges, 17 January 1939.
66. CAB 23/97, p. 39. Cab.1(39) Conclusion 9, p. 1.

67. Draft enclosed, ibid., p. 37.
68. Ibid., p. 1.
69. Ibid., pp. 1–2.
70. Ibid., p. 2.
71. Ibid.
72. CAB 23/97, p. 62. Cab 2(39) Cabinet Minutes, 25 January 1939, p. 10.
73. CAB 23/97, p. 63. Cab 2(39) Cabinet Minutes, 25 January 1939, p. 11.
74. PRO CAB 27/624, p. 133. Thirty Sixth Meeting of the Cabinet Foreign Policy Committee, 26 January 1939.
75. Cab 23/97, p. 175. Cab 5(39) Cabinet Minutes, 2 February 1939, pp. 6–7.
76. Ibid., p. 7.
77. Ibid., pp. 7–9.
78. Ibid., p. 9.
79. Ibid., pp. 9–10.
80. Ibid., p. 10.
81. Ibid., pp. 10–11.
82. Ibid.
83. Ibid.
84. Ibid., p. 13.
85. PRO CAB 23/100, p. 128. Cab.36(39) Cabinet Minutes, 3 July 1939, p. 18.
86. Halifax Diary, 19 October 1945, quoted in A. Roberts, *The Holy Fox, A Biography of Lord Halifax* (London, 1991), p. 297.
87. CAB 23/97, p. 182. CP 5(39) Cabinet Minutes, 2 February 1939, p. 13.
88. CAB 23/100, pp. 130–1. Cab.36(39) Cabinet Minutes, 3 July 1939, pp. 20–1.
89. R.P. Shay Jr, *British Rearmament in the Thirties: Politics and Profits* (Princeton, 1977), p. 246.
90. This misconception persists, a recent study maintaining, with incorrect figures, that: 'This sort of expenditure did put great strain on the economy. In June 1939, Britain's gold reserves fell to £300 million, which represented a drop of £800 million from April 1938.' F. McDonough, *Neville Chamberlain, Appeasement and the British Road to War* (Manchester, 1998), p. 42.
91. Shay, *British Rearmament*, p. 280.
92. Sayers, *Financial Policy*, p. 229.

8 'Not a Damned Bit Good'

1. It is still maintained that where the economic and financial activities of the British government concerned wider policy, they were driven by narrow national self-interest. It is argued here that self-interest was certainly evident but hardly patriotic. F. McDonough, *Chamberlain, Appeasement and Britain's Road to War* (Manchester, 1998).
2. PRO T 160/885/F17545. Arrangements Leading up to Lord Stamp's Survey of War Plans in the Economic and Financial Spheres. Letter, Anderson to Simon, 8 May 1939.
3. Ibid. Memorandum by Salter et al., 'Economic Defence'.
4. Ibid. Anderson to Simon, 8 May.
5. Ibid. Memorandum by Hopkins, 17 May 1939.
6. Ibid. Draft proposal for Simon, 10 June 1939.

7. Ibid. Wilson to Simon, 14 June 1939.
8. Ibid.
9. There were other attractive reasons for choosing Stamp, who chaired the CEI and was a former civil servant and a director of the Bank of England. As such he was 'a principal link between the academic world and business and Whitehall', and not a potentially hostile outsider. Wilson wrote to him appreciatively, noting that 'the Prime Minister, the Chancellor, the Lord Privy Seal, and the President of the Board of Trade are in agreement with the plan and have blessed you for coming to look after it for us'. This genial tone continued when Wilson explained that Stamp's work would begin with 'a little meeting in this room of yourself, Henderson, Clay, Hoppy, Phillips and myself'. L.G. Wickham-Legg and E.T. Williams (eds), *Dictionary of National Biography, 1941–1950* (London, 1959), p. 818; T 160/885/F 17545. Letter, Wilson to Stamp, June 1939.
10. T 160/885/F17545 Memorandum by Salter et al., 'Economic Defence'.
11. Ibid. Wilson to Hopkins, 12 June 1939.
12. Ibid. Rucker to Bridges, 22 June 1939.
13. Ibid. Bridges to Wilson, 1 July 1939.
14. Ibid. Wilson to Bridges, 4 July 1939.
15. PRO CAB 89/1. War Cabinet. Survey of Economic and Financial Plans. Proceedings P(E&F). 1st to 70th MTGS 1939. Vol. 1: Survey of War Plans in the Economic and Financial Spheres. Second Informal Meeting.
16. PRO CAB 89/3. War Cabinet. Survey of Economic and Financial Plans. Memoranda P(E&F), 1–14. 1939. Vol. 1: Survey of War Plans in the Economic and Financial Spheres. Memoranda furnished by the Treasury, Reference W.P. (E&F) 2nd Meeting, Conclusion 2, 11 July 1939.
17. Ibid., p. 12.
18. Ibid., pp. 16–17.
19. Ibid., p. 17.
20. Ibid.
21. PRO CAB 24/288, p. 122. CP 167(39) Economic Advisory Council. Committee on Economic Information, Twenty Seventh Report. Defence Expenditure and the Economic and Financial Problems Connected Therewith, 20 July 1939, p. 5.
22. Ibid., p. 6.
23. Ibid., pp. 6–7.
24. S. Howson and D. Winch, *The Economic Advisory Council, 1930–1939: a Study in Economic Advice during Depression and Recovery* (Cambridge, 1977), p. 149.
25. CAB 24/288, p. 124. CP 167(39) Committee on Economic Information, Twenty Seventh Report, p. 9.
26. PRO CAB 24/287. CP 149(39) Cabinet. Note on the Financial Situation. Also appended to Cab 36(39).
27. Ibid.
28. Ibid., p. 1.
29. Ibid., p. 2.
30. Ibid., p. 4.
31. Ibid., p. 5.
32. Ibid.
33. PRO CAB 23/100, p. 117. Cab. 36(39) Cabinet Minutes, 3 July 1939, p. 7.

34. Ibid., p. 9.
35. Ibid.
36. Ibid., p. 10.
37. Ibid., pp. 10–11.
38. PRO CAB 24/287. CP 148(39) The Financial Situation. The German Financial Effort for Rearmament. Note by the Chancellor of the Exchequer. Also appended to Cab 36(39).
39. Ibid., p. 6.
40. Ibid., p. 2.
41. Ibid., p. 6.
42. CAB 23/100, p. 121. Cab.36(39) Cabinet Minutes, 3 July, p. 11.
43. Ibid.
44. Ibid., p. 12.
45. Ibid.
46. Ibid.
47. Ibid., p. 13.
48. Ibid., p. 14.
49. Ibid., p. 15.
50. Ibid., pp. 15–16.
51. Ibid., p. 16.
52. Ibid., p. 17.
53. MD Book 206, p. 92. Telephone Conversation with the Bank of England, 10 August 1939.
54. Ibid.
55. Ibid., Book 206, pp. 290F. Telegram. For the Acting Secretary of the Treasury from Butterworth. Strictly Confidential for Immediate Delivery, 24 August 1939.
56. Ibid., pp. 290F–G.
57. Ibid., p. 290G.
58. Ibid., p. 290H.
59. Ibid., p. 290I. Telegram. For Immediate and Personal Delivery to the Acting Secretary of the Treasury, 24 August 1939.
60. Ibid., p. 293. Telephone Conversation with the Bank of England, 24 August 1939.
61. Ibid., pp. 293–4.
62. PRO T 160/877/16003. Brief for Chancellor, 21 August 1939.
63. MD Book 206, p. 307. Telephone Conversation between Hanes and Lochhead, 24 August 1939.
64. Ibid., p. 308.
65. Ibid.
66. Ibid., p. 309.
67. Ibid., p. 349. Telephone Conversation between Lochhead and Morgenthau, 25 August 1939.
68. Ibid., pp. 314O. Paraphrase of Telegram received from American Embassy Paris. For the Treasury, 26 August 1939.
69. Ibid., pp. 314O–P.
70. Ibid., p. 327. Telephone Conversation between Hanes, Lochhead and Butterworth, 25 August 1939.
71. Ibid.

72. Ibid., pp. 290D–E. Telegram. For Treasury from Butterworth, 24 August 1939.
73. Ibid., p. 426L. Telegram. For Treasury from Butterworth, 28 August 1939.
74. Ibid., p. 426M.
75. Ibid.
76. Ibid., p. 521K. Telegram. For Treasury from Butterworth, 30 August, 1939.
77. CAB 89/1. Survey of War Plans in the Economic and Financial Spheres. Twenty Fourth Meeting. Conclusion, 3 August 1939.

Conclusion

1. Keynes' support for aspects of the government's rearmament policy is well known. However, this does not amount to a vindication of fourth arm policy, as Keynes internationalism left him blind to many of its most dangerous failings. It has been observed that 'Keynes and the Treasury were broadly at one regarding international monetary policy after 1931'. G.C. Peden, *Keynes, the Treasury and British Economic Policy* (Basingstoke, 1988), p. 26.
2. A.J.P. Taylor, *The Origins of the Second World War* (Harmondsworth, 1963), p. 7.
3. Milward contends that in the war: 'British Strategy opened the gates of supply to the whole world and ensured from the very start that the economic effects of the war would be world wide. The maximization of production in Britain would mobilize the resources of a world economy which was wallowing in unemployment and stagnating trade, and sinking rapidly into another severe depression.' The second sentence serves as an accurate description of the British economic role after 1931. However, in war, unlike depression, the United States was the chief beneficiary of British policy. A.S. Milward, *War, Economy and Society, 1939–1945* (Harmondsworth, 1977), p. 42.
4. Ambassador Kennedy observed that 'Mr Hull's Trade Agreements program is completely out of the window'. Quoted in E. Gilman, 'Economic Aspects of Anglo-American Relations in the Era of Roosevelt and Chamberlain' (unpublished Ph.D. Thesis, University of London, 1976), p. 263. Gilman's excellent account of trade tensions during the 'Phoney War', has been criticised by Reynolds on the grounds that 'he takes the State Department's suspicions too much at face value', having 'overlooked' a speech by Chamberlain in defence of the Agreement and liberal practice on 31 January 1940, which constitutes 'an important piece of contrary evidence'. Reynolds notes that: 'It seems important, therefore, that Anglo-American economic competition should not be exaggerated or misunderstood.' D. Reynolds, *The Creation of the Anglo-American Alliance 1937–41: a Study in Competitive Co-operation* (London, 1981), p. 317, fn 87; p. 78. This criticism is harsh: Gilman simply relates the full force of the State Department's Anglophobia whilst doing justice to the conflict in official British minds between liberal principles and the now unavoidable imperatives of economic survival. Gilman, 'Economic Aspects', pp. 263–302.
5. Paradoxically Keynes, a latecomer to the joys of autarky, was optimistic, even after the collapse of France. In a memorandum entitled 'Foreign

Exchange Control and Payments Agreements', which set the agenda for a meeting of the chancellor's Exchange Control Conference, he explored this new area of interest. He saw the need for Schacht-style payments agreements as 'one of the most important instruments at our disposal for the long term financing of a long war', although he acknowledged that 'I write this in a state of considerable ignorance . . . I have never seen the text of a payments agreement'. Nevertheless, he was confident that the extension of blockade to 'almost the whole of continental Europe' would eliminate 'the possibility of scarcity of supply and high prices in the international markets. On the contrary, in commodity after commodity there is a prospect of a hideous unsold surplus and a market collapse. Reasons of internal politics and internal economy will turn most overseas countries, when they have fully tumbled to the new situation, into suppliants for our custom, passionately anxious to find a market on almost any terms for their overwhelmingly burdensome domestic surplus.' He concluded that 'whilst we must not abuse our strength, it would be foolish to overlook it'. Keynes Memorandum, 29 July 1940. D. Moggridge (ed.), *The Collected Writings of John Maynard Keynes* Vol. 23, *Activities, 1940–1943: External War Finance* (Cambridge, 1979), pp. 6 and 8–9.
6. C. Barnett, *The Lost Victory: British Dreams, British Realities 1945–1950* (London, 1995), pp. 106–7.
7. Ibid., p. 107.
8. R.G. Hawtrey, *The Gold Standard in Theory and Practice* 2nd edn (London, 1931), p. 2.
9. Ibid., p. 3.
10. Barnett, *The Lost Victory*, p. 108.
11. Ibid., p. 397.
12. W.D. Rubinstein, 'Cultural Explanations for Britain's Economic Decline: How True?', in B. Collins and K. Robbins (eds), *British Culture and Economic Decline* (London, 1990), pp. 67–8.
13. C. Barnett, *The Audit of War: the Illusion and Reality of Britain as a Great Nation* (London, 1986), p. 144.
14. Ibid.
15. P. Kennedy, *The Rise and Fall of the Great Powers: Economic Change and Military Conflict from 1500 to 2000* (London, 1988), p. 408. Kennedy's argument that the US economy 'was merely underutilized because of the Depression', with idle American resources simply waiting for employment on weapons contracts is now orthodoxy. Ibid., p. 429.
16. R.G.D. Allen, 'Mutual Aid between the U.S. and the British Empire', *Journal of the Royal Statistical Society* 109 (1946), pp. 267–8.
17. Ibid., p. 268.
18. Development of a Canadian armaments industry could have served a useful political purpose. Canada's Liberal government opposed closer military involvement with Britain, but 'the Canadian military establishment . . . more clearly than most saw that Canadian public opinion would ultimately accept, even demand, the overseas commitment of armed forces'. Mackenzie King could scarcely have resisted lavish inward investment at Britain's expense which would have tied Canada more closely to Britain's war effort. Such a move was expected in the United States, and Roosevelt, uneasy at

the possibility of a vast Canadian industry falling into the wrong hands, illustrated his fears in conversation with Morgenthau by reference to the example of the Napoleonic turncoat Bernadotte. J.A. English, 'Not an Equilateral Triangle: Canada's Strategic Relationship with the United States and Britain, 1939–1945' in *The North Atlantic Triangle in a Changing World: Anglo-American–Canadian Relations, 1902–1956* (Toronto, 1996), p. 152.

19. Allen, 'Mutual Aid', p. 268.
20. K. Feiling, *The Life of Neville Chamberlain* (London, 1946), p. 323.
21. PRO CAB 23/93, p. 123. Cab. (18)38 Cabinet Minutes, 6 April 1938, p. 22.
22. B.E.V. Sabine, *British Budgets in Peace and War, 1932–1945* (London, 1970), p. 300.

Select Bibliography

Unpublished primary sources

United Kingdom

Public Record Office, Kew:
Board of Trade Papers
Cabinet Office Papers
Foreign Office Papers
Prime Minister's Office Papers
Treasury Office Papers

United States of America

National Archives, Washington DC:
Department of State. General Records, RG.59
Franklin D. Roosevelt Library, Hyde Park NY:
The Henry J. Morgenthau Jr Diary
The President's Personal File
The President's Secretary's File

Published primary sources

Command papers

Cd 8462 of 1917, Dominions Royal Commission, *Final Report of the Royal Commission on the Natural Resources, Trade and Legislation of Certain Portions of His Majesty's Dominions*
Cd 9032 of 1918, Committee on Commercial and Industrial Policy, *Interim Report on Certain Essential Industries*
Cd 9035 of 1918, Committee on Commercial and Industrial Policy, *Final Report of the Committee on Commercial and Industrial Policy after the War*
Cd 9182 of 1918, Committee on Currency and Foreign Exchanges [Cunliffe Committee], *First Interim Report of the Committee on Currency and Foreign Exchanges after the War*
Cmd 3897 of 1931, Committee on Finance and Industry [Macmillan Committee] *Report*

Collections

Documents on British Foreign Policy, Second and Third Series
Foreign Relations of the United States, Various Volumes
Franklin D. Roosevelt and Foreign Affairs, Second Series, D.B. Schewe (ed.)

Newspapers and periodicals

The Economist
Journal of the Royal Statistical Society
Lloyds Bank Limited Monthly Review
New York Times
National Review
The Times

Secondary sources

Dictionary of American Biography
Dictionary of National Biography

Aldcroft, D.H. 'Economic Growth in Britain in the Interwar Years: a Reassessment', *Economic History Review* Second Series 20 (1967), pp. 311–26.

Aldcroft, D.H. *The Interwar Economy: Britain, 1919–1939* (London, 1970).

Andrew, C. and Dilks D. (eds) *The Missing Dimension: Governments and Intelligence Communities in the Twentieth Century* (London, 1984).

Atkin, J. 'Official Regulation of British Overseas Investment, 1914–1931', *Economic History Review* Second Series 23 (1970), pp. 324–35.

Barkai, A. *Nazi Economics: Ideology, Theory, and Policy* (Oxford, 1990).

Barnett, C. *The Collapse of British Power* (London, 1972).

Barnett, C. *The Audit of War: the Illusion and Reality of Britain as a Great Nation* (London, 1986).

Barnett, C. *The Lost Victory: British Dreams and British Realities, 1945–1950* (London, 1995).

Bell, P. *Chamberlain, Germany and Japan, 1933–1934* (Basingstoke, 1996).

Beloff, M. *Imperial Sunset* Vol. 2, *Dream of Commonwealth, 1921–1942* (London, 1989).

Bialer, U. *The Shadow of the Bomber: Fear of Air Attack and British Politics, 1932–1939* (London, 1980).

Blum, J.M. *From the Morgenthau Diaries* Vol. 1, *Years of Crisis, 1928–1938* (Boston, 1959).

Blum, J.M. *From the Morgenthau Diaries* Vol. 2, *Years of Urgency, 1939–1941* (Boston, 1965).

Boadle, D.G. 'The Formation of the Foreign Office Economic Relations Section, 1930–1937', *Historical Journal* 20 (1977), pp. 919–36.

Bond, B. (ed.) *Chief of Staff: the Diaries of Lt. General Sir Henry Pownal* Vol. 1, *1933–1940* (London, 1974).

Bond, B. *Liddell-Hart: a Study of His Military Thought* (London, 1977).

Bond, B. *British Military Policy between the Two World Wars* (Oxford, 1980).

Boyce, R.W.D. *British Capitalism at the Crossroads, 1919–1932: a Study in Politics, Economics and International Relations* (Cambridge, 1987).

Boyce R. and Robertson, E. (eds) *Paths to War: New Essays on the Origins of the Second World War* (London, 1989).

Bullock, A. *Hitler: a Study in Tyranny* (London, 1954).

Burk, K. *Britain, America and the Sinews of War, 1914–1918* (London, 1985).

Butler, J.R.M. *Lord Lothian (Philip Kerr) 1882–1940* (London, 1960).

Cain, P.J. and Hopkins, A.G. *British Imperialism: Crisis and Deconstruction, 1914–1990* (New York, 1993).

Carr, W. *Arms, Autarky and Aggression: a Study in German Foreign Policy, 1933–1939* (London, 1972).

Carroll, B.A. *Design for Total War: Arms and Economics in the Third Reich* (The Hague, 1968).

Chalmers, M. *Paying for Defence: Military Spending and British Decline* (London, 1985).

Charmley, J.D. *Neville Chamberlain and the Lost Peace* (London, 1989).

Charmley, J.D. *Churchill's Special Relationship: the Anglo-American Alliance, 1940–1957* (London, 1995).

Chester, D.N. and Willson, F.M.G. *The Organisation of British Central Government, 1914–1964* (London, 1968).

Churchill, W.L.S. *The Second World War* Vol. 1, *The Gathering Storm* (London, 1948).

Clarke, S.V.O. *Central Bank Cooperation, 1924–1931* (New York, 1967).

Clarke, S.V.O. *Exchange-Rate Stabilization in the Mid-1930s: Negotiating the Tripartite Agreement* (Princeton, 1977).

Coghlan, F. 'Armaments, Economic Policy and Appeasement: Background to British Foreign Policy, 1931–37', *History* 57 (1972), pp. 205–16.

Costigliola, F.C. 'Anglo-American Financial Rivalry in the 1920s', *Journal of Economic History* 37 (1977), pp. 911–34.

Costigliola, F.C. *Awkward Dominion: American Political, Economic, and Cultural Relations with Europe, 1919–1933* (Ithaca and London, 1984).

Cowling, M. *The Impact of Hitler: British Politics and British Policy, 1933–1940* (London, 1975).

Dallek, R. *Franklin D. Roosevelt and American Foreign Policy, 1932–1945* (New York, 1979).

Dilks, D. (ed.) *The Diaries of Sir Alexander Cadogan O.M., 1938–1945* (London, 1971).

Dilks, D. (ed.) *Retreat from Power: Studies in Britain's Foreign Policy* Vol. 1 (London, 1981).

Dockrill, M.L. and McKercher, B.J.C. *Diplomacy and World Power: Studies in British Foreign Policy, 1890–1950* (Oxford, 1996).

Douglas, R. *In the Year of Munich* (London, 1977).

Douglas, R. 'Chamberlain and Eden, 1937–1938', *Journal of Contemporary History* 13 (1978), pp. 97–116.

Drummond, I.M. *British Economic Policy and the Empire, 1919–1939* (London, 1972).

Drummond, I.M. *Imperial Economic Policy, 1917–1939: Studies in Expansion and Protection* (London, 1974).

Drummond, I.M. *London, Washington, and the Management of the Franc, 1936–1939* (Princeton, 1979).

Drummond, I.M. *The Floating Pound and the Sterling Area, 1931–1939* (Cambridge, 1981).

Drummond, I.M. *The Gold Standard and the International Monetary System, 1900–1939* (Basingstoke, 1987).

Drummond, I.M. and Hillmer, N. *Negotiating Freer Trade: the United Kingdom, the United States, Canada, and the Trade Agreements of 1938* (Waterloo, 1989).

Duncan-Hall, H. *North American Supply* (London, 1955).

Edgerton, D. *Science, Technology and the British Industrial 'Decline', 1870–1970* (Cambridge, 1996).

Eichengreen, B.J. *Sterling and the Tariff, 1929–1932* (Princeton, 1981).

Eichengreen, B.J. *Golden Fetters: the Gold Standard and the Great Depression, 1919–1939* (Oxford, 1992).

Feiling, K.G. *The Life of Neville Chamberlain* (London, 1946).

Feinstein, C.H. *National Income, Expenditure and Output of the U.K. 1855–1965* (Cambridge, 1976).

Feinstein, C.H. (ed.) *Banking, Currency and Finance in Europe between the Wars* (Oxford, 1995).

Ferris, J.R. *Men, Money and Diplomacy: the Evolution of British Strategic Policy, 1919–1926* (Ithaca, 1989).

Fry, G.K. *Statesmen in Disguise: the Changing Rôle of the Administrative Class of the British Home Civil Service, 1853–1960* (London, 1969).

Gardner, L.C. *Economic Aspects of New Deal Diplomacy* (New York, 1981).

Gardner, R. *Sterling–Dollar Diplomacy: the Origins and Prospects of Our International Economic Order* (New York, 1969).

Gibbs, N.H. *Grand Strategy* Vol. 1, *Rearmament Policy* (London, 1976).

Gilbert, M. *The Roots of Appeasement* (London, 1966).

Gilbert, M. and Gott, R. *The Appeasers* (London, 1963).

Gilman, E. 'Economic Aspects of Anglo-American Relations in the Era of Roosevelt and Chamberlain' (unpublished Ph.D. Thesis, University of London, 1976).

Green, F. 'The Military View of American National Policy, 1904–1940', *American Historical Review* 66 (1961), pp. 354–77.

Grigg, P.J. *Prejudice and Judgement* (London, 1948).

Hall, H. 'The Foreign Policy Making Process in Britain, 1934–35, and the Origins of the Anglo-German Naval Agreement', *Historical Journal* 19 (1976), pp. 477–99.

Hancock, W.C. *Survey of British Commonwealth Affairs* Vol. 2, *Problems of Economic Policy 1918–1939 Part 1* (Oxford, 1940).

Hancock, W.K. and Gowing, M.M. *British War Economy* (London, 1949).

Harrison, M. (ed.) *The Economics of World War Two: Six Great Powers in International Comparison* (Cambridge, 1998).

Hauner, M. 'Czechoslovakia as a Military Factor in British Considerations of 1938', *Journal of Strategic Studies* 1 (1978), pp. 194–222.

Hauner, M. 'Did Hitler Want a World Dominion?', *Journal of Contemporary History* 13 (1978), pp. 15–32.

Hawtrey, R.G. *The Gold Standard in Theory and Practice* 2nd edn (London, 1931).

Hawtrey, R.G. *A Century of Bank Rate* 2nd edn (London, 1962).

Hillgruber, A. 'England's Place in Hitler's Plans for World Dominion', *Journal of Contemporary History* 9 (1974), pp. 5–22.

Hobsbawm, E.J. *The Age of Extremes: the Short Twentieth Century, 1914–1991* (London, 1994).

Holland, R.F. *Britain and the Commonwealth Alliance, 1918–1939* (London, 1981).

Howard, M. *The Continental Commitment: the Dilemma of British Defence Policy in the Era of Two World Wars* (London, 1972).

Howson, S. *Domestic Monetary Management in Britain, 1919–1938* (Cambridge, 1975).

Howson, S. *Sterling's Managed Float: the Operations of the Exchange Equalisation Account, 1932–1939* (Princeton, 1980).

Howson, S. and Winch, D. *The Economic Advisory Council, 1930–1939: a Study in Economic Advice during Depression and Recovery* (Cambridge, 1977).

Johnson, F.A. *Defence by Committee: the British Committee of Imperial Defence, 1885–1959* (Oxford, 1960).

Kaiser, D.E. *Economic Diplomacy and the Origins of the Second World War: Germany, Britain, France, and Eastern Europe, 1930–1939* (Princeton, 1980).

Kennedy, P. *The Realities behind Diplomacy: Background Influences on British External Policy, 1865–1980* (London, 1981).

Kennedy, P. *The Rise and Fall of the Great Powers: Economic Change and Military Conflict from 1500 to 2000* (London, 1988).

Keynes J.M. *How to Pay for the War* (London, 1940).

Kimball, W.F. 'Beggar My Neighbour: America and the Interim British Financial Crisis, 1940–1941', *Journal of Economic History* 29 (1969), pp. 758–72.

Kimball, W.F. 'Lend-Lease and the Open Door: the Temptation of British Opulence, 1937–1942', *Political Science Quarterly* 86 (1971), pp. 232–59.

Kindelberger, C.P. *The World in Depression, 1929–1939* (London, 1973).

Kottman, R.N. *Reciprocity and the North Atlantic Triangle, 1932–1938* (Ithaca, 1968).

Kreider, C. *The Anglo-American Trade Agreement* (New York, 1942).

Lake, D.A. *Power, Protection, and Free Trade: International Sources of U.S. Commercial Strategy* (Ithaca, 1988).

Lammers, D. 'Fascism, Communism, and the Foreign Office, 1937–1939' *Journal of Contemporary History* 6 (1971), pp. 66–86.

Leith-Ross, Sir F. *Money Talks: Fifty Years of International Finance* (London, 1968).

Liddell-Hart, B.H. *The Other Side of the Hill: Germany's Generals, Their Rise and Fall with Their Own Account of Military Events, 1939–1945* (London, 1948).

Liddell-Hart, B.H. *Memoirs of Captain Liddell-Hart* Vol. 2 (London, 1965).

Louis, W.R. *The Origins of the Second World War: A.J.P. Taylor and His Critics* (New York, 1972).

Louis, W.R. *In the Name of God Go! Leo Amery and the British Empire in the Age of Churchill* (New York and London, 1992).

Macdonald, C.A. 'Economic Appeasement and the German Moderates, 1937–39', *Past and Present* 56 (1972), pp. 105–35.

Macdonald, C.A. *The United States, Britain and Appeasement, 1936–1939* (London, 1980).

McCulloch T. 'Anglo-American Economic Diplomacy and the European Crisis, 1933–1939' (unpublished D.Phil. Thesis, University of Oxford, 1978).

McDonough, F. *Neville Chamberlain, Appeasement and the British Road to War* (Manchester, 1998).

McKercher, B.J.C. '"Our Most Dangerous Enemy": Great Britain pre-eminent in the 1930s', *International History Review* 13 (1991), pp. 751–83.

McKercher, B.J.C. *Transition of Power: Britain's Loss of Global Pre-eminence to the United States, 1930–1945* (Cambridge, 1999).

McKercher, B.J.C. and Aronson, L. (eds) *The North Atlantic Triangle in a Changing World: Anglo-American–Canadian Relations, 1902–1956* (Toronto, 1996).

Marwick, A. 'Middle Opinion in the Thirties: Planning Progress and Political "Agreement"', *English Historical Review* 79 (1964), pp. 285–98.

May, E.R. 'Nazi Germany and the United States: a Review Essay', *Journal of Modern History* 41 (1969), pp. 207–14.

Megaw, M.R. 'The Scramble for the Pacific: Anglo-United States Rivalry in the 1930s', *Historical Studies* 17 (1977), pp. 458–73.

Meyers, R. *Britische Sicherheitspolitik* (Reading, 1972).

Middlemas, K. *Diplomacy of Illusion: the British Government and Germany, 1937–1939* (London, 1972).

Milward, A.S. *The German Economy at War* (London, 1965).

Milward, A.S. *The Economic Effects of the Two World Wars on Britain* (London, 1972).

Milward, A.S. *War, Economy and Society, 1939–1945* (Harmondsworth, 1977).

Minney, R.J. (ed.) *The Private Papers of Hore-Belisha* (New York, 1960).

Moggridge, D.A. *British Monetary Policy, 1924–1931: the Norman Conquest of $4.86* (Cambridge, 1972).

Mommsen, W.J. and Kettenacker, L. (eds) *The Fascist Challenge and the Policy of Appeasement* (London, 1983).

Morris, J. *Farewell the Trumpets: an Imperial Retreat* (London, 1978).

Newton, S. *The Profits of Peace: the Political Economy of Anglo-German Appeasement* (Oxford, 1996).

Offner, A. *The First World War: an Agrarian Interpretation* (Oxford, 1989).

Orde, A. *The Eclipse of Great Britain: the United States and British Imperial Decline, 1895–1956* (Basingstoke, 1996).

Ovendale, R. *Appeasement and the English Speaking World: Britain, the United States, the Dominions and the Policy of 'Appeasement', 1937–1939* (Cardiff, 1975).

Overy, R. 'German Pre-war Aircraft Production Plans: November 1936–April 1939', *English Historical Review* 90 (1975), pp. 778–97.

Overy, R. *War and Economy in the Third Reich* (Oxford, 1994).

Overy, R. *The Nazi Economic Recovery* 2nd edn (Cambridge, 1996).

Overy, R. and Wheatcroft, A. *The Road to War* (London, 1989).

Parker, R.A.C. 'Economics Rearmament and Foreign Policy: the United Kingdom before 1939: a Preliminary Study', *Journal of Contemporary History* 10 (1975), pp. 637–47.

Parker, R.A.C. 'Britain, France and Scandinavia, 1939–1940', *History* 61 (1976), pp. 369–87.

Parker, R.A.C. 'British Rearmament 1936–1939: Treasury, Trade Unions and Skilled Labour', *English Historical Review* 96 (1981), pp. 306–43.

Parker, R.A.C. 'The Pound Sterling, the American Treasury and British Preparations for War, 1938–39', *English Historical Review* 98 (1983), pp. 261–79.

Parker, R.A.C. *Chamberlain and Appeasement: British Policy and the Coming of the Second World War* (Basingstoke, 1993).

Peden, G.C. *British Rearmament and the Treasury, 1932–1939* (Edinburgh, 1979).

Peden, G.C. 'Sir Warren Fisher and British Rearmament against Germany', *English Historical Review* 94 (1979), pp. 29–47.

Peden, G.C. 'A Matter of Timing: the Economic Background to British Foreign Policy, 1937–1939', *History* 69 (1984), pp. 15–27.

Peden, G.C. 'The Burden of Imperial Defence and the Continental Commitment Reconsidered', *Historical Journal* 27 (1984), pp. 405–23.

Peden, G.C. *Keynes, the Treasury and British Economic Policy* (London, 1988).

Peele, G. and Cook, C. (eds) *The Politics of Reappraisal, 1918–1939* (London, 1975).

Post, G. Jr *Dilemmas of Appeasement; British Deterrence and Defense, 1934–1937* (Ithaca, 1993).

Postan, M.M. *British War Production* (London, 1952).

Puckler, Count *How Strong is Britain?* (London, 1939).

Reynolds, D. 'Competitive Co-operation: Anglo-American Relations in World War Two', *Historical Journal* 23 (1980), pp. 233–45.

Reynolds, D. *The Creation of the Anglo-American Alliance, 1937–1941: a Study in Competitive Cooperation* (London, 1981).

Reynolds, D. *Britannia Overruled: British Policy and World Power in the Twentieth Century* (London, 1991).

Rhodes, B.D. 'Reassessing "Uncle Shylock": the United States and the French War Debt, 1917–1929', *Journal of American History* 55 (1969), pp. 787–803.

Roberts, A. *The Holy Fox: a Biography of Lord Halifax* (London, 1991).

Robbins, K.G. *Munich 1938* (London, 1968).

Robbins, K.G. and Collins, B. *British Culture and Economic Decline* (London, 1990).

Rooth, T. *British Protectionism and the International Economy: Overseas Commercial Policy in the 1930s* (Cambridge, 1993).

Roskill, S. *British Naval Policy between the Wars* Vol. 1, *The Period of Anglo-American Antagonism* (London, 1972).

Roskill, S. *Hankey, Man of Secrets,* Vol. 2 *1919–1931* (London, 1972).

Rowland, B.M. (ed.) *Balance of Power or Hegemony: the Interwar Monetary System* (New York, 1976).

Sabine, B.E.V. *British Budgets in Peace and War, 1932–1945* (London, 1970).

Salmon, P. 'British Plans for Economic Warfare against Germany, 1937–1939: the Problem of Swedish Iron Ore', *Journal of Contemporary History* 16 (1981), pp. 53–71.

Sayers, R.S. *Financial Policy, 1939–1945* (London, 1956).

Schatz, A.W. 'The Anglo-American Trade Agreement and Cordell Hull's Search for Peace, 1936–1938', *Journal of American History* 57 (1970), pp. 85–103.

Schmidt, G. *The Politics and Economics of Appeasement: British Foreign Policy in the 1930s* (Leamington Spa, 1986).

Schroeder, P.W. 'Munich and the British Tradition', *History* 19 (1976), pp. 223–43.

Seal, A. (ed.) *The Decline, Revival and Fall of the British Empire: the Ford Lectures and Other Essays* (Cambridge, 1982).

Shay, R.P. Jr *British Rearmament in the Thirties: Politics and Profits* (Princeton, 1977).

Skidelsky, R. *Politicians and the Slump: the Labour Government of 1929–1931* (London, 1967).

Speer, A. *Inside the Third Reich* (London, 1970).

Stevenson, J. and Cook, C. *The Slump: Society and Politics during the Depression* (London, 1977).

Strange, S. *Sterling and British Policy: a Political Study of an International Currency in Decline* (London, 1971).

Taylor, A.J.P. *The Origins of the Second World War* (Harmondsworth, 1963).

Taylor, A.J.P. *English History, 1914–1945* (Oxford, 1966).

Thomas, G. *Geschichte der deutschen Wehr-und Rüstungswirtschaft (1918–1943/5),* W. Birkenfeld (ed.) (Boppard am Rhein, 1966).

Wark, W.K. *The Ultimate Enemy: British Intelligence and Nazi Germany, 1933–1939* (London, 1985).

Watt, D.C. *Personalities and Policies: Studies in the Formulation of British Foreign Policy in the Twentieth Century* (London, 1965).

Watt, D.C. *Too Serious a Business: European Armed Forces and the Approach to the Second World War* (London, 1975).

Watt, D.C. *Succeeding John Bull: America in Britain's Place, 1900–1975* (Cambridge, 1984).

Watt, D.C. *How War Came: the Immediate Origins of the Second World War, 1938–1939* (London, 1989).

Webber, G.C. *The Ideology of the British Right, 1918–1939* (London, 1986).

Wendt, B.J. *Economic Appeasement: Handel und Finanz in der britischen Deutschlandpolitik, 1933–1939* (Düsseldorf, 1971).

Wiener, M. *English Culture and the Decline of the Industrial Spirit, 1850–1980* (Cambridge, 1981).

Williams, D. 'London and the 1931 Financial Crisis', *Economic History Review* Second Series 15 (1962–63), pp. 513–28.

Young, R. 'Spokesman for Economic Warfare: the Industrial Intelligence Centre in the 1930s', *European Studies Review* 6 (1976), pp. 473–89.

Zitelmann, R. *Hitler: Selbstverständnis eines Revolutionärs* (Hamburg, 1987).

Index